Social Work and Community in a Private World
Getting Out in Public

Robert Fisher
University of Houston

Howard Jacob Karger
University of Houston

 LONGMAN

An imprint of Addison Wesley Longman, Inc.

New York • Reading, Massachusetts • Menlo Park, California • Harlow, England
Don Mills, Ontario • Sydney • Mexico City • Madrid • Amsterdam

Social Work and Community in a Private World: Getting Out in Public

Longman, 10 Bank Street, White Plains, N.Y. 10606

Executive editor: Pamela A. Gordon
Associate editor: Hillary B. Henderson
Editorial assistant: Jennifer A. McCaffery
Production editor: Linda Moser/Professional Book Center
Production supervisor: Edith Pullman
Cover design: Celine Brandes
Compositor: Professional Book Center

Library of Congress Cataloging-in-Publication Data

Fisher, Robert
    Social work and community in a private world : getting out in
public / Robert Fisher, Howard Jacob Karger.
        p.   cm.
    Includes bibliographical references and index.
    ISBN 0-8013-1421-6
    1. Social service.   2. Public welfare.   3. Social policy.
4. Social workers.   I. Karger, Howard Jacob.   II. Title.
HV40.F545   1997
362.3'2—dc20   96-17906
                                                          CIP

1 2 3 4 5 6 7 8 9 10-MA-0099989796

For my mother, Eve Schneiderman Fisher,
whose support and expectations helped get me out in public.

Robert Fisher

For my father, whose toiling gave me the opportunity to get an education,
and whose arguments made me think harder.

Howard Jacob Karger

Contents

Preface

This is a very important and challenging time to be studying and practicing social work. The world is in a dramatic state of transition, responding to changes rooted in the global economy, new communication technologies, and a worldwide reactionary political climate. This flux creates immense problems. Events in places as disparate as Rwanda, Bosnia, and the streets of urban America give one a sense that society is disintegrating; the attacks of neoconservative public officials on social welfare policy and the very idea of "government" reinforce this perception. The barriers to progressive change seem immense and are growing second by second. Fortunately, new contexts always produce new openings for social change. For social workers and their clients to make the most of the opportunities offered by this contemporary transition, they must understand the nature and causes of the new conditions and the new roads to social change. To advance progressive social change, this book offers an analysis of contemporary life, a model for contextualizing social work practice, and an argument for how the new context relates to social work theory, practice, policy, and research. Furthermore, the book proposes a different way of understanding the importance of macro theory, community organization, generalist practice, policy, and research—all critical components of "getting out in public." By emphasizing the need for social workers to expand public life and promote a progressive conception of the public good, we hope to broaden the lens of social work beyond its current foci, which are primarily on a depoliticized personal and family therapy and exclusive conceptualizations of cultural identity and professional interest. We believe that the profession can continue to change and grow, and as it does, enjoy a brighter and better future. Moreover, we think that the concept of getting out in public expands the trajectory of social change beyond individual and direct service practice and beyond the community—whether physical or cultural—in ways more congruent with the challenges of contemporary life in the twenty-first century.

This book proposes that as the societal context for social work practice becomes increasingly asocial—that is, focused on private needs and institutions and divorced from social concerns—public life declines, and the conception of a public good becomes increasingly conservative and exclusionary. The task of social change increasingly falls to oppressed and disempowered people working with and being served by activists and professionals who possess the skills, understanding, and long-term commitment to the values and goals of social justice and social change. As Freire (quoted in Rees, 1991) said, "In order for the oppressed to be able to wage the struggle for their liberation they must perceive the reality of oppression, not as a closed world from which there is no exit, but as a limited situation which they can transform" (p. 7).

At first glance, the vision of social work as social change may not suit the career goals or professional image of many current or future social workers. Nevertheless, we agree with Homan (1994) that "human service workers are social change agents, at least the good ones are. . . . [While] most workers are not full-time community change agents . . . all workers will be confronted by the challenge to seek changes in the way things are" (pp. 38–40). What all social workers share in common, and what brings people into the profession, is a concern for people and social problems. The vast majority of social workers want to effect change. One of the goals of this book is to make change more possible by examining the barriers to social change both within and outside the profession, and by stretching social workers' views of what the contemporary context requires to effect progressive social change.

CONTEXTUALIZING SOCIAL WORK
IN A PRIVATE WORLD

The best social work training contextualizes practice. It trains social workers—both within and beyond the classroom—in skill development and social science knowledge of the changing structures and processes of society. The applied nature of social work, among other features, distinguishes it from other ways of knowing and from disciplines such as history and sociology. But equally important is the need to contextualize practice, informing a single intervention with a larger understanding of the relation of power to society. In part, this contextualizing is what sets social work apart from other ways of acting and from other helping professions such as psychotherapy or medicine. It is also what distinguishes social work education more than any other aspect: education for social change links skill training with a larger contextual understanding of society. Analysis of social problems and conditions affects which skills get used and for what purpose.

In their study of community organizing training institutes, Robinson and Hanna (1994) describe how programs, such as the Midwest Academy and the Industrial

Areas Foundation, the training institute founded by Saul Alinsky, effectively teach the skills of organizing. In training sessions lasting from a few days to a few weeks, participants learn the training institute's organizing method. Robinson and Hanna (1994) conclude that, in general, these institutes do their work exceedingly well, much better than community organization training in schools of social work. But schools of social work offer a critical component of community organization that these institutes, by their short-term nature and by their ties to a specific organizing approach, are unable to provide. The best schools of social work offer perspective, analysis, and theory about community organizing. These social work programs provide a larger view of the history, diverse practices, theories, and contemporary factors—such as politics, social problems, social movements, and social policies—that serve as a bedrock for a practitioner's understanding of community work. This foundation informs and mobilizes social work skills. It is this critical analysis of contemporary issues and problems that offers the practitioner the knowledge base to tackle issues more effectively. It is also this theory base that helps the practitioner to clarify and articulate the nature of a problem and its causes, to frame issues for the short and long term, to conceptualize organizational goals, and to plan strategies. Knowing the history and diversity of approaches to community organizing enables practitioners, especially those with little experience, to understand and evaluate their own work and to see other possibilities. Ultimately, the focus on skill development and the specific skill training that community organizing institutes offer can be found after formal social work training. But the perspective and knowledge of history, theories, diverse strategies, social policy, research, and organizational change—the larger contextualization of macro practice—is not easily available in workshops or institutes outside of schools of social work.

The need for contextualization is even more urgent for students focusing on micro, direct service practice. Students more interested in this area often complain that when they go into the field they lack specialized training in a highly specific clinical or psychotherapeutic methodology. Despite a heavy emphasis on direct social service skills, even the Master of Social Work degree does not prepare students for the range of micro skills necessary to be an effective counselor, caseworker, or therapist. Here again, a vast number of excellent training courses, workshops, and institutes provide intensive training in specific micro interventions. These workshops are regularly offered in every major city. But what students gain in their social work education, unavailable in workshops outside of the university, is the contextualization of practice—the larger picture provided by an understanding of social welfare history, theory, policy, research, diverse practice alternatives, and organizational politics. It is precisely this wider base that provides the framework, perspective, and overarching knowledge upon which casework, counseling, and therapeutic skills training must rest. Contextualization differentiates the social work approach to individual problems from a purely psychological approach. Moreover, contextualization is essential to affecting both individual and social change. Anchoring study and practice—whether macro or micro—to a structural analysis of social conditions and the goal of social change is what makes social work *social*.

The contextualization of practice is what university-level social work education provides best. Indeed, one of the fundamental arguments of this book is that effective practice in a rapidly changing world demands an even greater understanding of and emphasis on contemporary macro realities. Those interested in social change must not only base their practice on such knowledge, but given their advanced training, they must also assume the task of articulating their understanding of the contemporary context to clients, community members, and to the larger society.

To some, these statements may sound elitist. Is a college education the only means for understanding the world around us? Does one have to go to a school of social work in order to be able to contextualize a problem—to understand private troubles as public issues (to paraphrase C. Wright Mills [1959])? Social work education is certainly not the only means to develop a critical perspective and knowledge of history, contemporary politics, and public life. Social movements, for example, have always been profound training grounds for activists, instructing them in both skill development, critical thinking, and an analysis of the contemporary context. But one cannot gain a critical perspective, such as the one this book offers, simply by listening to the evening news or talk show radio. Given the increasingly skewed nature of power and social activism in the United States, critical social analysis is becoming an endangered species, more and more removed from the masses of people. What we hear and know is controlled through increasingly conservative media outlets, providing most people with a narrow conceptualization of social problems, their causes, and their possible solutions. Moreover, the analysis offered by the media is further skewed by the transformation of news into entertainment. The year-long media obsession with the O. J. Simpson trial illustrates the point. After almost 30 years of territorial dispute in the Middle East, in late September of 1995, the prime minister of Israel agreed to remove troops from key West Bank towns. This story was covered only after CNN News reported on the most recent haggling in the O. J. Simpson trial.

Critical social work education, on the other hand, can function as an antidote to this social myopia. When focused on social change, social work education can be an excellent means for (1) acquiring or further developing a broad and critical understanding of the public sphere that influences almost all aspects of daily life, (2) tying this contextualization to specific skills and work, and (3) developing an ideology steeped in critical analysis, values, and theory. Taken together, these factors can turn social workers into social change agents—drum majors for social justice (Lipsitz, 1988)—and turn social work education into education for social change. The reawakening of social work to the possibilities for progressive social change is a major reason for writing this book.

PUBLIC LIFE AND THE PUBLIC GOOD

This book is organized around the theme of restoring public life and advancing a progressive vision of the public good in a world that is becoming increasingly private and anti-public. These concepts are used widely in other social science disciplines as scholars, students, and professionals grapple with how to respond to the privatizing trends of the larger society and to contemporary attacks on progressive ideas, values, programs, and policies. At the outset, these concepts must be understood in relative terms. A *progressive public good* (inclusive, democratic, and egalitarian) is juxtaposed with a *conservative public good* (exclusive, dominated by hierarchical institutional and corporate oligarchies, and vastly unequal). Of course, just as the "personal is political," private and public life are intertwined. Our increasingly private world seeks to marginalize public life and undermine the very idea of a progressive public good. In a nutshell, this book argues that social change and good social work are dependent in a "privatizing" context on the expansion of public life (the social realm), the promotion of a progressive public good, and the legitimation of a politicized social work practice and agenda that seeks to help clients, stimulate public activism, and promote the general social welfare.

Although the book's early chapters flesh out these ideas, one critical point about the concept of a public or common good is worth emphasizing. Specifically, the concepts of public life and a public good are not fixed absolutes. Public life is an ongoing debate, a dynamic and democratic process about the values and goals of society. The public good is also a process that includes diverse voices and ideas. Hence, the ideal of a common good—the existence of a single good, common for everyone—is a naïve, narrow, and potentially undemocratic conceptualization of public life. It beckons for a social life free of conflict, diversity, tension, and divergent interests. In a society as economically, racially, ethnically, and culturally stratified as the United States, in a society where so many groups have been oppressed and excluded from the common good for centuries, it is, at the least, inappropriate to call for a common good among all segments of the society. We understand how groups such as the poor, women, blacks, gay men, lesbian women, and people with disabilities, could take offense at being told to drop their special needs and claims in the interests of advancing a common good. Clearly, the idea of a common good can be employed in a conservative manner to limit diversity and democratic discourse. This book argues, instead, for an expansion of public life, an expansion of the voices participating in defining the public good, and an expansion of our understanding about how the interests of the most powerful in society conflict with the interests of the poor, working, and middle classes. Certainly it is desirable for oppositional groups to find common ground in order to gain more power and clout and to affect social change. Certainly society seems to be coming apart at the seams; that is one reason the concept of a common good seems to have such salience today among both conservatives and liberals. But the answer to contemporary problems lies not in stitching inequality and oppression back together again, but rather in discovering and addressing what is causing the fraying of the social fabric. This can best be done in a society where public life is rich, where public discourse about social problems is expansive and open to diverse opinions, and where society is committed to the improvement of conditions for all its members, not just the rich and powerful.

ORGANIZATION OF THE BOOK

Nancy Amidei, social worker and advocate, tells the story about how when she lectures at universities on the need for social change and social action, faculty pull her aside and say, "We agree with what you said in your lecture. But it's not like when you were in school. Students are just not interested in social change any more." Then students pull her aside and say, "We agree with what you said in your lecture. But it's not like when you were in school. Faculty are just not interested in social change any more." We believe that social work educators, students, and practitioners are eager for a coherent analysis of the context and prospects of social change that builds on recent scholarship and debates in other disciplines.

Before discussing further what this book is, it is important to discuss what it is not. First, this is not a book about political social work practice *per se*. Instead, it is a book about the political context of social work practice and how this context affects social change efforts.

Second, this book is not designed to provide students with a definitive, concrete set of practice skills. That objective is beyond the scope of this volume. Instead, this book primarily provides a schematic for the skills necessary to understand—and practice in—the contemporary context of social work practice. Understanding the context of practice, however, is no substitute for the skills of social work practice. Although many skills are discussed here, this book is meant to complement skills-based courses.

Third, this is not solely a macro practice textbook. Instead, it addresses the need to integrate macro and micro practice within the general venue of social work practice. *Social Work and Community in a Private World* does, however, focus on macro analysis and practice because it seeks to balance the emphasis in most contemporary social work—even in what is called "generalist" practice—on a form of decontextualized micro practice. It seeks to provide material that will help social workers link themselves and clients to a better understanding of the social nature of individual problems, to social causes, and to the possibilities of social change.

Fourth, while this book is directed at social work students and practitioners, it is not an exclusively social work book limited only to the literature and debates of the profession. The authors incorporate contemporary social and political thought from almost all of the social sciences into a framework that speaks to the concerns of social work education and social work practice. By integrating new insights from contemporary social science literature with social work knowledge and issues, the authors seek to advance a politicized and contextualized form of social work practice that can expand the public realm and social change efforts in an era hostile to both.

Last, this is not a textbook that handles all sides of issues in an "objective manner" and therefore fails to present a strong point of view. The authors argue that all social work is—and should be—political and about social change. As social worker Michael Reisch (1995) emphasized in a keynote address to the National Association of Social Workers, "If you think you are not political, guess again!" But the book's point of view is not a narrow one, given the diverse views of the authors and the wide variety of topics addressed. This volume presents an argument for rethinking social work practice and education in terms of the challenges of our contemporary context. Moreover, it seeks to do so in a lively manner. Both authors believe that, where appropriate, scholarship should be passionate, engaged, and iconoclastic.

Part One: Private World and Public Life focuses on the new context for social work and social change. Chapter 1 details the nature of the new private global context in which social work is being practiced. It emphasizes how society and our conception of it have been transformed in the past generation and how social workers must both understand and challenge the asocial aspects of the new privatism. Practicing social work in a world organized around private individuals, private spaces, and private institutions is made much more difficult as the very concept of the *social* is declining.

Chapter 2 discusses the nature of contemporary public life, which, despite much media hype, did not pass away with the 1960s. Paradoxically, the new private context produces a public life organized mainly around issues of cultural identity such as gender, race, ethnicity, and sexual orientation. Building on new social movement and postmodern theory, organizations and groups are seen as laden with potential challenges—as seeds of a multicultural, social renewal and as efforts that fragment progressive social change. The chapter concludes with directives on how to "universalize the particular" and build "unity out of diversity."

Chapter 3 offers a framework for social work education and practice based on a "critical contextualization" of contemporary life. Specifically, this critical contextualization places issues of power and the potential for social change at the heart of an analysis that interconnects daily social work practice with the dynamic structures of society. This chapter goes beyond ecological and empowerment theory and proposes a framework of contextualized practice that is integrated (combining micro and macro methods), consciously political, energized by a social change ideology, and organized as much as possible in collective settings and around collective solutions. These core concepts inform the discussion of contextualized practice that follows in the book's second half.

Part Two: Contextualizing Social Work addresses selected research, policy, community organization, and organizational knowledge and skills required for undertaking progressive social work in the 1990s and into the twenty-first century. Chapter 4 discusses the nature of social work research and how it can better serve the interests of social change rather than the abstract idea of social science objectivity or its current fascination with quantitative analysis. As such, this chapter is concerned with using social work research to promote a progressive vision of the public good. For the public good to be advanced, all social work research, including research in micro, mezzo, and macro practice, must be contextualized and politicized. Through a discussion of various research methodologies, including ethnographic, historical, and action research, a new and more politicized approach to social work research is proposed. Finally, this chapter investigates the responsibility of social work researchers and practitioners to contribute to a public discourse on social change, public life, and the social welfare of American society.

Chapter 5 discusses how social policy and the conception of the public good are political and reflect the larger struggles for social change occurring in society. As such, this chapter examines competing definitions of the pubic good and shows how these definitions have molded public policy. Also discussed is the importance of the global economy in shaping domestic policy. Last, this chapter examines the contribution the social work profession can make to the promotion of social change, public life, and a progressive public good.

Chapter 6 analyzes the value and contribution of community organization and macro practice to social workers interested in understanding and modifying contemporary public life. Moreover, the chapter emphasizes that all social work practice must be grounded in a critical contextualization, regardless of the level of intervention or the methods employed. Consequently, all forms of social work practice can help build public life and advance social change. Despite the call in the third chapter for an integrated practice approach that favors no specific method, we find that social work education and practice have increasingly marginalized community organization practice. Integrated practice often ends up leaving out macro practice, or puts it in a subordinate role. Accordingly, chapter 6 emphasizes the importance of macro practice in rebuilding social life and making it an integral component in all social work practice. The proposed objective is not only to enhance the important role of macro intervention in a contextualized practice, but to suggest the macro dimensions of a truly integrated practice that moves social work beyond its narrow current focus on a decontextualized individual and family therapy.

Chapter 7 deals with issues of organizational change. Most social workers will spend much of their careers working in organizations and agencies. Social service organizations are under severe fiscal pressures in the new contemporary context, which often leads to the "deskilling" and "deprofessionalizing" of social service work. In such a context, social workers must learn skills to best advance the interests of their clients, their own professional goals, the needs of the organization, and the advancement of social change. This Gordian knot of organizational effectiveness in a postindustrial and postmodern context is answered here in part with an argument for a form of modified unionism. While acknowledging that unions are currently out of fashion, we argue for a form of modified unionism that best represents the interests of clients and workers while at the same time advancing new demands for increased democracy and workplace participation. This chapter also addresses the objective (noted throughout the book) of putting issues of class and culture into the social change equation. At the least, the seventh chapter raises critical questions about professional careers and agency life in our contemporary context.

USING THE BOOK IN COURSES

Social Work and Community in a Private World is written primarily as a supplementary text for a wide variety of social work courses related to macro practice, social policy, research, human behavior in the social environment, and generalist practice. The utility of this book for courses in community organization and practice, social change, advocacy, policy, and research is obvious: This book is a call to contextualize all of social work in an understanding of the macro/public world. Accordingly, it offers chapters related to community organization, macro social science theory, policy, research, and organizational change to support the argument of the seminal importance of social work arenas beyond the individual and family. The book can also be used for courses in human behavior and the social environment. It focuses on new theories of social analysis about privatization, globalization, postindustrialism, and postmodernism from a social science literature with which social work students should be familiar. And it ties these theories to the practice of social work and the struggle for social justice. Finally, we hope that faculty and students in generalist practice courses find this book valuable. It is our experience that generalist practice courses often end up focusing disproportionately on micro practice models, analysis, and skills. While this book focuses most heavily on the macro side of the ledger, it presents an argument for an *integrated politicized practice*, which includes both micro and macro practice content. Because it presents an argument for a better blending of micro and macro, because it recognizes the value of generalist practice, *and* because it argues for the seminal contribution of macro content to *all* social work, *Social Work and Community in a Private World* might prove a provocative and helpful supplemental text in generalist courses seeking more balance and social justice content. We also think the book will be of use to social work educators in general, especially those interested in curricula reform, and to field instructors seeking to making connection to the macro at their field placements. No matter where the book is used, however, our strategy is to be intellectually stimulating as we acquaint readers with what we assume will be many fresh ideas, conceptualizations, and analyses. The larger goal is to advance the cause of progressive social change. In these seemingly uncharted times, we hope the book serves as a rudimentary road map for a renewed progressive social work into the twenty-first century. In a small way, we hope by focusing on the public dimension we will help put the *social* back into social work.

ACKNOWLEDGMENTS

Social Work and Community in a Private World is a mutual and cooperative public act of critical social commentary by two activist intellectuals and social work academics. As with all public life, the process of writing was a dynamic give-and-take of often similar but occasionally divergent viewpoints. The careful reader will find some differences in perspective. Robert Fisher had primary responsibility for the initial writing of the Preface and Part One; Howard Karger for Part Two and the Conclusion. Nevertheless, this is definitely a jointly authored work. This final version reflects the critical interaction between the authors. Differences in perspective are to be expected when coauthoring a book that covers the range of social work subjects from theory to practice, and from policy to research. Moreover, it is to be expected when authors deal with controversial subjects, such as contemporary social conditions, politics, public life, and a "common" good. In the end, this tension became a central strength of the book, as each author was forced to clarify and modify positions.

There are several people who deserve acknowledgment for their help in the preparation of this book. Joe Kling will find his ideas throughout the first part of the book. David Stoesz took the time to review large parts of an earlier draft of the second part of the manuscript. His comments were invaluable. David Wagner read the entire manuscript with care and precision; the book is much better for his sharp and challenging criticism. Susan Robbins also generously critiqued parts of the manuscript. The participants at the "Community Organization and New Social Movement Theory" Conference did so as well, and Cheryl Hyde helped with the book's title. Although the late Harry Specht and Mark Courtney did not review the book, their *Unfaithful Angels* provided a jumping-off point and a stylistic model from which to proceed. The Graduate School of Social Work at the University of Houston and its dean, Karen Haynes, generously gave both authors a leave of absence to complete the book. Students in SOCW 7328: Critical Issues in Political Social Work—a required course for Political Social Work students at the University of Houston's Graduate School of Social Work—read an earlier draft with few complaints and much insight.

We are also grateful to the following reviewers who read the manuscript and provided helpful suggestions: Mahasweta M. Banerjee, University of Kansas; David P. Fauri, Virginia Commonwealth University; Robert McAndrews, Salem State University; Irene Queiro-Tajalli, Indiana University; Migdalia Reyes, San Jose State University; Steven R. Rose, Louisiana State University; Jennifer R. Stucker, Eastern Washington University; David Wagner, University of Southern Maine; Marion Wagner, Indiana University; Dolores Finger Wright, Delaware State University; Daniel Weisman, Rhode Island College.

I dislike "private" acknowledgments. They make unnecessarily intimate the public act of writing nonfiction. Nevertheless, relationships and connection do matter. The personal is political, and thanks are due. Juliet shouldered a disproportionate amount of family responsibility during the writing of this book. Since then I am back to doing my share, but she and the guys—Ian and Ace—are owed a few chits. Public life is about mutual responsibility; by my making this debt public, the kids are sure to hold me accountable.

Robert Fisher

Thanks to Saul for his good-natured patience in tolerating an obsessed father. A warm thanks to the Christinks for listening to my complaining and letting me use their computer monitor. Finally, thanks to Nigel Hall, a great editor and friend, who patiently listened to my rantings and ravings.

Howard J. Karger

part **I**

Private World and Public Life

chapter 1

Social Work in a Private World

$\mathbf{T}$he world is dramatically changing, experiencing an epochal transformation equal to that of the industrial revolution of the nineteenth century. While there are really never dramatic breaks with the past—the seeds and precursors of change always rest in a prior era—much of contemporary life seems very different and detached from that of only a few decades ago. Needless to say, as the world changes, so does the context for social work. The shift to an increasing privatization of life and society—so evident in the 1980s and the 1990s throughout the globe—and the challenges and opportunities this shift poses to social workers are the focus of this chapter. This is both a difficult and important time to be a social worker. The central struggles of the new privatized world revolve around the social problems and social needs we address on a daily basis. At the very moment that social need mounts, so do attacks on the value of social work and the worth and claims of clients. This chapter argues that effective social work practice requires an understanding of the vast changes underway, a deep contextualization of contemporary social work practice.

A PRIVATE NEW WORLD

We increasingly live in a private as opposed to a public world. A public world, Ryan (1992) offers, encourages "open, inclusive, and effective deliberation about matters of common and critical concern" (p. 259). Habermas (1989) further suggests that the public represents what is open to all, as opposed to being exclusive or closed. Or the public is tied to the state, such as a public building, which is not necessarily completely open to all but does house the government and is fundamentally about "promoting the public or common welfare of its rightful members" (p. 2). The pub-

3

lic is about the creation and maintenance of society and the existence in a social world larger than one's self or one's family. Public life is life at work, at school, in communities, and through national and international citizenship. The public realm is the world of contact with acquaintances and strangers, including a broad diversity of people. It is the *social* in social work.

In a multitude of ways, the world in which social workers live and work is increasingly moving away from the public, away from the social, and towards a preoccupation with the private. This is the new and challenging context for contemporary social work. How do we practice *social* work in a world increasingly antagonistic to the public sphere? How do we create empowered public citizens in a context that increasingly values independent and autonomous private consumers, workers, and family members?

For the purposes of this book, the privatization of life has one central feature: It reflects a society highly focused on and dominated by *private individuals*, *private spaces*, and *private institutions*. These developments are certainly not new. American society has always been highly individualistic. This is the core of Lockean political theory upon which our democratic civilization rests. In the 1830s, de Tocqueville (1969) found it to be the distinguishing feature of American life, especially when compared to the more collectivistic mentality of Europe. In terms of private space, for example, most people have always preferred the comfort of their own home to that of the street. Lastly, American capitalism has always been characterized by a strong skepticism about public institutions, such as government or public welfare programs, and a preference for private institutions, such as business or private charity. Capitalism has always been the engine that drives American society. What it has done well, American society has done well. What it has done poorly, such as address the public and social needs outside the world of profit, the society has done poorly (Warner, 1968; Bellah et al., 1985). The new privatization of life, however, is occurring with faster speed and wider scope than ever before. In the past generation, an extraordinary social, political, and economic transformation dramatically accelerated and expanded the privatization process, profoundly reshaping the context in which social workers live and practice.

Private Individuals

Sociologist David Riesman wrote in *The Lonely Crowd* (1950) of the penchant of Americans to act not on goals or ideas of their own but on the commitments and passions of others. He wrote of a society becoming increasingly "other directed" rather than "inner directed." More recently, social commentators (Sennett, 1974; 1990; Lasch, 1978; Bellah et al., 1985; Bookchin, 1987; Specht & Courtney, 1994) argue the opposite. Americans, and much of the rest of the world, are becoming increasingly self-absorbed with the private and the personal. They are moving increasingly away from a concern with the larger society, away from commitment to a public life. Bellah and his associates (1985) see this vividly in the contemporary penchant for psychotherapy—the sharing of a "first language of individualism" and the goals of self-actualization—by large numbers of the citizenry across the political spectrum. Reality is explained through a lens of individual will, personal life, and personal morality. "Be all you can be" promises a recruiting poster of the United States Army, an organization that seeks to subvert the individual will of soldiers to the Army's collective goals.

Sennett (1974) and Lasch (1978) see this penchant for the personal as a retreat into narcissism. Ironically, they argue, the obsession with personal needs and wants blocks its fulfillment as people become more distanced from and less grounded in society. Elshtain (1994) proposes that contemporary versions of individualized rights erode civil society, freeing citizens from all and any ties of mutual interdependence and reciprocal obligation. Political philosopher Hannah Arendt (quoted in Sennett, 1990) argued that the retreat into the personal, what she called "the fear of making contact," reflects "a lack of the will to live in the world" (p. 135). For Arendt, public life is like the act of giving birth, taking action in a world that must not be lived simply at it was received. As society seems to become more difficult, divided, and dangerous, the increasing fear of the social world causes people to turn inward to a preoccupation with themselves and their families. But the prominence and dominance of individualist strategies and visions throughout society continually narrow attention to the personal and private. Martin and O'Connor (1989) propose that the focus on individual rights, freedom, and opportunity discourages Americans from seeing how the social context impacts their lives. The fear of difference coupled with the concern for the personal—both exaggerated in the 1980s and 1990s—turn the private domains of self and family, of private intimate matters, into the *proper* arenas and concerns of life.

If the private domain becomes *the* natural and good arena, what does that say for public life? In the past, Sennett (1974) argues, as family became the preserve for the moral and good life, the public became the site of the immoral, the place where laws of respectability were broken. The private, the personal, and the family became a refuge from the horrors of society. Prostitutes were "women of the streets." Proper women did not go out unaccompanied in public. For men, the public world became a place to rid themselves of the constraints of the private world, to "lose themselves in public" as the phrase goes. The public is nasty or exotic, but always "other." If public life is the "open, inclusive, and effective deliberation about matters of common and critical concern" (Ryan, 1992, p. 259), what comes to pass for matters of concern in a private world are personal intimate ones. Public life becomes all about private life. The more immoral the better. For an illustration of this point, one only has to watch *Oprah* or *Geraldo*, or any of the other comparable television programs that engage millions daily in the most intimate matters of personal life that pass for, or at least take the place of, public deliberation about common and critical concerns.

As public activity takes on a private familiarity, most interactions take on an ersatz air of the personal and intimate. Department store clerks say, "You all come back and visit us soon," as if they were good friends whose house you had just dropped by. Or telephone solicitors refer to you by your first name, creating a familiarity in hope of softening you to the real intent of the call. Corporations welcome new workers into their "family." The moral behavior of presidents and other elected officials is often judged not by their competence, but their suitability as a friend or family member. A general sense of the public gets lost in such a discourse.

For some, attention to the self takes the form of Twelve-Step groups, counseling sessions, yoga retreats, or marathon runs. For most in this consumerist culture the drive for self- and family fulfillment transforms individuals from public citizens into private consumers. "Shop 'til you drop." L. L. Bean is open 24 hours, seven days a week. Shopping malls become the new public spaces. Seniors use them as safe places to exercise. Teenagers see malls as "cool" (in every sense of the word) places to hang around. And for others, malls are safe meeting places that replace the function of the more vulnerable public parks. When malls first opened in the 1950s, marketing research revealed that the average length of stay was approximately 20 minutes. Now on average people remain over three hours.

To be sure, people have always been concerned with personal safety and with meeting personal material needs. Contemporary Americans are arguably not more safety or acquisition oriented than a farmer, peasant, or worker of the nineteenth century, spending much of their waking and sleeping hours thinking about health and material needs and strategies to meet them. But with the increasing availability of goods, with the increasing decline of public life, and with the increasing power of advertising, consumption has become the hallmark of society. For example, consider the amount of space most newspapers devote to ads versus news. It matters how people spend their leisure hours—much more available to workers today than to their counterparts in the nineteenth or first half of the twentieth centuries. These hours can theoretically be devoted to citizenship as well as consumption. Bookchin (1987) argues that the current definition of a "good citizen" is one "who obeys the laws, pays taxes, votes ritualistically for preselected candidates, and minds his or her own business" (p. 9)—and, we add, goes shopping religiously.

Americans live and work in a world of individuals who, in their quest for self-fulfillment and their fear of society, turn inward and away from the social, and *ipso facto*, participate in the dissipation of a sense of public life and a public good. In the privatizing context, the public spaces necessary for public life are disappearing.

Private Spaces

The turning away from public life is equally visible in the places people inhabit and their relationship to each other. Spatial arrangements matter, although people tend not to think about them, especially in social work. For example, cities are spatially structured. The nature and patterns of physical facilities such as houses, streets, shopping and work areas, or the very form of a city, its neighborhoods and suburbs, impinge directly on social life and social work. "It is of course a truism that spatial relations are necessarily social," geographer Kevin Cox (1988, p. 71) argues. Edward Soja (1985) goes further, declaring that "spatiality situates social life" (p. 90). Spatial arrangements both reflect and produce social problems and determine the feasibility of social strategies to address them.

In the new, privatized context, public space declines as private space takes over. This trend is especially serious for the poor and working class citizens excluded from the new private spaces and for social workers interested in rebuilding a sense of the public and a progressive vision of the public good. Boyte (1992) describes public spaces as "environments that are open, accessible and involve a mix of different people and groups" (p. 6). They also are spaces, like city streets or public parks and beaches, that are "owned" by the people. They have a primarily public function, for people to gather, walk, jog, play, and talk *in public*. Private spaces, conversely, are intentionally designed as limited-access, closed places that are restricted to homogenous groups. This space can include the house or apartment where one lives, or increasingly proliferating private spaces such as gated communities or shopping malls. In all private spaces, there is a desire to provide a controlled space of order and clarity, one removed from an unpredictable and complex public space. "On the most physical level," Sennett (1974) writes, the private "environment prompts people to think of the public domain as meaningless" (p. 12). Private spaces are also designed to make money—malls or suburban developments—or to provide a closed, exclusive space for the reproduction of class relations, such as a restricted country club.

The decline of public space, or at least the ongoing tension in a capitalist society between public and private space, is not new. The United States, like most capitalist nations, appropriates space primarily as a private commodity. Parks, space for public buildings like libraries and schools, open "commons" for citizens are expensive *and* produce no income. They sell nothing; they must be supported by public taxation, by the people for the public good. City streets and sidewalks, historically, were the most basic unit of public space. Walking is a most public of acts. With the invention of the automobile, one of the most private means of transportation, the city street was transformed from a public milieu to an "artery" for motion. Walking in public becomes an anachronism. As the automobile has come to dominate American life, so has the detachment people feel to the milieus they travel through. "One ceases to believe one's surrounding have any meaning save as a means toward the end of one's own motion" (Sennett, 1974, p. 15).

To the extent that the environment has meaning beyond being a thoroughfare, it usually beckons fear, danger, or distaste. Office workers in Houston, Dallas, and Montreal, for example, walk downtown from one corporate structure to another in the privacy and protection of an underground tunnel system connecting the "fortified cells of affluence" in which they work (Davis, 1992, p. 155). The tunnels are the new public spaces, where people interact, shop, and eat on their lunch hours. Owned by private firms, they are closed to city problems and citizens of the street. They are not public spaces. New private spaces keep "street people" and diversity out; controlled private spaces sacrifice diversity and real public interaction. Sidewalks, parks, even libraries are left to the poor and the marginalized.

Judd (1994) argues that "the enclosure of commercial and residential space is becoming a defining and ubiquitous feature of American cities" (p. 2). Increasingly, enclosed private spaces replace older, open public space throughout our cities. Shopping malls, walled and gated communities, skyscrapers that turn away from the city streets—these are the spaces in which people increasingly work, live, and play. They offer safe havens and guarded spaces in an unfriendly world. Security is important to the new private spaces. Witness the proliferation of private police patrols in neighborhoods that can afford them, electronic security systems for houses and cars, and gated communities with police attendants. But fear proves itself omnipresent. Surveys show that suburbanites in Milwaukee are as frightened of violent crime as those living in the inner city of Washington, where the level of mayhem is 20 times greater (Davis, 1992).

People who once lived in relatively densely settled cities have left them for more private suburbs. They live and work in areas characterized by freeways, shopping malls, detached single family housing, and postindustrial business areas devoted primarily to finance, banking, and information processing. They enter the city only occasionally, pay little or no taxes to it, and are free of its political control. What used to be a nation of city dwellers is now a nation of suburbanites. Cities, the areas most affected by social problems and in need of social change, are avoided and ignored. "Are cities dead?" became the Nietzchean-like question of the early 1990s. More than half of commuting trips in the contemporary metropolis are suburb to suburb rather than suburb to central city. And even those who work in or occasionally visit the central city for an opera or symphony, do so under the sealed protection of automobiles, underground parking garages, and tight security (cited in Kling, 1993, p. 37). This "disaggregation" of space spreads life outward with a centrifugal force that removes concern with the urban center and with those who remain there. Mike Davis (1992) captures the condition brilliantly in his book on Los Angeles:

> In Los Angeles, once-upon-a-time a demi-paradise of free beaches, luxurious parks, and "cruising strips," genuinely democratic space is all but extinct. The Oz-like archipelago of Westside pleasure domes—a continuum of tony malls, arts centers and gourmet strips—is reciprocally dependent upon the social imprisonment of the third-world service proletariat who live in increasingly repressive ghettoes and barrios. In a city of several million yearning immigrants, public amenities are radically shrinking, parks are becoming derelict and beaches more segregated, libraries and playgrounds are closing, youth congregations of ordinary kinds are banned, and the streets are becoming more desolate and dangerous. (p. 227)

The private spaces focused on selling products must mask "the authoritarian control characteristic of enclosed, privatized space" (Judd, 1994, p. 2) by packaging themselves as their exact opposites. As a result, private malls simulate city life beyond their walls, creating "an analogous city" inside a "sealed realm" (Boddy, 1992, p. 125). They become "authentic reproductions" of old city marketplaces without the messiness, diversity, and public interactions of real public space: carnivals without the spontaneity, history without pain or struggle, public life packaged for private spaces. For developers, these enclosed malls provide a degree of security, surveillance, pedestrian flow, and climate control not possible outdoors. Citizens are transformed into happy, safe consumers, as long as they refrain from acting in a manner deemed unfavorable to the conducting of business. Despite their public appearance, these are, after all, private spaces, designed and controlled by corporations for the express purpose of making money.

The same is true for gated communities, which offer people a sanitized, historical version of community. Or for suburbs in general, which historically provided an escape from the problems of urban life and substituted private for public space: lawns for public parks, backyards for city streets, and malls for downtowns. "Like the suburban house, which rejected the sociability of front porches and sidewalks for private backyards, the malls looked inward, turning their back on the public street" (Crawford, 1992, p. 21). Increasingly, Sorkin (1992) writes, people live in ageographical spaces, cities and towns and neighborhoods that all look and seem the same. They live with increasingly loosened ties to any specific space. These "analogous" spaces are similar to television in their structure. Television homogenizes difference, provides a conceptual grid of boundless reach in which all combinations make sense. It makes a coherent view of the social order difficult to picture, just as it blends all of this difference together. Skyscrapers, houses, factories, enclosed and strip malls seem almost to float in a non-place, urban realm. A universal sameness of place occurs. Plasticized strip malls, the ubiquitous fast food eating places, and franchise capitalism provide an interchangeable, departicularized reality all over America (Sorkin, 1992).

The more time people spend watching television in the "privacy" of their living rooms, driving in private cars, talking into cellular phones, communicating through electronic mail, and living in "detached" housing and independent living spaces, the more they fall prey to the domination of private space. Contrary to the belief that new communication inventions such as electronic mail and the Internet foster a public communication hitherto unknown, these technologies actually involve private acts done in the privacy of a home or office. Users of these systems choose the people with whom they "interact." Ultimately, it is a highly private form of potentially public communication. There are good reasons why many prefer the new private spaces and lifestyles. But there are costs as well, not only for those left out and kept out of the skyscrapers, atrium hotels, malls, affluent suburbs, and computer networks, but also for the millions who feel cut adrift from a sense of community and bereft of connection to a social world whose very nature transcends, and thereby adds to, individual life.

Sorkin (1992) proposes three central components of the new private spaces that dominate contemporary life. First, there is a loosening of all ties to specific space. The new private spaces replace delight in specific places with universal sameness. Second, there is an obsession with security. New levels of manipulation and surveillance over the citizenry proliferate with new modes of segregation, and the citizenry increasingly adopts new modes of security and protection. Space becomes fortressed, whether at work in a multinational tower or at home. Third, private space becomes one of simulations. New shopping areas often idealize the past, simultaneously asserting connection with a past city life they are helping to obliterate. Like advertising, they create an image while being absolutely oblivious to the real needs and traditions of inhabitants.

However, as people remove themselves from public life, as they are distanced from the real public, they lose what is vital—the social mix and the surprises of democratic space—the very things that gave city life its human connection. Public urban life requires physical proximity and democratic public realms. Public space affords the unique opportunity to grapple with difference. With less public space, people find a highly limited discourse in the new privatized spaces, limited in both range of vision and variety of participants. The divided city—separated by class, race, ethnicity, and neighborhoods—has always posed extraordinary challenges to its inhabitants and to those social activists who wanted to change it. As space becomes more privatized, the gulf deepens and *social* life declines.

Private Institutions

One of the most significant international developments in the 1980s and early 1990s has been the rise of the "privatization" strategy. As a result of pressures from profound economic and social changes that began in the early 1970s, the very idea of public social programs, not to mention the socialist or welfare state, was delegitimized. In the Reagan-Bush era especially, but continuing in the United States into the 1990s, "big government" became *the* problem. Neoconservatives and, to a lesser extent, neoliberals sought to dismantle the welfare state as much as possible (Piven & Cloward, 1982). A highly publicized example of this trend was found in New York City under former Mayor Ed Koch. Margaret Thatcher's efforts at privatization in Britain and Helmut Kohl's attempts to dismantle the social democratic welfare state in the Federal Republic of Germany symbolize this phenomenon in Western Europe (Barnekov, Boyle, & Rich, 1989). More recently, privatization is nowhere more in evidence than in Eastern and Central Europe, where nations are being pushed into a form of "shock therapy" capitalism that includes the nearly complete dismantling of the state and the termination of crucial, public sector social supports for citizens. This same phenomenon exists in Sub-Saharan Africa, where the combination of drought and the demands for economic reforms made by the International Monetary Fund (IMF) and the World Bank have pushed whole populations to the brink of starvation (Karger, 1995).

The argument is that in the new global economy, nations cannot afford costly social programs. The intent of "privatization" is to dismantle the state as much as possible to reduce "social costs" on the corporate sector and the affluent, those, in theory, responsible for stimulating the economy. If nations do not adopt such policies, if capitalism is not "unbridled," then investments will supposedly go elsewhere. These are clear strictures from the World Bank, the IMF, and global corporate investors. Not only in the United States and Europe, but in Asia, Africa, and South America, the context of privatization forces almost all social and political agendas away from social welfare conceptualizations toward laissez-faire, capitalist ones.

This strategy for "survival in the global economy" has swept across the globe, dominating not only national policy but local, urban options as well. Adopted early on by "sunbelt" cities such as Houston, Texas, this trend has emerged in most

American cities, formerly social democratic cities in Western Europe, formerly communist cities in Eastern Europe, and third-world cities. Accordingly, neoconservative politics and, to a somewhat lesser extent, neoliberal agendas seek to return cities to a "golden age of free enterprise." Social problems are ignored as much as possible as new business agendas of unfettered capitalism come to dominate global, national, and local decisionmaking. Cities as disparate as New York, Cleveland, London, and Vienna reprivatize by cutting public programs, turning public programs over to for-profit, private interests, and by ignoring festering social needs (Fisher & Kling, 1994). The problem of worsening poverty in the United States, for example, is deemed unsolvable; it is labeled the product of an "underclass" subculture and blamed on the victims of poverty and government programs.

Privatization refers not only to transferring governmental operations and roles over to business, but also to the reorientation of political, social, economic, and cultural institutions to corporate needs, values, goals, and leaders. Barnekov et al. (1989) propose that privatization "reflects a general policy orientation rather than a finite set of policy alternatives" (p. 4). This policy direction contains four key elements. First, priority is placed on economic considerations in almost all aspects of domestic activity. Second, wherever possible private markets are preferred over public policies in terms of allocative social choices. Third, if public intervention is deemed necessary, it must supplement private market processes and include maximum private sector participation. Fourth, public programs are expected to be modeled on the methods of private sector businesses.

Given the pressures of transnational capital, applause for the privatization strategy dominates the global discourse. As Paul Starr (1987) put it, "Some supporters tout privatization as a sovereign cure for virtually all ailments of the body politic. They prescribe it as a tonic for efficiency and economic growth, an appetite suppressant for the federal budget, a vaccine against bureaucratic empire-building, and a booster for individual freedom, including the opportunities of disadvantaged minorities" (p. 1). E. S. Savas, former assistant secretary of Housing and Urban Development in the Reagan years, both reflects and helped create this attitude. For Savas (1987), "privatization is the key to both limited and better government: limited in its size, scope, and power relative to society's other institutions; and better in that society's needs are satisfied more efficiently, effectively, and equitably" (p. 288).

Under such a framework, government becomes the problem, and champions of social programs become the enemy. Why are the poor impoverished? Because government programs create dependency (Murray, 1984). Why is the American economy in its third decade of economic crisis? Because government taxation increases the national debt by destroying entrepreneurial incentive and risk taking (Gilder, 1981). Why are key American corporations not more competitive in the global economy? Because government regulations foist unrealistic and costly programs on the backs of business (Friedman, 1962; Gilder, 1981). Public schools, the U.S. Post Office, and most public social services, especially those directed at providing income support for the poor, are all said to be not only ineffective but wrongheaded. The public sector and advocates of allocative programs are seen as doing more harm than good.

In fact, there is more than a grain of truth in some of these suppositions. Government defense expenditures in the 1980s did dramatically increase the federal debt. Bureaucracies can be autocratic and inefficient, whether they are public or private. But the argument for privatization conveniently forgets the different missions and roles of the public and private sectors. The mission of the public sector is to serve the public good, the general welfare. This is why elected officials are sometimes called "public servants." The public sector is the primary sector of a polity that has some resources to affect significant social change, and at least in theory, has the mission to do so. The private sector has a very different mission. It is designed to make profits, not address social problems. Unlike the public sector, it is not accountable to the citizenry and is responsible only to investors and stockholders. How can corporations be expected to address social problems in a highly competitive economy in which they are under severe economic pressure to restructure and downsize their operations? Social policy and programs are not the business of the private sector.

But the argument for dismantling the public sector and turning problems over to the private and voluntary sector was, and remains, a ruse. This strategy is fundamentally a political rationale for shedding government's social responsibility, decreasing taxes on the wealthy and powerful, selling off valuable state-owned industries or land, and deregulating trade and investment. Ultimately, such policies have a corrosive effect on public life and the very fabric of society. Problems in the privatized context mount, unattended and unaddressed. For those with fewer resources, opportunities to address the problems decline. Instead, they see a diminution of jobs that pay living wages to the unskilled; a shortage of adequate and sufficient housing for the working class, working class poor, and homeless; less available and adequate public services in the areas of health, education, and welfare; and a declining sense of safety and security in the streets (Fisher & Kling, 1994).

In the new, fee-for-service political economy, those who have the money to pay for quality services from private sources—whether it is private schools, private security systems, or private health care—are among the fortunate. People who must rely on the public are told that the public sector is being "restructured," and no longer has the resources to address such problems. Moreover, it no longer has the legitimacy. Such activity by public institutions is now deemed inappropriate. Recipients of public services, including the middle class, get less and less for more and more tax money. For vivid examples, one need only look at public schools or the continuing cuts in social welfare programs. These areas are not the primary or even secondary concern of the corporate designers of the privatization strategy. Profits and elite jobs come first. In the short run, this is good business policy—that is, cutting costs and regulations in order to maximize profits. In the long run, and more importantly, as social or public policy, it is absurd. What is startling is how effective the arguments for the privatization of institutions have been; they have become global common sense despite their obviously destructive aspects.

The lessons of history are clear. After the debacles of unregulated capitalism in the late nineteenth century and the 1920s, expansion of the public sector was required to clean up the social problems, curb the excesses of capitalist profiteering, and relegitimize the system (Fisher, 1994). Public sector programs have always played both an accumulation and legitimation function in capitalist economies (O'Connor, 1973). They help businesses accumulate capital in the form of government subsidies and supports, such as land grants, tax breaks, and defense contracts. They help legitimate the system through education and social programs, and through helping preserve order and harmony.

More recent scholarship on the role of the state (Gough, 1979; Piven & Cloward, 1982) argues that public programs are not simply handed down from above to pacify the masses and legitimate inequality. Social programs are also the victories of social movements and citizen resistance, programs that reflect the needs and demands of the powerless. The Wagner Act of 1935, which gave workers the right to collective bargaining, or the Voting Rights Act of 1965, which outlawed barriers to participation in the electoral process, demonstrate not simply the legitimation function at work, but a public sector whose policies were determined by the needs and demands of ordinary people, such as industrial workers and civil rights activists, organizing at the grassroots. Social policy can reflect democratic social struggle at work.

In the past, when either unbridled capital became excessively disruptive of society—controlling stock markets or the price of gold for the benefit of a few individuals—or when these excesses spawned mass disorder—deep divisions and conflicts with industrial workers—then new and more social democratic regimes came to power to address the instability and rising social problems. For example, throughout modern history, local traditions, culture, political leaders and resistances have tempered the free market capitalist city. Corporate liberal strategies of the early twentieth century, as exemplified in the National Civic Federation, sought to ameliorate the conflicts inherent in capital-labor relations. New York City, for example, modestly expanded the public sector, adopted public and social planning, enacted rent controls, and implemented public regulation of "the private search for wealth." Zoning, comprehensive urban plans, public parks, tenement housing codes, rent control, children's labor laws, and protective services were the progressive hallmarks of the day. In Western Europe, "Red Vienna" of the 1920s established a thorough system of social democratic policies and services to end decades of pain endured by workers lacking adequate housing, health care, and social services.

Over the course of the next few decades, most cities in Europe and, to a lesser extent, in the United States used state action to modify the impact of the private market. Pushed by grassroots resistance and political leaders, first in the 1930s and then in the 1960s, American governments at the national and local levels began to expand the planning and regulatory roles of the public sector and, in a limited way, responded to social justice inequities. By the early 1970s most nation-states and great cities of Western Europe and the United States remained fundamentally engines of capital. But throughout the Western industrial democracies, there was an active public sector, representing the contemporary struggle between the powerless and the powerful, between the interests of citizens and capital. The current proliferation and widespread acceptance of the privatization of government and institutions, which seeks to undo most of the progressive and hard-earned victories of the past two generations, illustrates the dominant position of conservative elites in the 1980s and early 1990s and the weak position of oppositional efforts. The affluent, powerful, and rightwing have been handily winning the social struggle of the past 20 years.

Later in this chapter, the authors will discuss the implications for social work of the increasing privatization of life: how the increase in individualism, private space, and the privatization of public institutions and services affects the practice of social work and the making of social change. But first, it is important to turn this discussion of the contemporary context of social work to the globalization of capital—the root of the new, privatized context, the reason why social struggle is now lopsided, and why practicing good social work is so difficult.

GLOBALIZATION: ECONOMIC DISTANCING FROM THE SOCIAL

The global order is currently undergoing an economic transformation not seen since the industrial revolution of the nineteenth century. While it is still unclear how this transformation will evolve, the first phase has pointed to a shift from an industrial to a postindustrial or information economy, a dramatic centralization of power worldwide among global corporations, an accelerating impoverishment of those people and regions of the world that do not fit into the upper echelons of the global economic restructuring, and a marked opposition to both the public sector and social matters.

The more obvious effects of the global political economy began in 1973 on the heels of the Organization of Petroleum Exporting Countries (OPEC) oil embargo and the impending defeat of the United States in Vietnam. Before 1973, the global order was relatively stable, dominated politically and economically by the United States. The period after World War II was to be, Henry Luce said, the beginning of the "American century" (quoted in Barnet, 1994). The booming and dominating American economy of the postwar era was able to triple the median family income between 1950 and 1970 (Barnet, 1994). However, the economic growth of the unchallenged American empire lasted less than a generation.

Around 1973, a number of factors coalesced to trigger the new, global political economy. For one, the OPEC embargo stalled the American economy. Second, the end of the Vietnam war vividly underscored the long-term drain of military expenditures on productive investment. As a consequence, the United States went off the fixed exchange rate of the gold standard. All of these factors occurred in a context of rising global economic competition and precipitated a crisis in capitalism of global proportions. Economic growth rates, corporate profits, and manufacturing fell off dramatically in almost every Western industrialized nation. To address the decline in profits that lay ahead for U.S. corporations, business leaders argued that a new political economy of unbridled capitalism needed to be introduced, one that minimized government regulation, lowered social expenditures, and negated the compromises made with labor unions since the 1930s. The era ahead was clearly going to be difficult for American business. If sacrifices were to be made, the members of the elite Business Roundtable proposed, they should not be made by those at the top of society. Profits and corporate salaries, the highest in the world, should not be cut. They proposed, instead, that the social welfare obligations of society needed to be curtailed to allow American businesses to compete more effectively worldwide (Fisher, 1994). This strategy, also known as economic restructuring or globalization, would soon become the ground rules for all nations and localities (Brecher, Childs, & Cutler, 1993; Brecher & Costello, 1994).

Globalization is not only a political response to economic changes; it also represents a dramatic shift in technology and information processing. As such, it embodies a new postindustrial context and a shift from an economy of industrial goods production to one of service production. Moreover, globalization entails the transformation of social life through computer and telecommunication innovations. Technological breakthroughs in transportation and communication alter the nature of work and the skills needed for employment in the high-technology, service economy. Because of these changes, the velocity of capital has increased exponentially in the new global economy, moving from investment sites through electronic mail, seemingly in the blink of an eye. In response, cities had to restructure, as downtowns withered and factory towns collapsed due to deindustrialization (Logan & Swanstrom, 1990). Businesses also had to restructure, through "downsizing" or some other euphemism. The results of this corporate strategy were the undermining of labor unions, the large-scale layoff of workers, and various other means of cost-cutting necessary to maximize profits in the new world economic order. The central issue for society became economic survival. A nation or city would be measured not by the quality of life it provided for its citizens or its commitment to promoting the social good, but by how it could cut costs to make it more attractive as an economic investment site for business.

"Privatization around family, status, and consumption produces its own distinctive politics: one which is antithetical to the solidarities of class and long-term commitments, and more amenable to the opportunism and search for the immediate 'fix' which capitalist interests have always found so congenial and easy to exploit" (Cox, 1988, p. 62). This philosophy fits with the 15-year lifespan of what used to be called "buildings" but now are "stores" on strips and at strip mall centers. This philosophy also fits with attitudes toward social problems and those in need. Whatever is quick, simple, easy, and least costly, is what will be done. This "free-enterprise" strategy, which foisted on the world global inequality and the centralization of capital, continues to increase dramatically.

The velocity of capital traveling though computerized systems transcends physical space, loosening capital investment from obligations and ties to communities and locales. Sandel (1988) argues that privatization ignores the "corrosive" affects of capitalism. Unrestrained capital mobility not only ignores the social, it disrupts community. Power rests in corporations unaccountable to society (Lasch, 1991). Not only has capital become distanced from the social, it has become almost unchained by government, even at the national level. The increased mobility of capital and the new types of international investment transcend the nation-state, eroding its power to control economic, let alone social, matters (Brecher, Childs, & Cutler, 1993). Stateless corporations, some of them with economies that rival the GNP of important countries, force nations to compete with each other for their business. Like the private ageographical spaces discussed earlier, these are corporations without ties to place. Of course, corporations are not as mobile as capital since physical moves remain expensive. Place matters somewhat to corporate investors. Nevertheless, as Martin Davis, former chairperson of Paramount Communications, put it: "You can't be emotionally bound to any particular asset" (Barnet, 1994, p. 754).

What this ultimately means is a near-complete distancing from the *social* at the very moment that these global entities are responsible for so much social change and damage worldwide. Economic globalization demands accelerated joblessness, declining tax bases, and the adoption of economic objectives over social ones and corporate over public needs. This strategy of global privatization ignores festering social and urban problems, which now, like almost everything else, are left to the so-called "marketplace." It represents the turning back of the oppositional movements and claims of the 1960s, deemed as too costly and as impediments to the shift in priorities of global capitalism. The new political economy that developed after 1973 was partially a catching-up to the economic and technological trends that had been in play since the 1950s, but which had not been felt because the cold war had proved so profitable. Politically, the strategy of global privatization represents not only an effort to promote a corporate and rightwing agenda, but relatedly, to delegitimate and defund progressive social change and proponents of social welfare programs (Starr, 1987).

At this stage, globalization is primarily the massing of private power on a global level. The concentration of wealth so evident in the United States in the 1980s and 1990s reflects worldwide economic trends. In response to the global changes discussed above, the new reality is characterized by heightened poverty throughout the globe, and a growing inequality between the winners and losers in the global transformation—the super rich and the trapped poor. As stateless megacompanies "search the world for bargain labor, sell their stock on exchanges from London to Hong Kong, and pin more and more of their hopes on customers in the emerging markets, most of them in Asia, they are walking away from the enormous public problems their private decisions create for American society" (Barnet, 1994, p. 754).

Curiously, as capital and power centralize in the new global economy, the function of both implementing its tasks and cleaning up its mess are increasingly decentralized, leading, paradoxically, to significant new forms of public life. Voluntary-sector social efforts proliferate worldwide to address problems as diverse as ecological disasters, inadequate public education, crime prevention, and AIDS. Total Quality Management (TQM) strategies spread in the workplace, part of the effort to decentralize decisionmaking around work strategies and performance. Public schools increasingly have site autonomy to develop participatory decisional structures that include administrators, teachers, parents, and business representatives. The voluntary sector expands exponentially, helping to address the needs of society through multitudinous nonprofit grassroots efforts. This proliferation is a mixed blessing, for while the tasks in the new global economy are handled on a more decentralized basis, power to make the essential decisions regarding the allocation of resources and organizational objectives is increasingly centralized. "Decentralization of production" accompanies "concentration of control" (Montgomery, 1995, p. 461).

Global capital devastates communities while it forces people back into them as a first line of coping and resistance to external economic forces. At first glance, community-based and voluntary-sector efforts seem to replicate the globalization strategy to centralize power and decentralize task structures. But grassroots efforts may yet prove the best means for meeting the challenges of contemporary privatization. They may be the seeds of resistance to the anti-social perspective and provide necessary opportunities for a public life in which people come to understand the value of a *public* good and *social* life. But such success will only occur if the communities people create tie their efforts to broader issues of economic and social change.

THE PROSPECT FOR SOCIAL CHANGE

It is difficult to wax optimistic about the prospects of social change in the contemporary context. Certainly the privatized trajectory of the postindustrial global reality has been set. Whether it continues is another matter. The concluding part to this chapter examines some of the barriers and opportunities within the contemporary context for social workers interested in social change.

First, the dominant discourse of individualism clearly makes social change and all collective efforts more difficult. Bellah et al. (1985) propose that the middle class can only talk in terms of individualistic achievement and self-fulfillment. Because Americans increasingly lack a language for the collective and community, people find it difficult to maintain commitment to others, either in a public sphere or in intimate relationships (Bellah et al., 1991). Even when people tend to form community, they often do so around discussion of personal needs (Twelve-Step groups) and personal salvation (churches). To the extent that discourse and language remain focused on individuals, so do discussions of problems and solutions. Witness contemporary debates about the nature of problems such as poverty, homelessness, AIDS, and so forth. When government is not being blamed, the victims are for their alleged individual shortcomings. They are lazy, unintelligent, mentally unstable, promiscuous, or simply tied to a deviant culture (underclass, homosexual, homeless, etc.). The discourse of individualizing problems dominates most contemporary debates and is functional for the agenda of global privatization, since if problems are individual in nature, then so must be the cures. Government programs, collective social policy, and social expenditures are dubbed the source of problems, certainly not the solution. In short, no social problems would exist if each person with a problem solved it individually.

Social work practice and education mirror this development, posing a barrier within as well as outside the profession. As Specht and Courtney (1994) (building on the work of Bellah, Lasch, and others) argue, the emphasis on the psychoanalytic and therapeutic in social work practice and education distances it from the immediate social world. Individualistic processes of counseling and therapy, individualized diagnoses of pathologies, and individual-based strategies for solving problems all perpetuate the individualistic trend and distance clients from the collective social world. Accordingly, students often come to schools of social work with primary training in psychology. Many want to be private practitioners, distanced from the poor and the public bureaucratic work of a welfare office or child protective services. They want to work with clients like themselves: middle class people who have insurance and can pay for private services. Public work looks more risky and less attractive. Students steer clear of courses or programs in community organization or macro practice, because at the least these avenues offer fewer professional opportunities. But to the extent that social work professionals also shun the public and retreat into the private, then the very work of *social* work is further devalued, delegitimized, and ridiculed.

Second, privatized and scattered spaces make building social and public solidarities more difficult. Community life has always been important as an assumed base of support for social work clients. Economic restructuring, more aptly labelled "destructuring," shatters community life and networks of social supports. Working with people who have little connection to the larger society makes social work more difficult. For social workers interested in community organizing, trying to organize in the private spaces of suburbia or shopping malls is not the same as organizing in working class neighborhoods or on the city streets of the past. People are not out there to be helped; they are inside private spaces and protected from the extant social world.

Moreover, as space disaggregates and people are separated by larger distances, the simple act of trying to bring people together physically to build a sense of public life is made much harder. To the extent that citizens and space are reduced to their market function—citizens become economic men and women, city space becomes shopping centers—the struggle to redefine citizenship in terms of social responsibility becomes more difficult. The decline of attachment to specific space (e.g., a neighborhood) and the geographic hypermobility of the population further contribute to a decrease in the sense of social ownership and public responsibility. Even the most basic ecological theories popular in social work observe that clients need a connection to their environment. Helping clients, not to mention building solidarity with them and promoting social change, has always been difficult work. As the environment becomes more dominated by others for private purposes and less known by both social workers and their clients, social work becomes even more challenging than before.

Third, the decline and delegitimization of the public sector, that is, the undermining of people's sense of the proper and important role of government in American life, pushes discourse on problems and solutions into an asocial focus on the individual and the family. Moreover, the decline and delegitimization of government forces social workers to rely on private funders for resources and promotes private solutions to serious public problems. In part, this reliance is based on the direct relationship in the United States between public sector social programs and private sector financial support for social welfare efforts (Wolch, 1990; Salamon, 1989). In those areas with more social democratic cultures, such as New York City, charity giving is also higher. In the United States, the liberal culture of public social responsibility tends to encourage more, not less, civic activism and support. Former President George Bush's concept of a "1,000 Points of Light" rests on the belief that the private sector will pick up the social responsibilities of a declining public sector. Bush's assumption was that private charities, such as the United Way and voluntary food banks, will simply replace public programs. They will not. In periods of economic contraction, when assistance is needed the most, charity giving is among the first things to decline. This occurred in the Great Depression and in the recession of the 1980s (Karger & Stoesz, 1994).

Equally challenging for social workers is the belief that private programs will solve social problems. It is clear that the private sector does not have the funds at its disposal, given its responsibility to its stockholders rather than the homeless or the unemployed, to address social problems in more than a token way. Schram (1993) argues that the penchant for private charity produced a mentality of "welfare by the bag." Widespread collective problems like homelessness and hunger are expected to be addressed by private individuals giving a can of tuna fish or beans, producing a bag of goods to tide over the alms recipient. Moreover, the very idea that government is the problem and the marketplace is the solution to social problems poses perhaps the greatest barrier to the mission of social work and social change. This policy is not only harmful in its failure to address social problems, it undermines democracy. Proponents of privatization argue that getting government off people's backs enhances democracy. The dismantling of the public sector in the United States, however, simply makes it more difficult for people to hold politicians and leaders accountable. Where can citizens go in a privatized context to make claims and demands or to engage in democratic debate? Suffice it to say that the barriers posed to democracy by the privatization of social life and institutions have harmful consequences ultimately to democratic citizenship throughout the world.

Globalization also creates worldwide pressures for the adoption of strategies of consensus and moderation and the rejection of conflict options. The argument is that for localities to be competitive in the global economy, social costs, such as protests or strikes, must be minimized. To polish its image and affect public life, business seeks to create partnerships, especially in the area of charitable giving. For social workers and agencies experiencing a decline in public funding, forming partnerships with those who have at least some resources becomes critical. Strategies of moderation and consensus ensue. No "rubbing raw people's resentments," as Saul Alinsky once proposed. The goal is to work together for the good of the whole. Working together now means focusing on community economic development instead of social action, for example, and working with banks and absentee landlords instead of targeting them. Moreover, the consensus line must be toed even by those who understand that the good of the whole is not what brings most businesses into partnership with social service agencies. Conflict and protest are relegated to being inappropriate icons of 1960s radicalism. By limiting the strategy options of social workers and their clients, funders profoundly influence their ability to effect social change. New "partners" may be willing to support "worthy" mainstream organizations, such as the Red Cross or the American Cancer Society, but be uninterested in "unworthy" welfare mothers or a Latino gay advocacy community center.

To the extent that the public debate on issues remains on the right, that is, focused on discussions on whether to revive orphanages, cut taxes for the rich, resume the ownership of semiautomatic weapons, and eliminate welfare programs and publicly funded television and the arts, then it is difficult to raise more progressive issues of interest to social workers and the people with whom they work. Having the political discourse stuck on the political right undermines the mission of social work and the goals of social change. Meanwhile, problems worsen and programs falter, which only contributes further to public suspicion of governmental efforts.

CONCLUSION

The goal of this book is to help contextualize contemporary social work and thereby assist social workers to become more effective agents of social change. This opening chapter has presented a bleak picture of the contemporary global context. Some of it may seem overstated. But our emphasis is intended to ensure that the difficulties ahead for social workers are understood fully and not minimized. That said, much of the rest of the book is about refashioning the social realm, meeting the challenges of privatization, redefining citizenship in terms of social responsibility, and expanding public life to include new, diverse voices throughout the globe.

This chapter therefore concludes with one essential opening for social change in the contemporary context (every context produces its own contradictions, which lead to new forms of social activism). *Domination is not permanent.* No ideology or group dominates forever or without challenge. As Eley puts it: "[hegemony] is not a fixed and immutable condition . . . but is an institutionally negotiable process in which the social and political forces of context, breakdown and transformation are constantly in play" (Eley, 1992, p. 323). While the contemporary global economy and its attendant strategy of privatization seem omnipotent, history teaches social change agents to know better. The Progressive Era of the early twentieth century, which gave birth to the first social work efforts, emerged from the conflicts and debates of a Gilded Age, tied like our own to laissez-faire capitalist economics and social-Darwinist social policy. The 1890s was a mean decade in American history; the period from 1900 to 1914, while limited in its achievement, was one of broad enlightenment and progressive fervor in comparison. More recently, the civil rights movement and the revolutionary spirit of the 1960s followed directly on the heels of McCarthyism and the fervent conservatism of the 1950s. With struggle and leadership, the *fin-de-siecle* context of the 1990s and beyond can also be altered.

Globalization, after all, is a two-way street. The push to a more private world includes its own contradictions and produces new forms of public life to voice new claims and address unattended problems. Public life seems in dramatic decline, but it is widely evident in the varied grassroots efforts produced by the contradictions of the new private context. Of course, the centralization of capital and the decentralization of opposition are, at present, a great mismatch. But the proliferation of grassroots struggles worldwide poses the potential to challenge the antisocial aspects of globalization and privatization on both the local and global level. This is especially true since globalization pushes people back into communities, the arenas where social workers do their best work. Manuel Castells (1983) insists that societies are not made up of "passive subjects resigned to structural domination. . . . People have affirmed their cultural identity, often in territorial terms, mobilizing to achieve their demands, organizing their communities, and staking out their places to preserve meaning, to restore whatever limited control they can over work and residence. . . ." (p. 350). These communities, Sara Evans and Harry Boyte (1986) argue, serve as free spaces of social change. These free spaces can become the sites of not only delivering services and building community, but also of challenging the global order. This process, of course, is difficult and not inevitable. Grassroots resistance must meet some serious challenges of its own, as discussed in the next chapter. One such challenge is the need to globalize grassroots connections, in transnational organizations such as Greenpeace and Amnesty International. Brecher and Costello (1994) call this building of global social change organizations and networks the "Lilliput Strategy." They argue that globalization is not a *fait accompli*, a done deal. The continued domination by those in power and the perpetual immiseration of most of the world's people at their hands can be altered on a global scale. What is needed is a globalization of the grassroots.

Social work can be at the center of contemporary social change. The current onslaught and the reaction against the social realm place the conflict over social service issues and the social welfare state at center stage. The daily issues and problems faced by social workers become in this new context the primary ones being debated in Washington and in state capitals. It is the central core of the truly public issues discussed on the evening news and talk show radio. These issues must also become the basis of contemporary social change. In such efforts, the skills and knowledge of social workers become not only critical but increasingly valued by those fighting for a more public and equitable society. The new private context politicizes social problems and all aspects of social work as perhaps never before, giving those who take up the challenge opportunity for significant leadership as social change agents, whether working as caseworkers, counselors, community organizers, or politicians.

Before becoming secretary of labor in the Clinton administration, Robert Reich (1983) suggested in *The Next American Frontier* that the economic decisions being made for the new global economy were really political choices entailed in the economic transformation. Leadership into the twenty-first century must devote itself, Reich (1983) wrote, "to helping our citizens perceive the consequence of public choices about economic change and to hold accountable those who make these choices in the first instance" (p. 275). This is a first step in understanding the contemporary context of social work, social problems, and social change. Doing social work around that understanding is the next step. The second chapter will address the nature and potential of contemporary public life, broadening the context to include not only things being done to social workers and their clients, but also examples and opportunities for social change.

chapter **2**

Building Public Life:
Theory and Practice[1]

The rebuilding of the social world begins with debunking myths about public life, understanding the variety of ways people build public life in the contemporary private world, and analyzing why these efforts succeed and fail. Current grassroots social work and citizen activism reflect and resist the new and increasingly privatized context. Global privatization forces social change to conform to the structure of decentralized organizational forms—for example, neighborhood health centers, domestic violence shelters, AIDS alliances, and community opposition to toxic waste dumping. At the same time, however, privitization promotes an opposition and alternative public life capable of challenging its antisocial aspects. This tension is the major concern of this second chapter: building public life in a private world.

In a lead article in the *New York Times*, titled "Does Democracy Have a Future," John Gray (1995) proposed that the question must be answered quickly because the current decline in "civil society," including the disappearance of a proper role for government, may lead to autocracy and economic ruin. "The social capital of trust and reciprocity that is invested in norms and networks of civil life may be a vital and contributing factor not only to effective government but also to economic progress" (Gray, 1995, p. 25). Building on the work of Robert Putnam (1994), who argued in *Making Democracy Work*, that a vibrant civil life is essential for both democracy and economic success, Gray forecasts that social dislocation, middle-class impoverishment, and urban desolation will worsen as a result of a diminished civil life. This will lead to a "Colombianization of the United States," wherein failing po-

---

[1] The following material on new social movements has appeared in a number of other works. Most recently, see R. Fisher and J. Kling (1994) "Community Organization and New Social Movement Theory," *Journal of Progressive Human Services*, (5), pp. 5–24. The author would like to thank Haworth Press for permission to reuse the material.

litical institutions and the absence of public life promote—as in that South American nation—an "ungovernable, criminalized and endemically violent society" (Gray, 1995, p. 25).

Conservatives are of a different opinion. Proponents of laissez-faire capitalism and a fee-for-service world are more enthusiastic about the potential of the contemporary context. They propose not only that the marketplace addresses social problems better than the public sector, but that it empowers people at the grassroots level. William Schambra (1991), a director in the Department of Health and Human Services in the Bush administration, suggested that:

> More and more, it is understood within the highest reaches of the federal government that our most urgent social problems—drug abuse, the spread of AIDS, infant mortality, teen pregnancy, homicide and violence—result precisely from a collapse in genuine local communities, and the structures that generate, collect, refine, and reflect local values and political beliefs. All too often in the past, we now see, the federal government contributed to this process by absorbing functions and authority from—thereby undermining—local communities. . . . I draw great encouragement from this sort of shift in policy focus—away from cumbersome, centralized bureaucratic programs, toward policy that is rooted deeply in the wisdom, values, and democratically determined wishes of the local community. (p. 6)

Despite neoconservative rhetoric that the private context empowers citizens by giving them more choice and relieving them of the constraints of government, the opposite appears true. Jack Kemp, former secretary of Housing and Urban Development in the Bush administration, argued for the advantages of giving working people power by turning them from tenants of public housing into homeowners. The essence of the HOME program, the centerpiece of the 1990 Cranston-Gonzales National Affordable Housing Act designed to increase the supply of housing for low-income families, however, was to dismantle and delegitimate public housing (Karger & Stoesz, 1994). This was similarly true for Bush's "1,000 Points of Light," a voluntary-sector charity approach to social welfare, which allegedly sought to free the American spirit by stressing voluntary community giving to support those in need. In reality, the attempt to privatize social welfare promoted an individualized system of "welfare by the bag," in which forms of assistance became "more fragmented, less accessible, less visible, and less likely to offer the poor resources that can effectively address the problems they confront" (Schram, 1993, p. 25). Gray (1995) and others are right about neoconservative "support" of democratic citizenship leading to a diminished public sphere and a reduced incentive for community participation. In the end, this "support" will further empower those who already hold corporate power and wealth, but could "Colombianize" the United States.

Critics lamenting the decline of civil life often miss the significant signs that a growing and vibrant civic life exists in the American grassroots. They need to look closer at how, despite the increasing globalization of capital and the privatization of life, a persistent heritage of democratic struggle since the late 1950s has carved out a civic culture and opposition that provides support and direction to social change agents. Wolch (1990) argues that the dismantling of the public sector and the transfer of many of its responsibilities to grassroots groups has "led to an explosion in the aggregate size of the voluntary-sector" (p. 209). Schambra (1991) sees the explosion but misinterprets its cause. The emerging efforts at the grassroots, whether in AIDS hospices, domestic violence shelters, or Alinsky-style community organizing projects develop not because they are now unrestrained by government control and finally free to become voluntary-sector "points of light." Instead, they emerge and proliferate because most communities and citizens find themselves less protected and less secure than before, forced to deliver services to those in need, and denied a voice in the new political discourse. Neoconservative policy contributes more to load-shedding of public responsibility and depoliticizing public life than to meeting human need and sustaining the democratic fabric. The fear of a depoliticized society reflected in contemporary critiques such as Gray's is therefore well-founded. The unchallenged domination of ruling elites and the politics of privatization, however, is overstated.

DEBUNKING MYTHS ABOUT PUBLIC LIFE

Myths about public life are among the first obstacles to overcome in the rebuilding of the public realm. In the privatized context, most of the information available about public life discourages it. Public life is what heinous politicians do. Public life is unsafe, especially in our reactionary climate. Public life revolves around symbols, soundbytes, and media manipulation. It is clearly better to mind private affairs and focus on the things that really matter—self and family. Myths such as these distort public life and discourage citizens from finding out about its true nature and the rewards of public involvement. Building on the ideas of Lappé and Dubois (1994), we offer a number of myths and truths about public life.

1. Public life is an elite affair, an exclusive realm of activity for presidents, appointed officials, and prominent civic leaders. This idea comes from a belief that public life is limited to the electoral or governmental arena. In truth, public life includes all activity outside of the private, including involvement in schools, social service organizations, and citizen action groups at the neighborhood level and beyond. History is not made simply by those at the top. Through participation in public life, ordinary people also make history.

2. Public life is dead. Although public life is under severe attack, aspects of the privatizing context push people into new public realms. For some commentators, participation in public life is widespread worldwide. The Kettering Foundation found that beneath the "troubled view of politics . . . [is] an American public that cares deeply about public life . . . , a foundation for building healthy democratic practices and new traditions of public participation in politics" (cited in Harwood, 1991, p. 5). In daily social change and service work, millions of people are deeply engaged in public life (Bellah et al., 1991). Paget (1990) estimates the existence of some two mil-

lion grassroots groups in the United States alone. Durning (1989) suggests that the developing countries are better organized than any time since European colonization, with widespread citizen action around a multitude of local concerns and needs.

3. Public life is unrewarding, unappealing, and a time-consuming waste that attracts mostly whining and hyper-critical types. This myth comes from efforts to distort the true nature of dissent and delegitimize grassroots claims. It reflects a complete lack of faith in the democratic process, which is indeed time-consuming, and an antagonism to democratic dialogue, which can be supportive but also must be critical. Moreover, public life enhances life. It is the arena in which people can learn a great deal about society and about themselves through serious engagement with social matters. In public life, people learn, often for the first time, that in consort with others they can make a difference. Participants in social change work report time and time again that the experience gives life new meaning and larger purpose. People can flourish with new-found commitment and engagement to something meaningful and larger than themselves and their private world. As one participant in a neighborhood women's project in Cambridge, Massachusetts, put it: "I would not have had the sense of what it felt like to be an active participant in history, in my life, in Cambridge, whatever, if I had not been in Bread and Roses. I felt like I took my first real risks in Bread and Roses" (Fisher, 1984, p. 165). Public life can be the opposite of unrewarding and unattractive.

4. Public life is about divisive conflict and oppressive power. Why ask for more conflict when there is certainly enough at work, on the streets, or at home? Aren't there enough people already trying to dominate others? Public life is about difference, and about learning to create a society by interacting with others who often have different opinions and experiences. Not all public life is about conflict, but neither is conflict in itself a bad thing. People learn and grow in conflict. In the privatized context, conflict is seen as disruptive and disharmonious. Conflict creates higher "social costs" to those in power. Social programs have to be implemented to address needs or prisons built to quiet disorder. But democracy demands dissent and opposition. Diversity and tolerance prosper from the public airing of difference. Neither conflict nor power are dirty words. As good community organizers say, the role of the social change agent is to give citizens a thirst for power. This is not the power to oppress others, but rather, the power to be able to affect change. Power is something people should want more of; otherwise, those who have it can continue to dominate and oppress. This thirst for power should not be romanticized, however. While strategies and tactics vary, the struggle for power is not always pleasant. Clearly there are risks involved.

5. Public life ruins people's private lives. It removes them from a focus on personal growth and the welfare of loved ones. That can be true, depending on the extent of the commitment to public work. But the model of the

public person who devotes all of his or her life to a cause is less appropriate now. With the lessons of the contemporary women's movement as a guide, people are learning how to balance, or at least be attentive to, both their public and personal lives. Many aspects of personal life are political, but an older model of political life tended to leave little room for the personal. Ideally, each informs and enriches the other. Moreover, many people find they have a more grounded private life from public participation, discovering, for example, a supportive group and community of friends brought together around common social concerns. These simply stated myths and truths about public life serve as an introduction to the complexities of public life in the contemporary era.

Whose Public Sphere and Public Good?

The public sphere includes those arenas and activities in which political domination and social power are inspected and challenged by democratic dialogue, institutions, and organizations (Habermas cited in Tananbaum, 1994). It is not limited to the realms of government, public institutions, and public opinion, all of which help determine what collective matters will be of general interest. On the contrary, the public sphere also contains various grassroots organizations, voluntary associations, and service centers—what Sara Evans and Harry Boyte (1986) call "free spaces." These free spaces have been an essential feature of American life, both in the past and the present. As discussed in the first chapter, this public sphere is essential to the definition of social problems and to their solution. It is also critical in determining the nature of social work practice in a given era. But a public world where citizens "confer in an unrestricted fashion about matters of general interest" (Habermas cited in Boyte, 1992, p. 341) has been replaced more by a contemporary political world manipulated by advertisers, technocrats, media moguls, corporate and interest group lobbyists, and politicians. Flacks (1990) contends that whereas the 1960s generation was interested in "making history" by participating openly and eagerly in public life, the more recent generation has been forced to focus on "making life" in a private sphere focused on the more personal and intimate aspects of everyday existence.

Public life and the public world traditionally meant a narrow bourgeois public sphere, one born in the eighteenth century and dominated by white Christian men from business and the professions. These men used the new innovation of the democratic process to challenge domination by a feudal, aristocratic elite. These men became the leaders of government, of public opinion, and of civil society. Ultimately, their definition of public life and the public good dominated contemporary visions. Their public debate spoke for and excluded other groups and ideas, attempting to consign middle-class women to the private sphere and the poor to invisibility. Of course, public life has always been contested terrain. Even with male bourgeois domination, there were always competing publics. Looking back to the public sphere of the early nineteenth century America, Ryan (1992) finds "not the ideal bourgeois sphere" of unchallenged affluent white male domination, but a "variegated, decentered, and democratic array of public spaces . . . in amorphous groupings of citizens aggregated according to ethnicity, class, race, pet cause, and party affiliation" (p. 264). Clearly, the public sphere was one in which "different and opposing publics maneuvered" for power and space and in which those publics with less power were subordinated and oppressed (Eley, 1992, pp. 325–26). The history of the public sphere and the definition of public needs has always been one of struggle, tied to issues of class, race, gender, power, interest, and justice. Discussion of the public sphere and definition of the "public good" is therefore really about the formation of diverse publics and diverse public goods "created through a turbulent, provisional and open-ended process of struggle, change, and challenge" (Boyte, 1992, p. 344).

The 1960s represented a rebirth and expansion of public life in America. African-Americans in the civil rights and black power movements, and white university students in the new left and antiwar movements, protested the inequities of American life at home and abroad. These movements "disturbed the equanimity and passivity of public discourse, shattered consensus, and revitalized a conception of politics based on participatory democracy" (Ryan, 1992, p. 259). Building on efforts to expand the public sphere and resulting from the sexist contradictions within them (Evans, 1979), the women's movement arose to demand inclusion in this expanding American public life and to challenge patriarchal assumptions of the public good. As Rosaldo (quoted in Ryan, 1992, p. 260) proposes, the basis and agenda of feminist theory rests more on "the denial of access to the public realm" than even questions of biological difference or reproductive functions. Women had participated in the past in the "variegated, decentered, and democratic array" of public life, but when social change groups were mixed, for example, it was almost always the men in these efforts who spoke to the outside world "in the first person for the community as a whole" (Eley, 1992, p. 314).

The new feminism demanded admission into the public realm. It called for the expansion of public life, debate, and policy to embrace and involve previously marginalized women and other oppressed groups. And it helped invent a new public agenda by not only adding a multitude of fresh issues to public life, but more specifically, it reconceptualized public life to include issues drawn from private experience (Ryan, 1992, p. 260). This reconceptualization of the public/private dichotomy has transformed public life and public discourse in the past generation. Claims to link the private and the public, the personal and the social, were advanced by prior feminist efforts over issues of reproductive rights, liberated sexuality, and cultural radicalism. But it was primarily the last generation of feminist activists and theorists who unlocked the public sphere to criticisms regarding sexuality, motherhood, and gendered divisions in the family, work, and society. Feminists argued that the creation of a truly open and democratic public life required the "dismantling of the patriarchal separation of private and public" (Pateman quoted in Eley, 1992, p. 318). The personal was political and the political was personal. Divisions between the public and private sphere simply served to marginalize the concerns and needs of women and other oppressed groups.

Not all agree. Some continue to draw a clear distinction between the public and the private. In its organizing training sessions, the Industrial Areas Foundation

(IAF), founded by Saul Alinsky, distinguishes clearly between the public world of business and politics and the private realm of family and friends. In public life, relationships are reciprocal and role-segmented; in private life, they are diffuse and unconditional (Skerry, 1993). Organizers and community activists are instructed not to mix the two. Keeping them separate enables IAF constituents to focus on their public needs and avoid efforts by public leaders to sidetrack public/collective matters into private/personal issues. Nevertheless, the relationship between the public world and private life should be drawn more opaquely. The public world of work and civic participation—a realm of difference, accountability, and open dialogue about matters of collective concern—always included personal elements. The private sphere of personal needs, family, loyalty, love, and intimacy always had public dimensions.

A central contribution of feminism in the last third of the twentieth century has been its profound influence on reconceptualizing public life to include private matters. This revisioning of public life spilled over to affect all social change efforts, both on the right and on the left. As Arato and Cohen point out, "demands for public access by once marginalized groups or insurgent social movements serve over time to accumulate and expand the rights of all citizens" (quoted in Ryan, 1992, p. 285). So it has been for the previously silent world of gay men, lesbian women, victims of rape and male violence, abused children, and people with disabilities, to name a few. With the new understanding of the connection between the public and private, a volcano of voices erupted, demanding admission to the public stage and demanding a public audience. For social change, this has been a mixed blessing, undermining older forms of public life oriented largely to issues of class and replacing them with new forms of social change connected more to issues of culture and personal identity.

NEW SOCIAL MOVEMENT THEORY
AND CONTEMPORARY PUBLIC LIFE

The expansion of public life worldwide to include a vast array of ideas, organizational forms, and agendas reflects the new forms of public life arising in the contemporary context (Wignaraja, 1993; Fisher, 1993). The extent and newness of contemporary activism demonstrates the potential and opportunities in social change today. The proliferation and vibrancy of contemporary projects counter arguments about the end of public life. Nevertheless, the fragmented, grassroots, and often parochial nature of these efforts undermines their potential for united political action against the pressures of global privatization. The challenge remains how to create unity out of diversity and how to encourage diverse public efforts while at the same time countering the fragmentation that eventually disempowers them. New social movement theory can be a helpful tool to better understand the problem and its solution. Moreover, new social movement theory offers insight into the nature of social change—past, present, and future. It defines the "new" by juxtaposing it against the "old" social movements (Fisher & Kling, 1994).

The "old" social change movements share critical similarities (Epstein, 1990; Fisher, 1992; Fisher, 1993; Scott, 1990). In the early twentieth century, social democratic movements and regimes in the United States and Western Europe arose to control the excesses of industrial capitalism. In the United States, probably the most prominent regime was the New Deal and the most prominent movement was the Congress of Industrial Organizations (C.I.O.). Based in the workplace, the locus of C.I.O. organizing was the industrial factory. Here, activists organized unions around class issues. The ideology—social democratic or communist—challenged capitalism and proposed a working class vision of the future. Old social movement activists targeted employers, the owners of the means of production. At the same time, organizers and labor leaders involved themselves and their unions in politics, hoping to win state power. Victories in the United States and Western Europe were the foundation of public policy and state action after World War II. The more communitarian, decentralized versions of these efforts, such as progressive social settlement houses, shared the old social movement vision and agenda.

Between 1946 and the late 1960s, labor-oriented, "old" social movements built a consensus around economic growth, welfare state expenditures, and U.S. imperial control. But throughout the Western industrial world beginning in the late 1960s, many factors surfaced to undermine the old social movements and regimes. The increasing globalization of the world economy undermined their ability—and that of their political representatives—to redistribute resources to constituents. As capital flow increasingly superseded state control in the emerging global economy, the welfare state faced increasing fiscal crises. The social democratic state lost support, while those associated with its development and implementation lost credibility.

The new postindustrial global economy put pressure on two inherent weaknesses in the old social movements. First, those in power within the movements, the corresponding regimes, and even many beneficiaries developed an increasingly parochial and self-serving agenda as prosperity weakened identification with the working class. Second, the old social movements may have achieved power as the voice for disadvantaged workers, but they also perpetuated the silence of others such as racial and ethnic minorities, women, young people just entering the work force, and the unskilled. Increasingly, these groups began to organize around their own needs, challenging the liberal democratic leaders and parties that gave only perfunctory attention to their interests and concerns. The new opposition emerged in insurgent grassroots associations over issues of democratic participation, personal liberty, civil rights, and quality of life.

The heirs of the old social movements found themselves hamstrung by a global economy, which escaped national regulation and control, and under attack from both the right and segments of the left for "statist" policies. For the generation that came to political consciousness in the years between 1960 and 1990, the practitioners of such old-style liberal politics came to be viewed almost as anachronisms (Flacks, 1990).

The new social change efforts, while emerging at different places and at different times throughout the globe, possess five characteristics that distinguish them from the old social movements. All of these have been replicated widely in social service agencies focused on or at least concerned about social change. First, they are community-based. Specifically, they are organized around communities of interest or geography, and much less often at the workplace or against the owners of capital (Offe, 1987). Castells (1983) defines this difference as organizing at the site of consumption rather than at the site of production.

Second, new social change efforts organize around constituencies and cultural identities, such as blacks, ethnics, women, gay men, lesbian women, students, ecologists, and peace activists. Labor becomes one constituency among many, not the main constituency group or even the first among equals (Brecher & Costello, 1990; Fisher, 1992). This shift to community-level, constituency-based organizing is the product of many factors, among them the change from an industrial to postindustrial economy. As Harvey (1985) argues, once the disaggregated parts of the fragmented society become "the basis for political action, then community consciousness replaces class consciousness as the springboard for action and the locus of social conflict" (pp. 120–21). Identity, community, and culture become the contexts through which people construct and understand political life.

The politics of culture is not new. American politics has often been marked by a multicultural politics of identity that restricted other identities from participating. Even though in the labor movement it was a class identity that legitimized working class struggle, the identity was mostly that of a white male worker of ethnic European descent. The new identity politics is different. Kling (1993) argues that from the early nineteenth century through the end of World War II, "class" and "citizenship" were accepted as the major identities uniting varying constituencies of working people to oppose existing conditions of oppression and to challenge unequal access to social opportunities and resources. "Class position" linked oppressed groups across differences of race, ethnicity, gender, and neighborhood. "Citizenship" tied groups together in a mutual exercise of common rights against injustice and legitimated the identification of working people with the larger democratic polity. A politics based on the primacy of class and the rights of citizenship informed almost all social change efforts (irrespective of race, ethnicity, and gender), whether based in the workplace or the neighborhood (Fisher & Kling, 1993). Since the late 1960s, class-based organizing has increasingly been replaced by identity politics and constituent organizing.

Third, the predominant ideology that informs new social movements is a neopopulist vision of democracy that rejects hierarchy, whether in small groups, the state, political parties and organizations, the family, or personal relationships (Amin, 1990). The organizational form is sufficiently small, loose, and open to "tap local knowledge and resources, to respond to problems rapidly and creatively, and to maintain the flexibility needed in changing circumstances" (Durning, 1989, pp. 6–7). Some have argued that these efforts are "nonideological," because proponents dismiss the old ideologies of capitalism, communism, and nationalism, and because they tend to be without a clear philosophic critique of existing systems. But others argue that the "neopopulist" principles and beliefs are what makes them new social movements (Boyte, Booth, & Max, 1986; Boyte & Riessman, 1986; Dalton & Kuechler, 1990; Fisher & Kling, 1988; Offe, 1987).

Fourth, the struggle over culture and social identity plays a greater role in community-based movements than in workplace-based efforts of the past. "After the great working class parties surrendered their remaining sense of radical political purpose with the onset of the cold war," Bronner (1990) writes, "new social movements emerged to reformulate the spirit of resistance in broader cultural terms" (p. 161). This new resistance includes feminism, black power, gay rights, ethnic nationalism, and victims' rights, among others. Nevertheless, culture and identity grounded in historical experience, values, social networks, and collective solidarity have always been central to social movements (Gutman, 1977). As class identity and solidarity become fragmented in the global privatizing context, and as workplace organizing declines in significance, resistance emerges increasingly around diverse cultural identity bases (Touraine, 1985). In an age where so many identities are undergoing rapid change and where so many communities are being destroyed and recreated, the assertion of identity not only replicates the decentralized form of global capital, it holds out a solid base for mobilizing resistance to it (Epstein, 1993).

Fifth, new social movement strategies focus on community self-help and empowerment (Gutierrez, 1990; Rees, 1991). As such, most community-based organizing seeks independence from the state, rather than state power. As Midgley (1986) points out, central to the rationale of community participation ". . . is a reaction against the centralization, bureaucratization, rigidity, and remoteness of the state. The ideology of community participation is sustained by the belief that the power of the state has extended too far, diminishing the freedoms of ordinary people and their rights to control their own affairs" (p. 4). Empowering individuals and community-oriented groups, usually through self-help strategies, is an essential feature of these efforts.

These are some of the major insights of new social movement theory. They help explain and critique postwar changes in social and cultural organization, including the emergence of global capitalism, the concomitant expansion of community-based citizen resistance, and the substitution of "empowerment" for the objective of winning and holding state power (Laclau & Mouffe, 1985). For example, social movement theory suggests that in a postindustrial, information-based world in which forms of power are no longer best reflected in workplace relations, people form organizations at the community rather than the factory level. Consequently, the struggle is over cultural identity issues rather than economic and class ones. Struggles in society become diffuse, spilling over the workplace and into the "life space" of neighborhoods and communities of interest. "These arenas, once considered solely part of the private domain of individuals and their families, have increasingly become the focus of new organizing efforts" (Capek & Gilderbloom, 1992, p. 38). The characteristic grouping of the new social movement form, Alberto Melucci writes, is one "submerged in everyday life," that requires "personal involvement in experiencing and practicing cultural innovation" (quoted in Capek & Gilderbloom, 1992, p. 39).

In terms of social work, the impact of the new social movement form of social change results in a proliferation of groups around a host of issues and cultural identities. Citizens get involved in public life through organizations as varied as Alcoholics Anonymous or a statewide gay and lesbian coalition. Social workers seek to meet the needs of the poor in homeless shelters, food pantries, social ministries, and city-wide homeless coalitions. Those more directly involved with identity groupings can be found working with organizations and agencies around issues of race, ethnicity, gender, or sexual orientation. These activities can take the form of advocacy work, community centers in an African-American neighborhood, a Chicano counseling center, an American Friends Service Committee immigration task force, a women's center or domestic violence project, an AIDS hospice, or anti-hate crimes efforts.

Social workers currently find themselves immersed in myriad issues that include homelessness and hunger, rape, battered women, infant mortality and children's rights, community public health advocacy, alcoholism, safe sex programs, and environmental destruction. Such has always been the case in social work. But in the past, efforts were less diverse since they were more tied to central sources of funding and social democratic ideology. The decentering of social work gives it greater diversity and creates a dynamic tension within the profession. Empowerment around individual issues and identity groups broadens the number of participants and the number of struggles being fought. Previously silent groups challenge the social work profession for acknowledgment and power. As reflected in the widespread adoption of the empowerment concept, social workers have begun to respond positively and eagerly.

POSTMODERN THEORY AND THE PUBLIC GOOD

Contemporary social change projects have directly affected the reconceptualization of a progressive public good. In the past, ideas about the public good tended to be defined from the top down and focused on either public distributive needs or private acquisitive issues. Historically, the search for a public good has ended all too quickly in dominant groups determining what is good for the public and in efforts to squash minority opinion. An essential feature of postmodern theory is the support it provides for the diversity of participants and viewpoints in public life. Postmodernists argue that public life must be expanded to include multiple publics, an argument that challenges older notions of an elite-dominated and -defined public good. But, because postmodern thinkers suspect all overriding value systems of curtailing individual choice and autonomy, they distrust and even deny the possibility of creating a new sense of a universal public good.

Postmodernist theory argues that the central base of participation in the new public life of the late twentieth century are subjective differences and cultural diversity. These subjectivities increasingly identify in terms of cultural identity—even multiple identities—that reinforces the claims of diverse groups. In addition, postmodern theory includes a sharp critique of contemporary life and a comprehensive view about the nature of power in society. All of these components are fundamental to late twentieth-century social change movements (Cocks, 1989).

For example, the postmodern critique of contemporary culture argues that social life no longer reflects social reality. Instead, the social world is increasingly presented as a virtual reality of signs and symbols that remove people not only from engagement with the social world, but also from a recognition of it. Instead of social reality, culture represents only "forms and images of cultural representation" (Chaney, 1994, p. 189). Signs such as advertisements, symbols such as designer labels, and soundbytes in political campaigns take over the social world as "maps" of current reality. Power determines what is real. As such, the power inherent in global privatization enforces a concept of reality that is private and focused on economic rationalization.

Postmodernism sees power as accessible to social change efforts because, like everything else, power is fragmented and subjective. Just as there are a variety of forms of social domination, there are also multiple forms of resistance to that domination, including the diverse cultural bases of new social change movements. Put another way, social change efforts are born in the interaction between subjectivity and subjection (Allen, 1993). Foucault (1982) argued that it was this pluralistic and multifaceted attack on localized forms of oppression that would serve as the basis of social change in a postmodern world. People are not simply sponges soaking up the dominant culture. Through various strategies, they fashion alternatives to it in their lives and in their communities. Hence, postmodernists encourage us to embrace the social fragmentation, both as a way of understanding the new social context and as a means for resisting it. Global privatization in postmodern theory is therefore not a *fait accompli*, but *the* dominant discourse in a public life swimming with many competing voices. Even though social change is understood as limited and time-specific, participation in public life is viewed as a responsible moral choice in a world where personal autonomy is threatened (Fisher & Kling, 1993).

The collapse of a political and cultural center—resulting partly from the organization of oppressed groups and partly from the impact of global capitalism—yields a fragmented political and cultural terrain. Modern thinkers, including Karl Marx and Max Weber, assumed that the forces of economic, political, and cultural centralization would eventually lead to the replacement of specific identities with generalized, bureaucratic, and class-oriented ones. But it has not quite worked that way. "As the modern public expands," Berman (1988) wrote, "it shatters into a multitude of fragments, speaking incommensurable private languages; the idea of modernity, conceived in numerous fragmentary ways, loses much of its vividness, resonance, and depth, and loses its capacity to organize and give meaning to people's lives" (pp. 16–17). It is the collapse of political and cultural centrality, in postmodern words "the crisis of narratives" (Lyotard, 1979), which produces the diversity of public life *and* fragments the very idea of a public good.

Because they embrace the fragmentation of social life, in order to both understand and change contemporary life, the inherent perspective of postmodern thinkers is antagonistic to a public good that speaks with a united voice. Carol Gilligan's (1982) widely popular book, *In a Different Voice*, illustrates in its very title an opposition to universalizing assumptions. As Harvey (1989) notes, "The idea that all groups have a right to speak for themselves, in their own voice, and have that voice accepted as authentic and legitimate is essential to the pluralistic stance of postmodernism" (p. 48).

Although postmodernism examines the nature of power and helps explain how the dominant culture oppresses individuals and groups, its fundamental belief in the subjectivity of human experience and its emphasis on cultural politics negates the view that there is a *single* public life or public good. For postmodernists, a concept such as the public good is subjective and culturally relative. According to these thinkers, the grand explanations of society—such as the modernist narrative of emancipation or the socialist one of equality—are now largely dead or at least without contemporary importance. Rather, it is the competing publics, with their differing conceptions of life and cultural politics, that represent current social change. A swirling brew of multiple publics has become the new public life. While these movements offer a form of resistance to global privatization, contemporary cultural politics also fragment a progressively minded public as much as it empowers social change.

The virtues and drawbacks of the postmodernist shift to "culture" are evident in the current emphasis of social work on "cultural competence" and "ethnic sensitive" practice. Increasingly, people of color in the United States are most vulnerable to the effects of global privatization. Hit hardest by social service cutbacks, people of color are quickly forced to develop self-help strategies. As the percentage of people of color and immigrants increases dramatically, clustering in urban areas hardest hit by the postindustrial transformation, progressive social workers and social work educators respond to their needs with an emphasis on oppressed cultural groups. Helen Northen (1982) emphasized early on that the "traditions of a culture or subculture" are fundamental to "effective functioning" (p. 52). As Lum (1992) clearly proposes,

> It is important for human services professionals to respond to the psychosocial needs of people of color. Minority knowledge theory, ethnic-sensitive helping skills, and knowledge of *cultural factors* [emphasis is ours] are essential ingredients in forming specific minority service delivery structures, training ethnic sensitive social workers, and implementing community outreach programs. (p. 2)

The dilemma posed for social workers by the highly diverse new social movements and the postmodern "turn to culture" challenges social work practice. If cultural pluralism becomes the operative ideology underlying social work practice, how do social workers interested in social change overcome the divisions between identity and cultural groups in order to address larger structural problems such as the global economy? How can contemporary public life become more united in order to effect progressive social change? Epstein (1993) writes of how splits in identity politics—along lines of gender, religion, and sexual orientation—undermined unity in the campaign against the Gulf War in San Francisco. Lehr (1993) describes comparable problems among gay activists, who divide over issues of class and politics, and thereby realize the limits of identity politics. A theme of this book is that public life can become more united around a progressive politics and agenda. People and groups are not limited to narrow identities. For many people, identity politics is a beginning, not an end. Gay men and lesbian women running an HIV center reach out to communities of people of color, where AIDS is spreading, and oppose city and state cutbacks in health services because social service cuts hurt all in need. Nevertheless, the dilemma is not a simple one. While the emphasis on cultural difference and building cultural competence makes progressive social workers more attentive to the cultural needs of oppressed groups, this emphasis tends to remove the lens of class and political economy at a time when class self-interest dominates the politics of global privatization. In addition, identity politics often neglects the shared social experience among oppressed people of diverse cultural backgrounds and orientations.

Whether social change will be effective in the 1990s and beyond depends on the ability of social change efforts to overcome these divisions (Brecher & Costello, 1994). The fragmented efforts of identity and cultural politics divide the opposition, Kauffman (1992) concurs, and "privileges difference over commonality" (p. 20). Despite its global proliferation, this splintering of efforts, resources, identity, and vision constrains contemporary public life. On the other hand, social activists convincingly argue how predictable it is that just as women, gays, lesbians, blacks, latinos, and people with disabilities rediscover their voice through building organizations and participating in the public sphere, critics on both the Right and Left suddenly fear the splintering of society into parochial camps. Certainly, the goals of critics on the Right and Left are not the same: The Right seeks to stifle social change; the Left strives to build a progressive movement. The Right has been especially nasty in this regard, attacking multiculturalism as the bane of Western civilization. In their wholesale attack on progressive social change, neoconservatives focus their opprobrium on multiculturalism to halt dissent, limit opposition, and deter demands for increased public support for oppressed people and the amelioration of social problems.

The fear of movement fragmentation by some progressives is made to seem dubious by the persistence of such claims throughout history and the current success of many efforts thought to be fragmenting social movements. John Dewey, for example, bemoaned in the early part of this century that "the loyalties which once held individuals, which gave them support, direction, and unity of outlook on life, have well-nigh disappeared" (quoted in Lasch, 1991, p. 368).

People often want and seek more secure anchors in public life. Often this search results in overlooking the virtues of a decentralized public sphere. For illustration, one only need examine the impact of the contemporary women's movement on issues of rape and battering. Or look at the impact of grassroots, self-help efforts on alcohol abuse and drunk driving. Or even recognize the increased visibility and legitimacy of gay, lesbian, disability, and environmental issues. For example, ACT-UP's notion of political struggle is a near perfect example of postmodern activism and one step removed from guerilla theater. Despite its fragmenting tendencies, ACT-UP has been successful in sharpening AIDS awareness, compelling public discussion about its nature and treatment, and making clear its meaning for the population as a whole (Fisher & Kling, 1993). Brecher and Costello (1993) argue that identity groups that share a sense of common history and fate are the essential building blocks to move beyond the new global economic order.

While cultural group resistance cannot and should not be quieted, the complaints of progressives about the decline of public life result from the limits of this form of social change. Even as the number of participants in grassroots social change movements increase, much of this effort is at a level of daily life unnoticed and undetected by the public outside of particular identity or issue groups. Moreover, because most of these efforts focus on culture, they tend not to be connected to larger issues of political and economic life. People and society outside the small group are not only unaware of the efforts, they are largely unaffected by them, especially when it comes to issues of political economy. What develops is something akin to multiple spheres of public life: the dominant one of global economic and political power rules while multiple publics at the grassroots spin about it. The peripheral groups sometimes target the center, but all too rarely do they affect the primary path of the dominant private world.

UNIVERSALIZING THE PARTICULAR

What can social workers do to strengthen public life and, thereby, the opportunities for social change? Debates and critiques increasingly propose to modify the fragmentation described by theories of postmodernism and new social movements by developing a shared progressive ideology. Any effort to "universalize the particular" and "create unity out of diversity" must fashion a sense of a shared public good among progressive groups. It must connect the public to the private and the social to the individual. Grounded in both late twentieth-century feminist theory and the social work values of social justice, equity, and redistribution, a vision of a progressive common good must include attention to both basic material needs and the needs of individuals for personal autonomy and privacy. "Without understood and secure parameters of individual self expression and personal ownership," Doyal and Gough (1991) write, "the *raison d'etre* for redistribution—the maximum development of the individual as a person—becomes lost" (p. 5).

Along with others (Doyal & Gough, 1991; Fisher & Kling, 1991; Epstein, 1993), we argue that the current challenge is to unite contemporary social change by integrating the differing and often competing claims of oppressed citizens. This may take the form of common programs, like that of the Rainbow Coalition in the United States or the Greens in Western Europe, which seek to bring the important issues of our time to a focal point. Or it might result in a new perspective, such as human needs theory (discussed below), that focuses on the public *right* to both basic physical survival and personal autonomy (Doyal & Gough, 1991). Political commentator Walter Lippmann once proposed that the test of democracy was not whether it produced self-reliant citizens engaged in democratic life, as de Tocqueville suggested, but whether it produced essential goods and services for all its citizens (quoted in Lasch, 1991, p. 366). Human needs theory includes both

Lippmann's emphasis on meeting basic survival needs and more personal individualistic objectives. As Doyal and Gough (1991) propose: ". . . since physical survival and personal autonomy are the preconditions for any individual action in any culture, they constitute the most basic human needs—those which must be satisfied to some degree before actors can effectively participate in their form of life to achieve any other valued goals" (p. 54).

A progressive and more united vision of the public good must ultimately be grounded in the view that the needs of *all* people should be met to the *optimum* degree. As Doyal and Gough (1991) frame it, the public right of physical survival for everyone would include adequate health and health care, nutrition, housing, nonhazardous work and physical environments, economic and physical security in childhood and adulthood, basic education, and safe birth control and childbearing. The public right to personal autonomy would consist of both freedom of agency and political freedom, including improved self-understanding, mental health, and personal opportunity. These ideas present only a rudimentary base for a reconceptualized public good. There are clearly other dimensions to a core universal ideology, not to mention the specific needs of particular groups. But the conception of a public good proposed by Doyal and Gough (1991) illustrates a synthesis that transcends the dualism of social versus individual needs. It also bridges the gap between class and culture and between the old and new social movement forms.

Bookchin (1987) similarly advances a new conception of social change based on a linkage between the personal and the social. Given the challenges to contemporary life wrought by global capitalism, Bookchin suggests that people seek self-definition *and* personal empowerment as means to render themselves socially operational. Civic re-empowerment becomes both a personal and social issue. It is about regaining private as well as public self-hood. And, it is the basis for retrieving personality and citizenship from a context that seeks to reduce people to beleaguered private selves and consumers. By becoming involved, the individual gets to act as a "truly social being" (Bookchin, 1987).

Emphasizing individual needs can be interpreted as a retreat into the personal, a reflection of the individualization and fragmentation promoted by both the privatized context and the postmodern sensibility (Sennett, 1990; Lasch, 1978). But it can also be understood as a resourceful strategy. Those engaged in social change in our private world fuse the personal with the social because the present context throws people back into the private, because groups formerly excluded from the public sphere find access and voice around matters previously considered private, and because this fusion legitimizes and strengthens resistance (Bookchin, 1987). People get involved for valid personal as well as collective reasons; they seek personal growth and empowerment as well as social change. Tying the two together—the individual and the collective—may yield a more integrated participation, a more sustained commitment to causes, and a more united social change effort.

Reconceptualizing public life around both social and personal needs has additional meaning for contemporary social change since it poses an alternative to the social fragmentation of our privatizing context (Doyal & Gough, 1991). First, it has the potential to demonstrate a common bond between all oppressed people. Second, a shared oppression offers a heightened potential for mutual sympathy and understanding. Third, universalizing needs and reformulating a truly public good makes united political action with common objectives more likely.

CONCLUSION

There is a vitality, breadth, and range to a public life influenced by the current emphasis on diversity and difference. At the same time, there is a fragmentation of community efforts and a shift away from issues of class, political economy, and the state, which undermines the ability of these groups to mitigate the effects of global privatization. As Epstein (1993) suggests, when difference and identity politics "take precedence over shared concerns" then the basis for effective political action and a broad movement evaporates. "The assertion of identity," she notes, "is only one side of an ongoing tension between the need for autonomy and the need for a more inclusive collectivity" (p. 318).

The real problem is not inappropriate strategies or poor organizational forms at the grassroots level. Nor is it an overemphasis on culture and identity as much as a problem of power inequity and economic dominance. Centralized economic and political power creates the new, privatized context. It also marginalizes and delegitimizes various groups, thereby forcing them into a defensive posture of protecting "their" history and "their" community. It can also lead people into believing that survival in a marketplace-driven world is all there is or can be. Nevertheless, practices and strategies do matter. Building bridges between diverse efforts and creating a more tightly focused conceptualization of the public good are the primary challenges to social change workers. To this end, we propose that social work should be grounded in at least four assumptions and practices that form the organizing themes for the book's remaining chapters.

First, social workers must accept and support multiculturalism, identity politics, and the new forms of public life. No efforts today can be successful without accepting and encouraging a public life that expresses the needs and goals of those people forced by the dominant culture to experience themselves as oppressed, marginalized, and different (Fisher & Kling, 1993). This acceptance does not mean blindly supporting all efforts, especially those lacking the potential to help build a unified front for social change. Identity politics can be reactionary as well as progressive. It is ultimately not enough to be multicultural and ethnically sensitive. In our increasingly reactionary context, social work must fight against racism, patriarchy, homophobia, and ethnocentrism in all forms.

Second, social workers must commit to the promotion of ideologies, philosophies, and value systems that connect grassroots efforts to a larger progressive politics grounded in issues of class/political economy and culture/identity. In societies vulnerable to fragmentation and the absence of a dialogue about the social world, the experience of oppressed people leads to the presentation of social needs and political programs in increasingly cultural and exclusionary terms. As Ernie Cortes, a lead organizer in the Texas IAF, states: "I don't think you organize around culture.

. . . I think that what we're trying to do is teach a civic culture" (quoted in Robinson & Hanna, 1994, p. 89). That new civic culture must spring from the cultural animus of contemporary activism, wherein political innovation, autonomy, and action are most evident. But the new civic culture must also emerge from the material needs of increasingly large numbers of people in the new world order, since most of the suffering today is related to physical needs and the struggle to survive. Cultural identification must be connected through political philosophy, party programs, social movements, and/or social change ideology to an understanding of the continuing, fundamental importance of contemporary class relations and global political economy. As Rivera and Erlich (1995) write, "When asked, communities of color are clear on what they need: jobs, housing, economic revival of inner cities, better health systems and education" (p. 250). These are questions of class and material survival, a fact better understood in the third world than in the first. The diverse public efforts that have proliferated widely throughout the world must go beyond their focus on identity and democratization to include an emphasis on economic equality and social justice. They must reintegrate old social change movement forms with new ones. Jobs with Justice organizes around issues of racism and gender discrimination at the workplace, but focuses on organizing workers around class interests. Effective feminist therapy understands the vicious impact of patriarchy on the lives of women, but addressing social problems among impoverished women requires a broad conception of politics and social change. Similarly, those efforts on the historic left and more tied to the old social change form must emphasize the concerns and demands of culture along with those of class in any new sense of a progressive public good (Young, 1993). Recent shifts in leadership in the AFL-CIO, or other union organizing drives, have been most successful when they built on the multicultural issues and orientations of their constituents.

Third, social workers must help develop broadly formulated issues and build organizational forms that unite diverse social change efforts. To counter the fragmentation and build organizational forms to challenge power in an era of increasingly centralized global power, social change must include efforts that build on community bases (whether geographic, cultural, or issue communities). These are the free spaces, the seeds of contemporary public life. But to challenge centralized power and to counter the causes of problems that almost always rest outside of the community, these efforts must result in networks, alliances, coalitions, political parties, and ultimately, transnational global associations. The fragmented forms of progressive public life share similar structures, goals, strategies, consciousness, and collective histories of oppression, even if that oppression and how it was challenged were different for each group. These shared characteristics, plus a critical analysis of the problems and opportunities posed by globalization, must serve as a base for building unity out of diversity and broader goals out of more specific ones.

Fourth, social change work must go beyond a sole focus on community life and become involved directly with state and social policy. Contemporary civil society — the public world outside of business and government—seeks largely to remain distant from the public sector, politics, and policy. Certainly the state, both the bureaucracies and the elected officials, has often been a force of coercion and oppression and an antagonist to social change. Nevertheless, the state has also been the site of significant class and identity group struggle over the nature and direction of society, and more specifically, the relationship between corporate capital and the public good. As mentioned earlier, it is also a primary site of contestation outside of the community for grassroots groups to affect larger issues. The result of turning away from the public sector, as both privatizers and many grassroots groups encourage, is to reject explicitly designs on the state and social policy and relinquish uncontested control to corporate power and cultural conservatives.

Despite the increasing powerlessness of nations in the face of global capital, the state still has an impact, is still the site where politicians and public bureaucrats act, and is still the arena for policy and program decisions affecting the individual and collective opportunities of citizens. It remains the best site to struggle over public issues, to make private issues public, and to challenge the dominance of global privatization. Building on the Catholic principle of "subsidiarity," Bellah et al. (1991) advise that "higher-level associations such as the state should never replace what lower-level associations can do effectively" (p. 262). Addressing domestic violence can be done better on a decentralized and autonomous basis, rather than through large federal programs. But the principle also implies that these higher-level associations, such as the public sector, have an "obligation to help when the lower-level associations lack the resources to do the job alone" (Bellah et al., 1991, p. 262). Power should ideally devolve to the grassroots where decisions can be more sensitive to diverse community needs and where participation in public life is most accessible and evident. But the state remains critical, not only in financially supporting and legitimating decentralized efforts, but in helping to encourage dialogue, challenge divisive local parochialisms, and serve as a large, centralized entity to impede, harness, and fight the power of global capital that opposes social change work. As Young (1993) and others propose, the new social movements in civil society have been too quick to throw out the old social movement idea of "struggling for state power." It may not be chic to do so in a context of postmodern public life and in a context of savage attacks on the public sector by advocates of global privatization. Certainly the right in the United States understands well the importance of the public sector. They attack the legitimacy of the state while, at the same time, those leading the attack work hard to control the state. These efforts are good indicators of the state's continued and potential significance.

Progressive activists in the third world understand that community needs and the demands voiced in civil society require public-sector attention and action. "At the core of the political methodologies of these new movements," Alvarez (1993) writes of community efforts in São Paulo, "is the mobilization of neighborhood residents to make collective demands on the state" (p. 194). Annis (1987), also writing about Latin America, remarks that these widely proliferated efforts not only connect the poor to each other, but also to "their governments in unprecedented ways" (p. 21). A central argument of this book is that in a global context where the leveraging of local capital is so critical, social change groups and agencies must work with their community bases to challenge the state. They must also be willing and eager (as the old social movements were) to seek, win, and hold state power. We believe they must do so in new, democratic, and pluralistic ways—those more akin to new social movement ideology. They must see as a fundamental component of their work not only the empowerment of individuals and collectives, not only the meeting of community needs, but also the larger vision of using the state to challenge the powerful interests of contemporary global privatization.

The next chapter focuses on the critical importance of grounding social work education and practice in a macro contextualization. Such a macro contextualization would include the knowledge and skills that emphasize both political economy and cultural identity. This framework for social work education and practice goes beyond narrow micro/psychological frameworks of social work, which mire social workers in concerns about self-efficacy and individual empowerment, and transcends narrow views of macro social work, which present the world too simply in structuralist terms. Perhaps more importantly, it refashions the concept of empowerment to include a fundamental understanding about power and struggle in the era of global privatization. We argue that political economy needs to be reintroduced and merged with more contemporary cultural forms of identification and resistance. To this end, we propose in chapter 3 the grounding of *all* social work education and practice in the knowledge and skills of macro contextualization.

chapter 3

A Framework for Contextualizing Social Work Practice

How can social work help rebuild the public realm, relegitimize the social sphere, and promote social change? How can social workers help clients to rebuild communities while the privatized context in which they work makes problems worse and their jobs harder? This question has always been the central dilemma for the social work profession. Of course, the answer rests beyond the reach of any single group in society. The question nevertheless remains: What can social workers do to best serve the needs of those they assist, fight against the forces that immiserate clients and communities, *and* help rebuild a sense of a progressive public life?

The first two chapters sought to provide essential knowledge for a critical contextualization of contemporary social work. Contextualization refers to knowing and understanding the connection between daily social work practice and the structural dynamics of society—its history, economy, politics, and social and cultural dimensions. Contextualization assumes that individual, family, and community problems are always tied to larger structural factors. At the heart of a critical contextualization is an analysis of power and inequality and a social change ideology that translates this critical analysis into action. The issue in this chapter is how to contextualize social work practice. In a nutshell, the core concepts of a contextualized practice framework (see Box 3.1) include: (1) integrating practice, (2) going beyond ecological and empowerment theory to focus on power, (3) putting macro contextualization at the base of social work practice, (4) building on the political nature of social work, (5) sustaining and galvanizing practice through social change ideology, (6) focusing social work processes on groups and on strategies toward collective solutions, (7) understanding the virtues and limits of community, and (8) going beyond culture to reinclude class as a critical element in social work practice. This chapter seeks to provide an understanding of the framework of contextualized practice through a full discussion of these core concepts.

**BOX 3.1   Core Elements for Contextualizing
Social Work Practice**

- An integrated social work practice
- Education for social work that focuses on power
- Putting macro social work analysis and practice at the base of social work practice
- Understanding the political nature of social work practice
- Inclusion of a social change ideology into social work practice
- Emphasizing collective processes and strategies in social work practice
- Connecting the community to social work practice
- Using class as well as cultural issues in social work practice

---

AN INTEGRATED PRACTICE

Specht and Courtney (1994), in their provocative *Unfaithful Angels*, argue that the problem in meeting human need rests in the individualistic nature of society. This individualistic focus is replicated in social work by the nearly unanimous and uncritical adoption of psychotherapeutic belief systems, analyses, and interventive strategies. It is this same turn to humanistic psychology and its emphasis on individual improvement—and individual failing—that Bellah et al. (1985), Sennett (1974), and Lasch (1978) attack more broadly in the larger society. Specht and Courtney (1994) argue that psychotherapy's basic belief in the perfectibility of the individual conflicts with social work's belief in the perfectibility of society. Over the past sixty years, they propose, social work has increasingly turned away from its *social* base toward humanistic psychology and private psychotherapeutic practice. It is this turning away from social problems, public work, and collective intervention that aids and abets the larger shift in society to privatism in all its forms. For Specht and Courtney (1994), psychotherapy is useless in dealing with the great social problems of the day, which is why they urge that "professionals who claim to do social work should not be secular priests in the church of individual repair" (p. 175). In short, micro intervention and practice is the problem, not the solution.

Instead of viewing the history of social work as becoming more individualistic in its practice, it is better understood as a dialectical tension in which certain eras are more individualistic and others more social. Nevertheless, the dominant trend in social work during the past twenty years has been to individualize problems and solutions and to privatize practice. These are largely byproducts of the recent shift to global privatization and the neoconservative politics of the era (Fisher, 1994; Leonard, 1990). It is deeply disturbing that the social work profession turned its attention almost exclusively in the 1980s and early 1990s to psychotherapy, "just when rising poverty, unemployment, and homelessness require a systemic response" (Lord & Kennedy, 1992, p. 23). While Specht and Courtney (1994) propose that social work has moved to individualized private practice over the past sixty years—others suggest that the current emphasis on private practice is more a product of the contemporary political economy and weakened social struggle—most critical theorists agree that the individualizing of problems and solutions makes good social work impossible. For them, it must be grounded in community life, macro practice, and structural analysis in order to be *social* work.

Communitarians such as Bellah et al. (1985), Etzioni (1993), and Specht and Courtney (1994) condemn individualism as the fundamental problem. However, the key issue is not individualism *per se* or even a focus on family therapy, but a decontextualized individualism that pushes people away from the social sphere. The problem of decontextualizing becomes one of removing individual and family circumstances from a connection to larger social forces. To the extent that this removal is achieved, the focus on the individual and family, within and outside of social work, reinforces the trend to the private and the asocial. To the extent that individualism, psychotherapy, family systems therapy, and direct service practice are contextualized, they begin to render stronger people, able to accept more responsibility not only for their own lives but for the world around them (Remele, 1994).

Individual needs are critical in social work and social change. After all, social structures are made by people interacting with each other. Impersonal macro conditions constitute the historical context within which people act, but as Lipsitz (1988) notes, "structural forces do not create movements for social change—people do" (p. 68). Even though social problems are rooted in structures of oppression, all problems cannot be simply blamed on the system. Carniol (1992) notes that "on the contrary, personal change is also central . . . we must work simultaneously on both liberating persons and liberating structures" (pp. 10–11). Individual change and larger social development must be linked (Withorn, 1984). The social dimension to individual intervention comes when social workers realize that "treating people as individuals and recognizing individual differences is quite different from understanding (diagnosing or assessing) problems as unique to people as individuals" (Longres & McLeod, 1980, p. 272). Because a social worker engaged in direct practice respects a person who receives Aid to Families with Dependent Children (AFDC) support, listens carefully to the welfare mother articulate needs and problems, and "starts where the client is at," does not mean that they must identify the individual as the source of the problems and solutions.

Drawing a connection between the personal and the social is smart strategy since intervention with individuals is the essence of most social work practice. A key lesson of current social change movements is that social change must be grounded in a linkage between the personal and political. A central challenge to social work is to connect the individual and the collective, the personal and the social. The goal is not to demonize individualism or psychotherapy or, conversely, to romanticize macro analysis and community practice. Micro level intervention should and will continue to have an important place in social work education and practice.

Specht and Courtney (1994) idealize community work, as if only community action and macro practice can save social work and return it to its founding principles. This view underestimates both the importance of individualism and the problems of communities. Remele (1994), in a study of psychotherapy and Catholic communities, proposes that there is nothing sacrosanct or inherently progressive in community activity, nor anything inherently reactionary in working therapeutically with individuals. The work of Eugen Drewermann (see Remele, 1994; Johnson, 1992), for example, argues for a therapeutic religion to empower clergy and undo the damage done to them by closed and oppressive church communities. Other commentators, including Sennett (1974) and Lasch (1991), see the idealization of community laden with parochialism, exclusiveness, and petty antagonisms towards different communities. The focus on community draws people into narrow neighborhood or small group concerns—larger than individual self-interest but primarily focused on community betterment—which often means exclusion of outsiders. "Maintaining community becomes an end in itself; the purge of those who don't really belong becomes the community's business" (Sennett, 1974, p. 261). Such parochialism deflects attention from the larger society and larger structural forces. "The more people are plunged into these passions of community, the more the basic institutions of social order are untouched" (Sennett, 1974, p. 309).

Paradoxically, these critics argue that building community can hurt the reawakening of public life. This view overstates the case. Community work and associations are essential to building public life in the contemporary context. But communities do have reactionary and oppressive aspects, especially when the rights of individuals for personal autonomy and the rights of "others" to be different are neither allowed nor tolerated. Turning away from individual work completely and adopting only macro practice as the true *social* work is both impractical and problematic. It certainly runs counter to building a progressive common good based on *both* collective material needs and personal autonomy. Moreover, it runs counter to the trend in social work toward practice integration. As Saxton (1991) proposes, "The split between casework and social action, between clinical social work and legislative activism is becoming passé as social workers recognize in practice that . . . the emphasis on one is dependent on, rather than exclusive of, the other" (p. 315). An integrated practice is essential to contextualized social work practice.

BEYOND ECOLOGICAL AND EMPOWERMENT THEORY

Where can social workers gain knowledge of an integrated practice that links the individual and the social? Much of social work has centered on the link between cause and function, social change and social service. More recently, ecological theory and the person-in-the-environment conceptualization contributed to social work practice by seeking to link the individual and the social. Briefly put, ecological theory is a social systems theory that focuses on the individual as seen and evaluated in the larger ecological context. Accordingly, ecological theory does not dichotomize social work narrowly into individual/adjustment, on the one hand, and macro/social change, on the other. Good person-in-the-environment theory sees the importance of "context" and the social change function of social work. At its best, it seeks to integrate the two levels of social work—micro and macro—into a more generalist approach. It recognizes that social change is not limited to community organization, and individual change does not occur only in social casework (Compton & Galaway, 1994).

While ecological theory is an important step in reconnecting the personal world to the social world, an integrated approach to social work that ties together the micro and the macro is not enough in the context of global privatization. Despite a concern for the "social," systems approaches contain a bias toward the "private troubles" of clients. In effect, they manage to separate—through both intervention strategies and inadequate critical contextualization—the personal and the social (Longres & McLeod, 1980). At the heart of an integrated practice must lie a critical contextualization that focuses on power, understood as potentially coercive *and* empowering, laden with the potential to both deny and support social change. The emphasis on the role of power is not found in systems theory or in most ecological theories. For these systems, everything is out there, in "suprasystems" or in the "environment" beyond the individual. Rarely are elements of the environment weighted for power differentials or inequities. Simply because people are eased into a better fit with their environment does not mean that they or the social worker understand the contextual and structural factors that shape their problems and their world. For example, the devastation of AIDS results not simply from the virus, but from homophobia, poverty, racism, and the lack of adequate health care for all but the most affluent. While it is important to help sick people by connecting them to welfare agencies and health care personnel, it also remains important to seek to combine individual intervention with structural work around AIDS.

Ecological theories come up short because they explain most problems as those of communication and linkage, of interaction and transactions between people and their environments. The individual is always at the base, and the emphasis is on determining how the environment can help the individual. The very formulation of the person-in-the-environment theory automatically focuses on the individual, not the environment. Hans Falck (1988) concludes from a literature review of systems and ecological approaches that "existing formulas to deal simultaneously with the individual and the environment, however named, are without exception, individualistic in nature" (quoted in LeComte, 1990, p. 33). The focus on the individual is also true for empowerment theories of social work practice.

Today, the concept of empowerment is arguably the dominant one in social work theory and practice. Because of its salience to social service practitioners, its appeal to almost all client populations, its ambiguous roots, and its adoption by activists across the political spectrum, empowerment has come to provide a coordinating theme for social work in the 1990s. As Barbara Levy Simon (1990) states:

. . . the subdivisions in the social work profession, including direct service/casework and macro practice/community organization have all explicitly incorporated the concept of empowerment into the very heart of their current work and value orientation and have come to view the empowerment of clients and constituents at both the individual and collective level as a central project of the overall profession. (p. 31)

At its best, empowerment theory seeks to provide an integrated and politicized basis for social work. It promotes "a dual working focus on individuals and their social and physical environments" (Simon, 1994, p. xiv). Empowerment also suggests that oppression and injustice can only be reversed "through changes in the distribution of power" (Gutierrez et al., 1992, p. 2).

The concept of empowerment is hotly contested political terrain outside of social work. Because of overuse, empowerment has become a hackneyed phrase. Therapists use it to describe a form of active insight, progressives use it to describe social change, and even the Republican Party used it in its "Contract with America." Although empowerment originated in the Left and in the 1960s social movements, neoconservatives have appropriated it. For example, neoconservative leaders William Bennett and Jack Kemp recently fashioned an organization called Empowering America, Inc., in which empowerment is defined in highly individualistic and marketplace terms. A conservative cable station is called "National Empowerment TV."

Within social work, the term is less contested but equally murky. For many social workers, empowerment has come more to be associated with psychological insight than social action. Moreover, while Simon (1994) and other progressives see empowerment as an extension of the left/liberal tradition in social work, other social workers see it as nearly synonymous with an individualistic, self-efficacy or strengths perspective. In a study of what social workers mean by empowerment, Gutierrez et al. (1992) discovered that (1) it is defined as combining micro and macro intervention, although this integration rarely occurs, and (2) it is seen primarily as a psychological process within individuals. Akins's (1985) definition is illustrative: "in a nutshell, empowerment is helping people assure or reclaim control over their own destiny—it focuses on the capacity of people to function in their own behalf" (cited in Cox & Parsons, 1994, p. 19). The current definition of empowerment clearly contributes to the individualization of social problems. For empowerment to be useful in social change, it must be contextualized in a larger political framework that understands power differentials and collectivizes issues and problems, thereby drawing micro practice into the larger canvas of social change.

Some may regard this discussion as nitpicking. What's wrong with Akins's (1985) definition of giving people the capacity to function on their own behalf? Tavris (cited in Kitzinger and Perkins, 1993) offers a simple example of how language that focuses on the personal occasions completely different responses. She notes how:

If a friend says to you, "Gee, I've been under a lot of stress lately," you could say, "What a shame; have you tried relaxing, jogging, watching funny movies, or taking naps?" But if your friend says, "Gee, I have a problem; I'm about to be evicted because I can't come up with the rent," you wouldn't dream of advising a nap, because it would be wildly inappropriate. (p. 10)

PUTTING MACRO CONTEXTUALIZATION AT THE BASE OF SOCIAL WORK

The dilemma facing most empowerment practice demonstrates the need to go beyond simple empowerment practice. To achieve the twin goals of integrating and politicizing practice, empowerment must be contextualized. The empowerment process is largely seen as linear even by those who see it as already tied to the contextualization of social problems. Beginning with an individual in need, the process helps the person from a strengths or self-efficacy perspective to get stabilized, and then links the personal to the collective and political. For example, a middle-aged woman who is homeless drops by a shelter on a very cold morning. She might receive extensive intake procedures, short-term shelter and food, and individual counseling. If the social worker were committed to an empowerment-based practice that connects the micro and macro, the woman might be referred to a shelter's resident council or a homeless advocacy effort once she is placed in a longer-term shelter or is back on her feet.

Time and time again, practitioners and even empowerment theorists say that once a person reaches some level of "stabilization" they leave the social work process. For these people, the social worker has worked effectively. As such, social workers rarely get the opportunity to help a client understand the larger structural factors that affect the problem or the collective nature of both the problem and its possible solutions. Clearly, addressing the client's immediate and specific needs is important. But while the social worker might seek to do more, the narrow, individualistic focus of most empowerment practice undermines its social change objectives. As social worker and activist Bob Hergenroeder relates:

> When I began this project [with a health care agency and AIDS effort] I was convinced that one's personal power and self-efficacy would only become visible at a point of personal stability, the point following one's successful passage through ill health, homelessness, loss of income, or a less than positive experience with any system of HIV services. On the contrary, what I experienced was that persons at that point want nothing other than to enjoy their completion and stability. Persons encountered far greater personal empowerment, were more willing to make their power visible, and were more likely to maintain a long-term use of personal power when they began their involvement while in the throes of personal need, anguish, and anger. (Hergenroeder, 1994, p. 3)

At a recent conference on empowerment at the University of Washington (Gutierrez & Nurius, 1994), social work practitioners and academics continually underscored the individualistic nature, linear process, and inability of most empowerment practice to connect with social and political forces. Speakers identified empowerment as an integrated, politicized social work practice but its linear process, which begins with individual intervention and then proceeds to the macro level, ultimately undermines the component of macro contextualization. As with the above example of the homeless woman and Hergenroeder's experience, many conference participants were unable to get clients to the macro part of the empowerment model. Once clients were helped, they moved on. If they did not get "stabilized," the intervention stayed focused on issues of personal need and development. This fact was especially curious, since many social workers at the conference emphasized how seminal the collective consciousness raising gained in social movements was for their own empowerment. It was their experience with macro-focused work—civil rights efforts, gay and lesbian issues, and feminist social movement organizations—that provided them with a clearer understanding of power, both individual and collective, and social inequity and oppression. Macro-focused work also provided them with the knowledge, skills, and the ideological framework for resisting injustice.

An informal subgroup at the conference created a working definition of empowerment emphasizing its integrative and political elements. Empowerment is "an integrative collaborative practice and process which struggles around confronting oppression, understands the structural basis of that oppression, and seeks as its ends social justice, equality, and the realization of human potential." This chapter argues that in order to achieve the ideal of a politicized and integrated empowerment-based practice, political education and critical consciousness must occur early in the process. All social work practice must rest on knowledge of structural foundations. A contextualized analysis teaches that individual problems are almost always social problems caused by structural factors (Longres, 1995). Contextualizing practice and education means that this structural analysis must come early, if not first, for both students and clients. In most cases, this analysis needs to happen in collective and group formats rather than in one-to-one or family counseling sessions. The macro connection—the collective and political nature of a person's problem—should be put at the beginning of the social work process rather than the end. This recommendation is not to bias micro practice in favor of macro practice but, rather, to propose a truly integrated practice that counters the current bias in social work towards a decontextualized micro practice.

If social work practice is to help empower clients, regardless of whether it is direct intervention or community organization, it must be grounded in a macro conceptualization of problems. For the past fifteen years, progressive macro practitioners have assumed that personal development and interpersonal issues are fundamental to good macro practice (Burghardt, 1982; Freire, 1970). But they have also understood that empowerment practice cannot simply be about helping people to *feel* more powerful. Social change is more than personal validation. Counseling a battered woman to feel more self-confident is helpful, but without a good understanding of her problem and its dangers, self-confidence alone would be irresponsible practice. Contextualized practice proposes that practice must include a structural understanding of the social and individual problem, offered ideally in a collaborative and collective process. In this way, power can be unmasked and made more visible. A macro contextualization at the base of all social work practice may seem novel, perhaps even threatening to some, only because micro practice theory is so dominant in the profession. Micro theory and practice will and should remain important. But to be most effective, to connect the individual to the larger problems posed by the contemporary context, social work education and practice must be built on a critical knowledge of macro analysis and practice.

POLITICIZED SOCIAL WORK

A politicized social work begins with the recognition that social work is fundamentally about power, public life, and social as well as personal change (Abramovitz, 1993; Haynes & Mickelson, 1991; Rees, 1991; Withorn, 1984). Although the word *political* is laden in our private world with mostly negative connotations, it comes from the Greek *polis*, which refers to an organized body. We have been referring to it as *the public*. Restoration of the public also means restoration of the political: public involvement, discussion, and action over public matters. Progressive and radical traditions in social work understand its political nature (Davis, 1967; Chambers, 1967; Wagner, 1990). Conservative traditions see political social work as essentially unprofessional and regard accommodating to the demands of those in power—who often set increasingly restrictive agency and social policy—as both professional and nonpolitical behavior. Agitating and advocating on behalf of clients and communities is seen by conservative thinkers as political and harmful (see Lubove, 1975; Bardill, 1993; Carniol, 1990). Certainly a decontextualized individual or family therapy that adjusts clients to the status quo is, in fact, political. Apolitical social work practice equals acceptance of current political realities. As Reisch (1993) proposes, "more than at any time in this century, politics and human services are inextricably connected. . . . Politics is no longer an activity that social workers can escape by hiding behind a veil of professionalism" (pp. 220–21). If practice remains depoliticized, it will continue to be blinded to the need for more political action and unable to respond to its own deepening crisis (Fabricant & Burghardt, 1992; Mahaffey, 1987).

An integrated knowledge and practice base has always been at the heart of the radical and "critical theory" traditions in social work. According to Burghardt and Fabricant (1987), "Radical practice begins with the fundamental premise that the circumstances of at-risk populations can be traced to political or economic relationships that exist in the larger social order" (p. 456). Those in the radical tradition perceive from the outset that individual "dysfunction" is almost always rooted in larger social factors that pattern individual behavior. A battered woman is seen as a victim of physical abuse rooted in a patriarchal society. A homeless person is not seen as a person with a behavioral dysfunction, but as a person who is homeless because of oppressive work, family, and class structures (who may or may not also have psychological problems) (Wagner, 1993). This vision leads to a more integrated social work practice opposing the dichotomization of practice into narrow skill or methodological specializations such as case work, group work, and community organization. The emphasis is on helping the person or group uncover the root of the problem.

Critical theory emphasizes that social work practice must be contextualized. In other words, it must be understood as related to power—its use, misuse, and inequities, and the struggles to change it. Practice must also be tied to political economy, class, and culture. This focus on collective power and oppression politicizes social work education and practice and moves it beyond simply empowerment practice. Without this focus, the profession of social work often plays a highly conservative role in society. Those in the radical tradition (Withorn, 1984; Burghardt & Fabricant, 1987) argue that social work is part of the larger conflicts in society, part of the struggle in public life over what the world should be like, who makes the decisions, and who benefits from them. In this struggle, social services have the potential to be a means of social control or of social change. They can replicate domination and oppression and reinforce the status quo. Or, they can serve as an important basis to change contemporary oppression and inequalities. Increasingly, as neoconservatives target social and public services, the political nature of social services is becoming clearer to a larger number of social workers. What once seemed radical now appears obvious.

For example, consider a health care social worker who is addressing the needs of a child with asthma. As mentioned earlier, contextualized social work links clients to an understanding of the social nature of individual problems, to their social causes, and to the possibilities for social change. A child suffering from asthma receives individual counseling from a health care social worker, who offers information on the individual prevention of asthma (e.g., taking of medications, disposing of dusty rugs in the child's bedroom) and perhaps referral to an asthma support group. But the epidemic growth of asthma is a serious collective and environmental problem tied to issues of power, policy, and social change efforts. Sitting in the waiting room at the public health clinic, the child's parent realizes that there are two dozen other kids there also having breathing problems. Contextualized social work practice would link the two problems, helping the child with her illness *and* empowering the parent with knowledge and resources related to the environmental causes and solutions of asthma. It is good social work, for example, to mention that the last 22 days of the summer have had ozone pollution levels at high levels, that the hospital has been full of children with respiratory problems, that something needs to be done about the quality of air and the willingness of people and their leaders to push for change, and that there is a long history of official denial of harmful air pollution levels. While the child's suffering occurs on an individual level, it also reflects a deep-rooted, collective social problem. Contextualized social work would raise these issues with clients *and* address the child's direct needs. How this is done obviously takes care and skill. There are various methods of raising structural issues that do not overwhelm clients or project onto them the social worker's own life experiences or politics. Collectivization of the process, discussed below, can be effective. But the important lesson here is that raising structural issues and helping clients make political connections are critical and legitimate elements of good social work practice.

THE ROLE OF SOCIAL CHANGE IDEOLOGY

Social workers constantly learn about new problems and needs in society. As such, they are always expanding their knowledge of contextual factors. But how do social workers mobilize and implement this knowledge and critical analysis? Withorn (1984) and Hyde (1992) suggest that this activity occurs best through ties with a social movement. The division between social service versus social change work disappears when practice is part of a social movement agency, such as a feminist domestic violence center. Social movements are able to contextualize practice because they supply, among other things, a social justice ideology that includes a critical analysis of the workings of the larger society. Movements also tie this understanding to daily life and the need for social change. We argue that contextualization and the politicization of practice occurs best in settings—including agencies, private practice, organizations, and social movements—fueled by a social change ideology.

Ideology offers a map that provides not only a clear understanding of the problems people face but also a blueprint for action. It remains essential to "move people to a set of ideas that critiques the current system, understands the importance of class and community, connects work to place and public to private spheres, and gets people to take risks and transcend what they thought was possible for themselves and their world" (Fisher & Kling, 1991, p. 82). We argue that ideological competence is essential to the creation of social work agencies and organizations able to articulate problems and help people reach a deeper understanding of the larger world affecting daily life.

Feminist social work practice is a good example of how social movement ideology helps to critically contextualize social work knowledge and practice. Why is the personal seen as political and the political seen as personal among feminists or gay and lesbian activists who are also heavily influenced by feminist practice, but not in the intimate discussions held on TV talk shows? Critics such as Lasch (1978), Sennett (1974), and Bellah et al. (1985) argue strongly that the personal reflects a turning away from the political. For them, the trend toward the personal depoliticizes social discourse and helps to undermine social and public life. Feminists do not agree (Van Den Bergh & Cooper, 1987; Withorn, 1984; Hyde, 1989; Hyde, 1992; Weil, 1986). Feminist social work practice is seen as a radical alternative to traditional social work. There are a number of central elements to feminist practice, similar to themes discussed earlier, such as integrative practice and empowerment ideology. But the concept that the personal is political "serves as an all-encompassing component of feminism" (Van Den Bergh & Cooper, 1987, p. 612). How can connecting the personal to the political be the basis of a radical practice that professes to alter nothing less than "relationships, processes, and institutions in American society"? (Van Den Bergh & Cooper, 1987, p. 611). We believe the connection is rooted in a social change ideology that provides a critical analysis of the patriarchal context in which women live both their personal and public lives. The critical analysis of patriarchy and women's emancipation from it rests at the base of feminist practice. This ideological base contextualizes and politicizes practice, whether it is feminist therapy (Miller, 1983) or feminist community organization (Hyde, 1992;

Gutierrez, 1990). The contextualization of feminist practice places personal and group experience in a larger political reality, collectivizes issues and problems, and grounds knowledge and practice—regardless of the level or method of intervention—in a critical understanding of the *social* base of women's experiences.

The work of Stout (1993) on the *social* problem of intimate femicide—men who kill female mates—emphasizes that "each day an average of four males kill female intimate partners in the United States" (p. 82). In her effort to determine who kills and why, Stout discovered that the typical offender has a strong need for power and control over his partner and has highly patriarchal attitudes toward women. In terms of intervention, feminist analysis like Stout's instructs that the need is not for family therapy; instead, the battered would be better helped by a feminist understanding of male violence against women as an extreme act of patriarchal power. In working with batterers, Stout proposes that the key is to get men to begin to address power issues of control and violence in their relationships.

Curiously, recent versions of feminist practice have become more private and therapeutic, and less public and political. Longres (1996) suggests that feminist and ethnic-sensitive approaches to social work practice are reflecting the demands of the contemporary conservative context, by being "more involved in subjective, clinical issues than justice and equity" (p. 8). Decontextualization also leads feminist practice away from a sharp analysis of power and oppression to a more narrow cultural critique. Without the ideological critique of oppression in patriarchal society and without a focus on the abuses of power in a gendered context, "difference feminism" credits gender inequality to "universal features of male and female psychosexual development rather than to the economic and social positions men and women hold, or to the actual power differences between men and women" (Pollitt, 1992, p. 801).

Without putting macro contextualization at the base of practice and without utilizing a social justice ideology to help practitioners frame issues, social work revolves largely around what C. Wright Mills (1959, p. 8) called "private troubles." It is critical contextualization that transforms private troubles into "public issues," connects the personal to the social, and politicizes the personal (Longres, 1995; Wharf, 1990). It is the understanding of patriarchy, racism, homophobia, ethnocentrism, and especially class inequalities that politicizes social work education and practice. It is the linkage of patriarchy and gender inequality to daily life that politicizes issues like sex and family life. Who vacuums the floors, does the dishes, and changes diapers is only political given the structural and political analysis of patriarchy and gender inequality. The role of a social change ideology is continually to emphasize structural factors and critically contextualize social work in an *abridged* and *energized* form accessible to daily practice.

Like political social work, ideology may at first sound foreign. But just as there is no value-free social science, ideology is present in all social work. Ideology can be implicit or explicit, and it can be the result of an elitist or democratic process. Many more comfortably refer to the "value base" of the profession, although "value base" is only part of a social worker's ideological map. To be effective, all good social work and social change ideology must ring true and speak directly to the needs and hopes of clients. If not, people turn away from it. That is why the value base of good social work and social justice ideology demands that all efforts begin with and rely on people's understanding of their own grievances. But an effective social change ideology must also go beyond people's daily experience. In order to effect social change, people must relate the sources of their problems to conditions beyond their immediate experience and to norms that conflict with some of the values and cultural traditions they have internalized (Fisher & Kling, 1987). Framing issues in a social justice perspective is essential to effective contextualization. Progressive social work offers students and clients a social justice ideology built on a critical analysis of problems and their solutions.

Rude (1980) argues that all effective social change efforts must include a dual ideology: an "inherent" popular view of politics and how the world works based on people's traditions *and* a "derived" external ideology of power and social change that ties daily issues and problems to events beyond personal experience. Together, these two visions provide an ideology of empowerment that legitimates grievances. They also help to mobilize citizens to action, as people come to see their individual issues in a larger perspective. For example, "nonviolent resistance" galvanized the ideology of the black, Southern, church-based communities in the 1950s and 1960s. The critique of patriarchy and sexism activated women in the 1960s and 1970s to see their lives differently and reopened the demand for women's participation in public life. At the same time, the critique built on the importance of private issues and personal connection. The interplay between popular and derived ideology is true today for all significant social change efforts.

Animated by a social justice ideology, all social work intervention is consciously politicized and contextualized. When rooted in a social justice ideology, the sharing of personal biography employed in empowerment practice directly connects to the social world (Freire, 1985; Longres & McLeod, 1980; Rees, 1991). The telling of a personal biography, whether in individual counseling, group therapy, consciousness-raising groups, or public life, begins to become *social* when people see themselves as part of a larger collectivity deeply affected by social forces. It is this connection to the social world that transforms apolitical biography into social analysis. The inclusion in personal biography of themes such as class, race, gender, ethnicity, religion, age, and sexual orientation pushes personal experience beyond the individual level. These themes connect the personal to social groups, social forces, and even social change. Without an ideology to make these connections, the narrative of personal life remains highly personal and private.

This is why Rose (1990) makes "contextualization" his "first principle" of an "advocacy/empowerment" model of clinical practice. For Rose, contextualization means connecting individuals to an understanding of the larger ideological/structural environment *and* to their own personal social context. Rose's model is a classic example in micro practice of the use of Rude's concept of inherent and derived ideology. "Starting where the client is" includes both the belief that clients know themselves and their personal world (inherent ideology) better than the social worker does. Added to this understanding, social workers bring to the dialogue external values and knowledge (derived ideology), that helps people "learn of their social historical existence" and understand themselves as "dynamic dimensions of a larger social contextual/ideologically constructed universe" (Rose, 1990, p. 46). The sharing of experience, knowledge, and world views between client and social worker brings "to consciousness both the unique experience of the individual and the social base for that individual's experience," and helps connect client troubles to structural factors and to a vision of social change.

COLLECTIVIZATION AND CONTEXTUALIZATION

Contextualization precedes empowerment in Rose's (1990) advocacy/empowerment model. Collectivity comes after it. Because Rose (1990) focuses on clinical practice and mental health work, collectivity is defined as the process of connecting the individual to others and to the larger society. The goal of collectivity is to counteract feelings of being alone, isolated, and different. It also seeks to establish a possible basis for advocacy work later on, but the primary objective of collectivity is to help individuals by connecting them to others.

In our use of the term, collectivization refers to the importance of collective settings, collective issues and problems, and collective solutions to empowerment. The framework we use for contextualized practice reads as follows: Real empowerment practice is integrated, tied to issues of power inequities, critically contextualized at the base, politicized, mobilized by social change ideology, and facilitated by collectivization. Empowerment can occur on an individual or a collective basis. But according to Longres and McLeod (1980), when social workers deal with individuals and families separately and when they separate clients from larger collectivities, "the weight is too strongly distributed in favor of working toward a resolution of private troubles" (p. 273).

In a seminal article based on work with women's and men's groups, Longres and McLeod (1980) argue that consciousness-raising connects the individualized problems of everyday life to the adverse conditions in the structure of society. This connection occurs best in settings that have an ideological focus, such as an agency committed to feminist concerns. In all consciousness-raising the conditions and struggles of the larger society must form a central basis of discussion. Perhaps most important, they argue that such discussion "is only possible within groups" (Longres & McLeod, 1980, p. 273). The key to effectively contextualizing problems is building groups of people with shared commonalities, who may, with the help of a social change agent, reveal to each other the structural basis of their individual problems and the potential for collective and individual change. Contextualization occurs more easily and profoundly as a collectively shared experience. While individual intervention has its place—people can learn a great deal in one-to-one counseling—it is intervention in groups and larger collective settings that more naturally contextualizes problems and connects people to an understanding of social change.

Contextualizing problems through group work is sensible for social workers unable to make connections in individualized treatment, unable to empower clients beyond personal stabilization, and barely able to deal effectively with clients on any level because of heavy caseloads and bureaucratic pressures. This point is supported in the literature (Longres & McLeod, 1980; Freire, 1970; Hyde, 1989) and in the more effective efforts at changing social services. According to Gutierrez and Lewis (1995), "The small group provides the ideal environment for exploring the social and political aspects of 'personal' problems and for developing strategies for work toward social change" (p. 108). Moreau and Leonard (cited in Mullaly, 1993) propose eight ways for the collectivization of social work practice; that is, to link individual and social experience by collectivizing the process. A sense of empowerment can also occur among students as part of the group consciousness-raising in the classroom setting. As one student, Maxine Seiler Vacek, in the political social work concentration at the University of Houston's Graduate School of Social Work notes:

> Not all social workers will have the opportunity to affect social change in dramatic ways such as union organizing, creating social movements, and rising to policy making positions within government structures. Nevertheless, I believe that it is the personal responsibility of each social worker to study and understand the structural constraints within our society which block opportunities for our clients' self-actualization. It is also the responsibility of each social worker to understand our political system as well as the methods and techniques which can be utilized to affect social policies and create real opportunities for social and economic justice in America. (Vacek, 1994, p. 13)

The use of collective settings for empowerment is vividly seen in social movement-related service agencies (Hyde, 1992). For example, the PIVOT Project in Houston, Texas, is a program for male batterers founded by Toby Myers, a feminist activist. The project is grounded explicitly in feminist ideology. The process of raising consciousness about male violence against women and grounding the personal experiences of male batterers in the larger social world of patriarchy and violence begins for these court appointed offenders in the first *collective* orientation session. Macro contextualization rests at the base of practice at PIVOT and not only comes early in the process but actually is basic from the outset. Some 50–100 men, and sometimes their female partners, listen to a critical analysis of the extent, nature, and causes of male violence against women. Some opportunity exists for questions, but this is fundamentally an orientation session to the critical analysis and feminist ideology that undergirds the project. The individual issues of each offender are seen not only as personal problems, but as collective ones resting on a base of patriarchy and violence. Contextualization occurs at the base of the group and the individual work that follows. During the process, individual needs get met in group and individual work, while problems are contextualized and collectivized. Here, social movement ideology serves to unmask oppression and fuel individual healing and collective action. Similar collective ways of contextualizing social justice can be found in other women's agencies, African-American efforts, and community organizing projects in the United States and worldwide (Hyde, 1992; Withorn, 1984; Morris, 1984; Freire, 1985; Fisher, 1994).

Collectivization must include collective solutions as well as collective processes. Social workers and society focus on individuals as the source of problems and solutions. Victims get blamed for both causing their problems and for failing to solve them. Because problems are seen primarily as reflecting individual cultural attitudes and behavior—promiscuity, immorality, laziness, and dependency—social service systems generally provide individual treatment and solutions. Depending on the client population, social service systems may also provide scrutiny, surveillance, and abuse (Wagner, 1993). Solutions are highly individualized in terms of process and objectives. A contextualized practice should lead practitioners to consider not only more collective processes but also collective as well as individual solutions.

In his study of homelessness Wagner (1993) asserts that the social structure forces the homeless to present and conceptualize themselves as atomized entities (individuals or families), distinguishing them to those with power as "worthy" of support and separating them from other homeless in order to gain resources critical to survival. In spite of such pressures, the homeless forged a collective consciousness that often placed collective needs and group solidarity ahead of personal gain. The homeless interviewed in Wagner's ethnographic study frequently asked, 'Why can't we all get housed?' or 'Why can't we all have services?' not just when they [as individuals] would get something" (Wagner, 1993, p. 180). If the problem is collective and a collective consciousness develops in a group structure, then individualized solutions and treatments undermine group solidarity. Wagner (1993) suggests distributing social benefits collectively: Income and resources for shelter and food should be disbursed to whole groups of people, not individuals. People could get a collective grant as members of a group or community, and funds could be allocated to hire organizers to help promote collective empowerment.

Here, again, is a call for the principle of subsidiarity; that is, let the most basic level of society address problems with the help of external supports from the public sector. There are precedents for these types of collective solutions in some New Deal and Great Society programs. Such measures met with initial opposition, and they would encounter even more in the contemporary context. But public debate around the need for collective responses to social problems would, at the least, help push the social dialogue in a positive direction, help challenge the seemingly unchallenged trend toward global privatization, and help force a debate within social work about the need for a better understanding of social problems and solutions. Contextualization teaches that a depoliticized social work practice cannot succeed; instead, social workers must identify collective, as well as individual, processes and strategies for social change (Fabricant & Burghardt, 1992).

COMMUNITY AND CONTEXTUALIZED PRACTICE

Community work is especially important as a natural site for collective cohesion, processes, strategies, and solutions. This is the goal of a communitarian movement gaining adherents in intellectual circles (Elshtain, 1994; Etzioni, 1993). A number of recent studies in social work also point in this direction. Specht and Courtney

(1994) call for a communitarian revival in social work focused on the delivery of community-based services. Fabricant and Burghardt (1992), while critical of a narrow communitarianism, agree that social service providers must become part of the communities they serve, and citizens and clients must be made part of the agencies in their communities. The organic connection between the building of community and the provision of social services must be renewed. In this process, shared connection strengthens the public discourse of individual and collective needs, and public life begins to be rebuilt. The current focus on the community seeks to respond to global privatization by sustaining public life at the grassroots level.

Admittedly, community organization and community work have changed in the past decades. The nature of urban life and the bonds that tie people together are different in the postindustrial, postmodern city than they were in the industrial metropolis where community organizing began. Delgado (1994) argues that community work has gone "beyond the politics of place" to focus on the politics of culture. Locality is critical to community organizing, but so are the bonds of race, ethnicity, language, religion, and so forth. The extraordinary work of Rev. Johnny Youngblood and his St. Paul Community Baptist Church parishioners, chronicled in Freedman (1993), attests to the power of focusing community work on both locality (the community of East New York) and cultures (male, African-American, and Christian) to effect change in the lives of neighborhood people and institutions. In the words of the Industrial Areas Foundation organizing institute, founded by Saul Alinsky, the community is where people learn about public life, social responsibility, and politics (Boyte, 1989; Skerry, 1993). Through Youngblood's efforts, St. Paul's is a "resource church" that serves as the epicenter of social renewal in a once-ravaged community of seemingly defeated people. "Folks bein' here is lookin' to believe in *somethin'*," Youngblood says, because "everything they got is fallin' down and crumblin' around 'em" (Freedman, 1993, p. 6). St. Paul's Church now sponsors a wide range of community services, helps win college loans and secure entry-level jobs at local banks for high school graduates, builds African-American men's groups at the church as well as a new school, shopping district, and a nationally touted low-income housing project (the Nehemiah program) in cooperation with the East Brooklyn Congregations and the Industrial Areas Foundation.

As global capital centralizes power, the revival of community-based approaches to social change might seem fruitless. But the community is an essential component of how people collectively deal with globalization. Michael Sandel (1988) suggests that increasing globalization requires the building and rebuilding of communities to provide a basis of stability and identity in a global context that challenges both. Without such community building, "we will find ourselves without any form of political community that expresses our shared identity, and knits us together in the families, schools, and neighborhoods that democracy requires" (quoted in Friedman, 1993, p.1; Sandel, 1988). The more the nation moves into a global economic model, the more people need community to give structure to everyday life. Community provides a base to stabilize and organize public life, to give people training in citizenship and social responsibility. Because global capitalism generally ignores its impact on community life and is fundamentally unaccountable, unrestrained, and corrosive to the traditional stability of the community, grassroots organizing becomes a means for dealing with the antisocial aspects of global privatization (Lasch, 1991; Sandel, 1988).

Curiously, many on the Left and the Right agree on this point. They both criticize the lack of civility or sense of a common good in society. They both seek societies with a better developed sense of civic duty, social cooperation, and mutual trust. And they tend to view the community as the basis of reviving public life and a sense of a commonwealth (Boyte, 1989; Bell, 1993). Clearly, any public philosophy for the contemporary era must recognize the value and importance of communities in helping to rebuild public life. But contextualized practice does not end with the community, just as integrated practice must not end with the individual. There are critical issues of power that need to be kept in mind if an equitable society is to be fashioned. These issues include challenging the absolute prerogative of private decisions, emphasizing social responsibilities as well as rights, refashioning the welfare state to support basic human needs, and limiting the power and scope of corporations and global capital.

The community is ultimately too narrow and too lacking in resources to perform such functions. And the focus on culture that many praise as an adhesive in an era when people no longer stick together is, by itself, not sufficient. Community and cultural identity are both too narrow to meet the challenge of global privatization. Communities need help from outside, and cultural issues, such as gender and race, need to be connected with those of class. Both objectives can be addressed in a renewed focus in social work practice against attacks on the welfare state and in support of cultural diversity. In this combined struggle, not only are the importance of class and the state reasserted, but they are tied to the contemporary identification around culture.

CONCLUSION: LINKING CLASS, CULTURE, AND COMMUNITY

Simple solutions are dangerous, and the path to social change is filled with land mines. As noted earlier, the task is not to find a single strategy to meet the challenges of global privatization; multiple strategies from multiple efforts are needed. Brecher and Costello (1994), Brecher, Childs, & Cutler (1993) and Amin et al. (1990) suggest the importance of linking grassroots organizations worldwide. This linkage would connect community groups increasingly organized around culture in the Northern Hemisphere with those focused on issues of class in the Southern Hemisphere. Linking grassroots efforts worldwide also underscores the need for social change activists to link issues of class and culture, not an easy task. Based on a long history of deception and abandonment of cultural efforts by class-based ones, multiculturalists argue against the centrality of class issues because they tend to exclude cultural concerns (Rivera & Erlich, 1995). Some recent structuralists, however, seek to bridge the gap by broadening the structural base to include not only economic but also cultural matters. Class becomes one identity, albeit an essential one, among many. Most important for social work, class returns to the equation of social change. As Ben Carniol (1990) puts it:

> . . . when it comes to social change, it is insufficient to work toward the dismantling of oppressive relations in gender, colour, sexuality, ability/disability, or other areas or in any combination of these. Unless the reconstruction of social relations also includes an *equal priority* [our emphasis] on dismantling the illegitimate power anchored to class privilege, the concentration of wealth into the hands of a privileged few will inevitably continue. (p. 138)

A reconceptualization of social work education and practice must link the struggle around political economy with that of cultural identity (Moreau, 1987; Coates, 1992; Carniol, 1992).

Reasserting the link between class and culture is important to social work practice because of its current turn away from poverty and class concerns (Specht & Courtney, 1994). This cultural focus often leaves class far behind cultural identity in terms of importance (Longres, 1995). The ongoing rebuilding of public life and a sense of a progressive common good must be tied to issues of political economy. Rebuilding must be connected to a critique of how inequities of power, unbridled capitalism, and class domination destroy public life. Otherwise, calls for the "cultural turn" play into neoconservative hands. According to William Kristol, a chief neoconservative strategist, "Our agenda now is to think about how to revitalize public institutions, how to strengthen the institutions of civic society—shaping the culture as opposed to reforming the politics" (quoted in Atlas, 1995, p. 54).

The neoconservative argument is that contemporary problems are largely cultural ones. The battleground has been moved away from economics, politics, and class to "culture wars" over values, identity, and voice. These are important struggles, which may yet strengthen the fabric of democracy. But the conservative focus on amoral people—usually the poor—who lack virtue and a sense of the common good only pushes the cultural debate down reactionary paths. This emphasis is being countered by progressive analyses of cultural issues such as race, gender, ethnicity, and sexual orientation. But contemporary social change also needs to debate issues of political power, class relations, and political economy. Neoconservatives assume that those aspects of society are fundamentally sound. We strongly disagree.

The primary issue of contemporary life is the unsoundness of current politics, class relations, and political economy. The fundamental issue is not one of a debased, individualistic culture, but, rather, globalization and the culture of privatism it nurtures. As Lasch remarks, "in a world in which there are no values except those of the market . . . [there is] an almost irresistible pressure on every activity to justify itself in the only terms it recognizes: to become a business proposition, to pay its own way, to show black ink on the bottom line" (cited in Judge, 1995, p. 35). Class remains critical to social change because class oppression is a global phenomenon. Without class consciousness and class alliances between the middle class and the poor, cultural conflict can neither challenge nor moderate global privatiza-

tion. Whether in agencies, organizations, schools, communities, or social movements, a contextualized practice requires linking struggles around class and cultural
oppression.

Although the social work practiced in traditional agencies is often conservative,
and the profession as a whole is vilified in society and even by some social workers, it nevertheless possesses the social justice ideology and historical experience to
play an important role in contemporary social change. Social work is grounded in a
social justice ideology that takes the side of the oppressed, seeks to universalize the
particular, and historically has paid careful attention to the conditions and needs of
the poor and working class. With a new attention to cultural matters that combines
the older forms of class-based social justice with the newer focus on identity and
empowerment, social work can link class and culture. One of the central goals of
politicized social work is the grounding of practice in both political economy and
cultural identity. A social work education and practice based on such a macro contextualization would be able to connect issues of poverty and political economy to
issues of race, gender, ethnicity, and sexual orientation. The argument for putting
macro knowledge at the base of practice includes the incorporation of class and
culture. It is this contextualization that provides the essential base for social change.

In contemporary society—and in social work education and practice—there is
a tendency to focus more on culture and less on class. It is hard work to keep focused on both, but they do go together. Class affects most things social in the
United States. Caryatis Cardea discusses the intersection of lesbian identity with
class around the issue of middle-class, feminist language:

> We are not taught in working-class homes to preface everything we say
> with the phrases: "I think," "I feel," "In my opinion," "I could be wrong,
> but". . . . We are often attacked for opinions we expressed, because we
> neglected to provide ourselves and our listeners, in the fashion of feminist
> process, with those verbal escape clauses. For the emphasis in middle-
> class language is not on the "I," but on the doubt-filled words "think,"
> "feel," "opinion". . . . The willingness of working-class lesbians to simply
> say what we want to say and take the consequences is an affront to the
> devotees of therapy. . . . Middle-class lesbians make clear their discomfort
> with . . . working-class dykes [who] do not negate their own statements
> (quoted in Kitzinger and Perkins, 1993, p. 147).

Cardea not only draws out the middle-class bias of much of feminism, but her
focus on identity gets at the dual tension of identity politics: the search for both
autonomy and a more inclusive collectivity.

Identity and multiculturalism have always been about power more than culture. Class has always been about oppression and the struggle against it. The current global economy pushes society away from "the ideals of multicultural unity
nurtured during more optimistic times" just as it exacerbates class relations by favoring the already rich and immiserating the poor and the middle class (Muwakkil,
1995, p. 16). Because the profession is well-connected to the constituencies and

sites of cultural resistance, social workers committed to building a progressive common good are better positioned than any other group in society to help shape class and culture into an ideology and movement for social change and public renewal.

A contextualized perspective can serve as the basis for a social work education and practice framework oriented to helping clients and promoting progressive social change. The remainder of this book discusses how other areas of social work are essential to forming a new framework for social work education and practice. Research contextualizes social work practice by advancing methodologies such as direct action, ethnography, and historical inquiry. Policy analysis reveals the political nature of contemporary social life and demands political responses to it. Macro practice inherently links education and practice to an understanding of social problems, strategies, and skills. Organizational analysis contextualizes practice at the agency level, pointing to the power and professional relations inherent in all organizational contexts. These elements broaden contextualization throughout social work education and practice. They link the process of social change to the various elements of social work education and practice. Whether students are taking a research course or practitioners are dealing with organizational problems at work, contextualization becomes an essential component. One important skill in this broader reconceptualization of social work practice is social research, which is examined in the following chapter.

part II

Contextualizing Social Work: Research, Policy, Practice, and the Social Service Workplace

chapter 4

Research: Contextualizing and Politicizing Social Work

A contextualized form of social work practice can form the basis for helping clients and promoting progressive social change. However, contextualizing social work practice involves more than just insight and astute political analyses; it also requires verifiable social change-oriented research. Properly gathered and analyzed, data can be a valuable asset in helping all practitioners raise awareness and facilitate action on a broad range of concerns.

This chapter examines the relationship between social work research, public life, and social change. As part of this investigation, the chapter probes both the function of social work research and its political dimensions. Also examined are the tenets and goals of politicized social work research. The authors contend that all social work research, including research in micro, mezzo, and macro practice, must be contextualized and politicized. This chapter also investigates the responsibility of social work researchers and practitioners to contribute to a public discourse on the common good. Finally, this chapter explores a sampling of research skills needed by social workers, including community needs assessments, ethnographic research, direct action research, policy research, and historical research.

William Reid (1987) described social work research as having three specific functions: (1) to use the perspectives and methods of science as a framework for practice activities; (2) to use research as a base for building knowledge for practice; and (3) to use research to secure situation-specific data for informing practice decisions, program operations, or efforts at social change. In analyzing these functions, Reid (1987) observes that:

> Despite progress on this and other fronts, the knowledge underlying direct practice in social work has hardly amounted to the hoped-for scientific base whose existence was often asserted. . . . That . . . could be applied as

well to the knowledge foundations of the macro level of social work practice, including community work, administration, and social action. Throughout its history, macro social work has drawn on the social sciences as sources of knowledge, but research-based knowledge relevant to practice at the macro level has been slow to accumulate and is probably even less substantial than that available for direct, or micro, practice. (p. 476)

Reid (1987) divides social work research into four categories:

- Studies concerned with the behavior, personality, and problems of individuals, families, and small groups.
- Studies that look at the utilization and outcomes of social services.
- Research studies that focus on the social work profession, including training and education.
- Macro research studies whose foci are organizations, communities, and social policy.

Herbert and Irene Rubin (1992) identify social action research as a distinct methodology within macro social work practice. They define action research as "the systematic gathering of information by people who are both affected by a problem and who want to solve the problem. It is a fact-gathering endeavor as people learn about the problem, a mobilization endeavor as people learn to share the problem, and a capacity-building endeavor as people work to solve the problem" (Rubin & Rubin, 1992, p. 156).

Several problems are created by defining social action research as a subspecialty within social work macro research. First, isolating social action research into a separate category allows less politicized research to continue unabated. Specifically, by devolving much of the responsibility for social change-oriented research onto social action research, traditional social work research is allowed to continue without having to prove its social utility.

The very act of separating social action research from traditional research functions in much the same way as segregating social change from traditional social work practice. In both instances, this separation leads to the creation of a social change ghetto within the social work profession. Within this ghetto are progressives and radicals who refuse to accommodate to the prevailing norm of micro-level practice. The role of this outsider group is to serve as the conscience of the social work profession and publicly meet the profession's social change obligations. This action is done at a relatively low cost, since macro social change-oriented students and practitioners compose at present only a small fraction of the social work profession (see chapter 6). By pointing to the subspeciality of social action, traditional social workers can remain unhampered in their pursuit of direct practice goals while still voicing their historic commitment to social justice and social change. As argued in chapter 3, good social work integrates micro and macro practice; it is inappropriate to limit social action research only to macro subjects.

Another problem is that in the same way social change and community organization are relegated to a low status within the profession, social action research is shuffled to the back of the research bus (Reid, 1987). Thus, many traditional researchers do not consider social action research "real research," but social advocacy and ideology masquerading as social research. Missing from this equation is the insight that all research is inherently political.

CRITIQUES OF SOCIAL WORK RESEARCH

Social work research has been scrutinized by a variety of rigorous critiques, albeit on an erratic basis. Although these criticisms of social work research methodology have not been of one voice, common themes emerge. One such consistent theme has been the inordinate value placed on quantitative over qualitative approaches to social work research (Karger, 1983; Ruckdeschel & Farris, 1981). Some of these critics (Heinemann, 1981; Ruckdeschel & Farris, 1981) assert that there are alternative ways of "knowing," and quantitative research represents only one avenue. These critics also argue that social work has borrowed methodologies from the hard sciences, some of which are ill-equipped to study the complex and dynamic interaction between human beings and the social environment. While most critics skeptical of positivism (highly quantitative research) acknowledge a role for quantitative research in social work, they believe that it is not the only methodology congruent with good science. What these critics propose are new constructs based on alternative assumptions about what constitutes valid research (Haworth, 1984).

Quantitative research has been the dominant influence in social work research for several decades. Many researchers who are strong advocates of this method (Hudson, 1982; Geismar, 1982; Schuerman, 1982) are inclined to see nonquantitative methods as preliminary and exploratory, rather than as alternative ways of knowing. Because of this bias and the demands of many academicians for social work to be a "hard" science (that is, it is generally believed that the hard sciences are more prestigious), qualitative methodologies generally occupy a lower position on the methodological hierarchy. By aping the hard sciences, social work has turned its back on the valuable qualitative contributions that have emerged from disciplines such as anthropology, history, and sociology (Glaser & Strauss, 1967; Chambers, 1992). Skeptics of positivism such as Joseph Vigilante (1974) and Martha Heinemann (1981) argue that social work research is wedded to an obsolete and narrow empiricism. The differences between positivists and skeptics cannot be bridged by facts, discussions, or arguments alone. These divergent viewpoints on research are based on fundamental differences in the perception of reality and how best to understand it.

The research debate also contains a political dimension (Austin, 1976; Heinemann, 1981; Karger, 1983). For example, whatever the merits of the qualitative approach, traditional quantitative researchers comprise the majority and hold positions of power. As such, they control the debate by determining the kinds of research taught, rewarded, funded, and published (Reid, 1987). Many social work doctoral students who have proposed alternative, nonquantitative research designs know well the power wielded by quantitatively oriented social work methodologists.

At one level, the scope of social research is heavily influenced by the methodology employed. For example, quantitative research methods are ill-equipped to examine intricate processes of change in large communities or organizations. Because of this limitation, many quantitative researchers are hesitant to tackle this complex unit of analysis. Instead of choosing a research methodology to fit a problem, too often researchers choose a problem to fit a methodology. Because complex social interactions cannot be easily translated into quantitative terms, potential research studies involving social change are often bypassed by students and other researchers looking for defensible methodological studies. As a result, much of current social work research is atomistic, disjointed, and contributes little to understanding and rectifying social and community problems.

Moreover, the kind of research undertaken is also determined by the flow of money. Specifically, the choice of methodologies employed is highly influenced by the kind of research that funding agencies will subsidize. For the most part, traditional funding agencies (e.g., government, foundations, voluntary and for-profit organizations, etc.) prefer to pay for highly quantitative research. Given this reality, most academics searching for research money are forced to shape their research agendas—and their methodologies—to fit the requirements of funding agencies.

Despite the emphasis on positivism, little real quantitative research actually goes on in social work. Moreover, there is a dearth of systematic research even in areas that lend themselves to highly empirical research. For example, child welfare researchers cannot even identify the exact number of children who have been killed by abuse, the precise number of children in foster care (Costin, Karger, & Stoesz, 1996), or the cost of providing such services, let alone the effects of child welfare services on the well-being of children. Nor have quantitative social work researchers seriously pursued data on the damage routinely afflicted on the minority poor and their communities. In fact, advocacy for those populations can be accomplished using relatively simple descriptive data. In short, social work researchers have failed to gather systematically the data that any occupational group would find essential to the pursuit of its work. The failure of quantitative researchers to use their skills in promoting the public good is not without consequence. One alternative to the male-dominated research paradigm has been proposed by feminists.

The Feminist Critique of Research

Feminists have adopted a different perspective in their attempt to politicize the traditionally male-defined field of social research. Nan Van Den Bergh and Lynn Cooper (1987) argue that feminists are opposed to the false dichotomy that exists between research and practice. Moreover, a feminist model of research suggests alternatives to the positivist approach to scientific inquiry. Van Den Bergh and Cooper (1986) call for research to be developed in line with the needs of underserved or oppressed populations: "An extraordinary amount of social science knowledge has been formulated from studies done by and on white males and generalized to the experience of all persons. Feminist researchers see a need to engage in research with an activist perspective in order to engender social change" (p. 14).

Feminists argue that social research should be guided by the principle of empowerment. Therefore, instead of designing research studies to be aloof or intrusive, social research should focus on the needs of the community and become an integral part of individual and community empowerment. Feminist research is therefore seen as an inclusive rather than exclusive enterprise. Through adopting an inclusive orientation, some feminists have argued that the distance between the researcher and those being researched will be narrowed. This approach would incorporate participants in important areas of the research process, such as the determination of study questions, decisions regarding methodology, and the analysis and interpretation of data (Van Den Bergh & Cooper, 1986).

Other feminists (Hooyman & Bricker-Jenkins, 1986) argue that the research process is dominated by a patriarchal system that controls both the questions asked and the definitions of social problems. In this way, social problems are falsely objectified as "facts." For Nancy Hooyman and Mary Bricker-Jenkins (1986), translating facts into social problems is neither rational nor scientific. Instead, it is a subjective process shaped by values, interests, and ideologies. They argue that instead of rational truths, there are multiple truths. The process of discovering these truths comes about through a personalized "naming" process, rather than by using the language, categories, and analyses of others. In opposition to the rational, linear thinking, and analytical processes valued by modern patriarchal cultures, feminists emphasize spirituality, multidimensional thinking, and synthesis (Ellsworth et al., 1982).

THE POLITICAL DIMENSIONS
OF SOCIAL WORK RESEARCH

Debates around the validity of quantitative and qualitative research methodologies skirt several important points. First, all social work research is inherently political and ideological. The choice of research topics, the questions asked, and the scope and funding of research are all politically and ideologically determined. "Safe" research can be either qualitative or quantitative. Conversely, socially useful, controversial research can employ either qualitative or quantitative methods. What makes research socially worthwhile is not the methodology used—which is really only a tool—but the quality of the research, the political goals that inform it, and the topics or areas that are investigated. For example, quantitative yet socially important research can be designed around factors that cause the powerlessness of the poor, the development of statistical indicators to measure the success of various community interventions and social change strategies, and indicators to measure community needs and aspirations. The possibilities are endless.

Second, the method employed in social research is far less important than the goals. Periodic debates pitting positivist against qualitative methodologies have done a disservice to those concerned with the social mission of research. Specifically, these philosophical debates have helped to camouflage the key question in research—its ultimate social mission—by promoting a false dichotomy between research methods. Instead of examining whether research should be guided by a political criteria that promotes social justice, human needs, and the public good, these philosophical excursions have focused on methodological concerns. Because of this narrowness, these debates have contributed little to clarifying the real mission of social work research.

To rule out a research methodology because it is quantitative or qualitative is to mistake the means for the ends. What is important in socially responsible research is not its methodology, but its goal. All social work research should be driven by a common goal: the promotion of social change for the public good. Hence, the only legitimate criterion for choosing a particular methodology in social work research should be its fit with a particular research problem.

To repeat an earlier point, social workers should not solely embrace social action research *per se*. Instead, all research should be designed for social action, including research in micro, mezzo, and macro practice. To accomplish this goal, all research in social work must be designed around the goal of promoting the public good. Replacing social action research with a larger conceptualization is not simply a semantic distinction. Devising a separate category for social action research inadvertently reduces its influence by encumbering it with the sole responsibility for social change, removing the obligation for social change from mainstream social work practice, and thereby further ghettoizing social action. It is also antithetical to the social justice ideology and mission of social work. In effect, social work research should aim to foster social change.

Some Tenets of Politicized Social Work Research

A dynamic form of politicized social work research must combine several important components. First, it must connect individual problems into the political economy of modern capitalism. For example, nonpoliticized social research views individual, group, and social problems as somehow removed from the context of economic and social relations. The problems of the poor are seen as personal deficits that can only be remedied through individual solutions, often in the form of remedial education, teaching proper work habits, and focusing on changes in self-concept. The primary emphasis of this research is on changing the client rather than addressing social problems. Even when the effects of the political economy are acknowledged, dysfunctional behaviors are viewed as resistant to change. Hence, nonpoliticized research is, in fact, ideological since it helps protect the economic system from scrutiny by placing problems within an individual context.

Research on addiction and chemical dependency reflects similar contradictions. Instead of locating at least part of the addiction problem in the social sphere, researchers focus either on the brain (a chemical deficit that makes one prone to addiction) or on the psychosocial background of the individual. Little blame is put on a society that tolerates high levels of economic insecurity, removes people from any real sense of community by emphasizing the private sphere over the public sphere, replaces meaningful social interaction with consumption, and offers psychotherapy and cable television as substitutes for anomie. Instead of systematically pursuing the causes of addiction within the social sphere, most social researchers are content to study the behavior of victims. By focusing exclusively on the individual, social researchers bow to ideological pressures and thereby condone the social conditions that lead to the problem.

Second, politicized social work research must operate in the service of the community. One criterion of social work research must be its social usefulness. Given finite resources, social research that is atomistic, fragmented, and contributes little to promoting social change can be counterproductive to creating a research agenda that operates in the best interests of those it serves. Fiscal and human resources consumed by meaningless research become unavailable for socially productive research. Furthermore, socially responsible research is compromised when research is judged by the intricacies of its methodology rather than the virtue of its goals.

Third, to serve communities, research findings must be made accessible to lay people. Instead of writing solely for other researchers, social workers must make their findings available as well to the general public, to communities, and to social change organizations. Research must not only be made available to communities but should also be designed to help these communities pursue social justice goals.

Finally, politicized social work research must be motivated by a desire to help give a voice to the voiceless. By emphasizing social responsibility, politicized research would be driven by the goal of empowering poor, vulnerable individuals and communities. Good research returns power to individuals and communities by giving them knowledge of their situation and insight into the causes of their problems. Incorporating communities into the research process empowers organizations or individuals by teaching them research skills and how to bring about changes based on information. Rubin and Rubin (1992) argue that, "When people who are affected by a problem develop the skills to learn about it, they are empowered" (p. 157). Politicized research empowers people by demystifying and democratizing the research process. As experts share knowledge, individuals and community members learn that research is neither sacrosanct nor infallible. Research is therefore understood for what it is—approximations of social reality in the service of explicit or implicit political goals.

SOCIAL WORK RESEARCH AND THE PUBLIC GOOD

Many social workers in the early twentieth century understood the relationship, if not the responsibility, between the enterprise of research and the promotion of the public good. These social work researchers took seriously not only the obligation to translate their research into the public arena, but to develop research projects that advanced the public good. Their goal was partly realized through the creation of social surveys.

Social action research found its earliest expression in the social survey movement of the early 1900s. Spurred on by increasing problems in poverty, homelessness, child labor, and economic exploitation, the social survey movement had its genesis in the period known as the Progressive Era (Reid, 1987). Motivated by advocacy rather than scientific objectivity, the intent of the social surveys were transparent. Zimbalast (1955) noted that, "The social survey movement was first and foremost a means of publicizing the needs of the community in as compelling a manner as possible, so as to galvanize the populace into taking remedial action. Facts were gathered and analyzed as a means to this end" (p. 170).

Led by the breakthrough Pittsburgh study of 1908, which focused on conditions of poverty and economic exploitation in Pittsburgh, social work reformers later developed social surveys that targeted exploitative industries such as garment manufacturing, bookbinding, mining, and meat packing (Zimbalast, 1977). Widely disseminated in newspapers and magazines, these studies provided ammunition for important social policies, including protective labor laws for women and children. The social survey movement was so influential that the leading social work journal of the early 1900s changed its name from *Charities and Commons* to *Survey* (Reid, 1987). Although the social survey movement was no longer a major force in social welfare by the early 1920s (Reid, 1987), it set the precedent of using social work research as a tool to inform and guide public opinion.

Russell Jacoby (1987) has pointed out that many progressive intellectuals have abandoned the public arena for an academic life where they communicate more with each other than with the public. The academic milieu housing social work research supports this behavior. For example, many social scientists view good research as divorced from instrumental ends such as the creation of public policies or strengthening social movements. Like the hard sciences, "pure research" in the social sciences is expected to be grounded in the innate value of epistemology. While applied research—in which many social workers are engaged—has some merit in academic circles, it usually occupies a lower position in the research hierarchy.

Survival in the academic world, especially for faculty but also for students, requires adherence to a fixed set of rules. To ensure a successful academic career—promotion, tenure, and professional recognition—most academicians must comply with a given set of rules, expectations, and behaviors. The key to academic success is the publication of "legitimate" research in refereed journals, book chapters, and scholarly monographs. To ensure the perpetuation of this academic culture, scholarly work is judged by referees—professional peers—who share similar views on what constitutes good research. Too often, however, the quality of this research is judged by its methodological purity rather than its contribution to knowledge or to the social good. Academicians produce research—sometimes at a breathtaking pace—to satisfy colleagues who decide on their future. Those academics who refuse to conform are either eliminated early on or frozen within an academic rank.

This closed academic system produces its own reality. For example, the academic value of social science research is frequently judged by its erudition rather than its clarity. In other words, research is often judged by the intellectual distance that separates it from the more mundane concerns of everyday life. Research that is esoteric, convoluted, and comprehensible only to a handful of scholars is increasingly becoming the benchmark for academic success. Conversely, social science research that is simple, direct, and easily understood is often judged as being superficial and unworthy of reward. Indeed, social science research that is disseminated widely because of its clarity, immediacy, or poignancy is often branded too "journalistic" to be considered as a serious academic accomplishment.

By adopting standards that reward arcane over socially responsible research, social scientists—including many social work researchers and practitioners—have made themselves irrelevant to a public discourse on social policy and societal priorities. Spurred on by an obsessive concern with the dazzle of methodology, it is not surprising that few social work researchers contribute to a public discourse on social problems for which they are supposed to be experts. An example of the trivialization of social research is illustrated by doctoral dissertations in social work, many of which are descriptive and emphasize methodology over theory.

Writing primarily for each other, social work researchers are replicating a pattern similar to many sociologists who became so preoccupied with methodological issues that they lost sight of the important questions. While sociologists were painstakingly refining their quantitative methodologies, the discipline was becoming increasingly irrelevant to the discourse on public policy. The halcyon days of the 1960s, when sociological research played a major role in developing poverty policy, were long gone by the middle 1970s. In its place, was a discipline that had lost stature and by that the interest of potential students. Instead of being a formidable intellectual force on American campuses, sociology has become in many universities a service department offering primarily undergraduate introductory and survey courses. To be fair, the impact of sociology was also diminished by the shift away from "soft" or nonvocational, and often politicized disciplines, a trend that began in the mid-1970s.

Social work researchers must focus their energies on finding ways to engage in a public dialogue that is integrated with sound social science research. The dearth of academicians—including social workers—involved in the public discourse on social policy has left a lacuna increasingly filled by ideologues, political pundits, or quasi-academics like Charles Murray. Many of these are "action researchers," who are writing in the service of right-wing causes and organizations. Others demonstrate little concern with social science theory, scientific method, or evidence that contradicts their political agenda. Sadly, while half-baked opinions masquerade as social truths, bright young social scientists are hunkering down to write books and articles largely irrelevant to the public policy issues of the day.

If social work researchers, both students and faculty, are to engage in a dialogue on public life, the rules governing academic success must be changed. Instead of rewarding research based solely on its methodological merit, work should also be judged on whether and how it contributes to the social good. Specifically, how does this research fit into the larger context? How does it contextualize problems, linking the individual, family, group, or community to history, place, culture, and power? Moreover, instead of writing for other academics, social work researchers must write both for scientific consumption and for a larger audience. For example, much of the social work research can be written in a style that is understandable to general lay readers. Or, at least pieces of that research can be groomed and rewritten for general consumption. By using executive summaries, synopses, press releases, and other avenues for the widespread dissemination of information, high-quality social work research can find its way into newspaper columns, radio and television talk shows, news bulletins, magazines, and so forth.

Social work researchers can also influence the public discourse on social problems in other ways. One approach is to engage in collaborative research efforts with communities and their leaders, which can be mutually beneficial. Manuel Pastor (1995) provides two scenarios that illustrate the benefit of this cooperation.

> You're a community leader trying to fight the siting of a toxic waste facility in your neighborhood. You have a strategy for organizing your neighbors, but you need access to research that demonstrates that your community has been the site of more than its fair share of such environmental negatives. Who does research in environmental racism? How do you find these people and begin working with them?
>
> You're a professor beginning work on labor market outcomes for African-American and Latino youth in Los Angeles. You have census data, but you want to learn more about community-initiated job training programs and make sure that your research is useful for activists working for change. How do you reach out to community groups to both learn from their activism and offer your services? (p. 9)

Various forms of collaboration between community activists and social researchers have gone on for a number of years. For example, a matching service for researchers and activists—the Poverty and Race Research Action Council (PRRAC)—was set up to organize day-long meetings to link these two groups. These meetings are intended to facilitate networking between activists and researchers, help air problems between them, and identify the advocacy groups' immediate research needs (Pastor, 1995). In Los Angeles alone, 1,500 activists and researchers became part of this network (Pastor, 1995).

A similar dialogue was sponsored by the Applied Research Center of the University of California–Berkeley. The goal of this conference was to study examples of successful collaboration between social change organizations and researchers, exchange information about the diverse research needs of community organization work, and to plan pilot collaborations among researchers and activists. Perhaps one of the more interesting ideas to come out of that meeting was a project to establish a set of standards around community research that could lead to the greater accountability of researchers toward the communities they are studying. These standards could also be used as grant conditions by funders (Applied Research Center, 1993).

As an applied discipline, social work also has a unique responsibility to produce competent social science research that is actively engaged in the struggle around defining and achieving a progressive public good. Rather than aping the methodological fetishism and public isolation of other social science disciplines, the social work profession can choose a middle ground that combines high-quality, scientific research with a cogent sense of social responsibility. In this way, social work can help fill the vacuum left in the public discourse around social problems, while at the same time establishing a model for other social science disciplines. Sound social science research is not incompatible with socially responsible research. Nor is research that is comprehensible to the lay reader necessarily superficial. While the balance between good science and social commitment is often difficult to achieve, it is a worthy goal.

SKILLS IMPLICATIONS: VARYING FORMS
OF SOCIAL WORK RESEARCH

Engaging in any form of systematic social investigation requires the development of specific research skills. The types of research methodologies suitable for social change encompass the vast range of techniques available to the social sciences. While it is beyond the scope of this book to engage in an in-depth examination of all forms of research that are suitable for social change activities, the following sample represents a skeletal framework of possible methodologies.

Community Needs Assessments

Community needs assessments are important tools for planners, researchers, and social activists. In general, a needs assessment can be defined as the systematic process of finding and identifying the needs of a group of people or a geographic, cultural, ethnic, or special interest community. According to Evelyn Slaght (1994), "The purpose of a needs assessment is to document the extent of a social problem and the gap between need and response" (p. 143). Mark Homan (1994) lists three primary goals for needs assessments: (1) to decide if there is a need for action, (2) to help design or direct an already contemplated action, and (3) to confirm what is already known and therefore justify an action already decided upon. Needs assessment surveys can also be used to solicit members by asking respondents if they are willing to work with an organization on issues they rated as important.

Different approaches used in needs assessments include social surveys, the development of social indicators (e.g., health, employment, and educational indices), and community forums. The methodology chosen depends on the information needed, how this information will be used, the time and resources available, and the level of client participation being sought (Austin & Lowe, 1994). Accordingly, community needs assessments can range from informal needs assessments carried out by volunteer staff in nontraditional organizations to formal and well-funded longitudinal studies.

A needs assessment can include large populations (e.g., entire cities, counties, or states), or it can examine the unmet needs of smaller units such as neighborhoods, a church congregation, or even agency workers (Homan, 1994). Needs assessments are difficult to undertake since needs are subject to different definitions, even within the same community or organization. Nevertheless, the results of needs assessments often dictate which programs will be funded or developed and the level of resources that will be allocated to meet the needs of communities (Austin & Lowe, 1994).

One of the most difficult, costly, and time-consuming components of a needs assessment involves the collection of data. Meenaghan et al. (1982) lists eight methods for gathering information in needs assessments: (1) general population surveys (interviewing a sample of community residents), (2) target population surveys (interviewing members of a select group), (3) service provider surveys, (4) key informant surveys (interviewing knowledgeable community members), (5) secondary data analysis (investigating available statistics on the target population), (6) examining social indicators, (7) reviews of administrative or managerial agency records, and (8) gathering information from other agencies. Some analysts (Homan, 1994; Netting, Kettner, & McMurtry, 1993) suggest that data collection is best accomplished by using existing data. Volumes of community data are available through numerous sources such as the U.S. Census Bureau, county records, and newspaper morgues.

The use of secondary data to create social indicators (indices of the relative well-being of a community) can be a useful tool in developing a needs assessment. Social indicators can give communities a better picture of their needs, strengths, and deficits, and provide a comprehensive picture of community life (Carley, 1981). As such, the needs of a community may become evident when examining specific social indicators such as health, educational level, crime, mortality, or family income (Carley, 1981). In addition, social indicators can be useful reference points in comparing conditions within and across communities. Finally, social indicators can be a useful tool in lobbying social agencies and legislative bodies.

One excellent source for constructing social indicators is U.S. Census Bureau data. Collected every ten years and periodically updated, the Census Bureau provides detailed data broken down into neighborhood tracts. This data can yield valuable community information including population numbers, gender breakdowns, employment status, educational levels, the racial and ethnic composition of a community, average family incomes, types and costs of housing, high school dropout rates, the percentage of residents that rely on public assistance, the age of neighborhood residents, and even the health status of the community (Kahn, 1994).

An increasingly common method for gathering information is the creation of focus groups. In general, focus groups are group interviews in which the researcher tosses out broad questions and then lets the group present their views. The group will normally talk for a while and then converge on a topic that interests members. The researcher will listen to the discussion and then move the group to other topics. To be successful, participants in focus groups must feel free to express their opinions openly (Morgan, 1988). Focus groups are used throughout society, ranging from providing ideas to television networks on program lineups, to advising the Republican and Democratic parties on which issues to address in their party planks.

Another technique frequently used for needs assessments is community, citywide, or national surveys. Information on the preferences, perceptions, and needs of whole communities or organizations can be derived from surveys in which all participants are asked a uniform set of questions. Although responses are often superficial compared to focus group interviews, surveys can examine a broad range of opinions. Often, surveys are used to complement or verify the opinions arising from focus groups (Rubin & Rubin, 1992).

The following components are typically considered necessary for the successful design and implementation of a needs assessment:

- Determining the time and money available for the study.
- Identifying the target population, which among other things can include, a geographic neighborhood, a social agency, or a cultural, racial, ethnic, gender, age-based, or disabled community.
- Defining the range of services to be examined.
- Selecting the methodology for collecting and evaluating data, including the method used to interpret the data.
- Ranking of needs based on instances of agreement.
- Getting feedback from participants as to accuracy.
- Writing and presenting the results of the study.

Apart from shedding light on the general needs of a community, a well-executed needs assessment will address questions such as, "Is the community or neighborhood worse off economically, socially, or politically than a more mainstream community or neighborhood? If so, what services are needed?" "Are the needs of the community adequately reflected in the current provision of services?" "What are people in the community concerned about? What are their goals?" The answers to these and other questions help address social problems, give voice to people's needs and hopes, and allow social workers to work toward a better match between community needs and the provision of services.

Ethnographic Methodologies

According to Wagenaar (1981), the goal of ethnographic research is "to determine the underlying rules, norms, and assumptions governing everyday life" (p. 132). Used primarily by sociologists and anthropologists, ethnographic research is an important tool for understanding communities and individuals. Qualitative ethnographical studies can yield valuable insights into the causes and the nature of social problems. These studies can also be useful in discovering indigenous strategies, tactics, and solutions to address those social problems. Ethnographies can take a variety of forms, ranging from active participant observation to a highly detached scientific approach. In all cases, it is "close-up research," in that the investigators must have face-to-face interaction with their subjects.

From de Tocqueville's (1969) nineteenth century tour of America to Bellah et al.'s (1985) insights into the character of the American middle class, ethnographical studies have influenced public thinking and social policy. Using ethnographic research, anthropologists such as Oscar Lewis (1965) helped develop the culture of poverty concept—for better or worse—that shaped poverty-related, social policies throughout most of the 1960s. Erving Goffman's (1965) groundbreaking book, *Asylums*, provided fuel for the deinstitutionalization movement that would emerge in the early 1970s. William Foote Whyte's (1966) *Street Corner Society* informed a whole generation about life on the streets. And Margaret Mead's ethnographies helped shape foreign aid policy to developing nations in addition to whetting the public's appetite for Peace Corps service overseas.

One example of ethnographic research in social work is David Wagner's (1993) investigation of homelessness, *Checkerboard Square*. Wagner's study of the homeless was conducted in two phases. The first phase involved in-depth interviews with the homeless or formerly homeless. These subjects were asked to give detailed information about their lives—how they became homeless and for how long they were homeless—and they answered a variety of questions about the politics of homelessness. In phase two, Wagner and his associates spent two years and countless hours interacting with the homeless and observing street-level, social networks.

Contrary to stereotypes, Wagner did not find social isolation, but a tight-knit community made up of surprisingly empowered homeless people and service providers who, although they slept at home, were still part of the community. Wagner's findings might have eluded most kinds of quantitative research that center on the observable—the health of the homeless, their diet and caloric intake, the length of time without a permanent home, and so forth. While quantitative measures of well-being are important, they cannot provide audiences with an intimate look into the realities faced by the homeless. Nor can they describe the strengths of this group. On the other hand, through close-up investigation, ethnographers can capture some of the texture and context of the group or community being studied. While clearly time-consuming, ethnographic research can capture the subtleties of human interaction while providing glimpses into the realities faced by different groups and cultures.

Research findings have generally come under close scrutiny in recent decades. While traditional social scientists question whether a sample can actually represent a larger population, postmodernists and others believe that all research should be understood as essentially interpretative and subjective, based on the context of the study and the researcher's social characteristics (Wagner, 1993). Postmodernists argue that the social context of the researcher and the concomitant reality of time and place make all research, including ethnography, subjective. Influenced by ideology and personal characteristics, the researchers' frame of reference is the lens that determines what they look for and, consequently, what they will find. Hence, when studying a complex phenomenon, feminists will throw the light of research investigation on gender issues, gays and lesbians on sexual identity issues, and people of color on race issues. This differential focus does not imply that ethnographic research is invalid. On the contrary, social phenomena are far too complex to have a single causative explanation. For social scientists, the mystery of a phenomenon is uncovered by examining multiple causes and explanations. Lenses of class or cultural identity serve to inform, not conclude, good social research.

Ethnographic research is congruent with the shift to a more culturally oriented and polyvocal discourse about social problems and solutions. Ethnography,

Spradley (1979) writes, describes a culture "from the native point of view" (p. 3). The goal of ethnographic research is to learn from those being studied and understand customs, perspectives, and behaviors "within the context of their culture" (Thornton & Garrett, 1995, p. 68). To this extent, ethnography helps empower previously silenced groups, gives voice to their problems and proposed solutions, expands discourse about the nature and variety of the public good, and reorients the research project by making the subjects of research, rather than the researchers, the agents of social change.

Historical Research

History derives its coherence from being a discoverer and interpreter of the past. Historians turn to the past to seek precedents or to examine the evolution of problems, ideas, institutions, social movements, or events. Modern historical research looks at the diverse cultural, social, and intellectual forces that have shaped society. Despite its roots in the humanities, historical research is primarily concerned with uncovering, evaluating, and interpreting facts. Good historical research is as empirically based as the positivist research done in other social sciences.

Elton (1967) argues that traditional historical research is the servant of its evidence; researchers are to ask no specific questions until they fully absorb the data. In Elton's view, historians are merely conduits through which the evidence speaks. Other historians have a different perspective. E. H. Carr (1987), for example, distinguishes between the facts of history and the facts of the past. The former are selected and interpreted by historians who reconstruct and explain the past; the latter are without limit and unknowable in their entirety (Tosh, 1991). As Carr (1987) puts it, "The facts of history cannot be purely objective, since they become facts of history only by virtue of the significance attached to them by the historian" (p. 120).

Historical research is more like that in sociology, social anthropology, political science, and economics, rather than literature (Dunkerley, 1988). Sociologists cannot undertake a study without considering its historical implications, and historians cannot fully understand social history without sociological insights. Consequently, the boundaries between these social science disciplines are somewhat artificial, and an interdependence exists between history and other social sciences, including social work (Dunkerley, 1988). As such, all disciplines occupy important places in the continuum of knowledge. Despite this disciplinary interdependence, historians have often had an uneasy relationship with the quantitative social sciences.

One reason is that traditional historians typically think of what has been, rather than what is now. Social researchers generally reverse that order (Floud, 1985). The gap between history and social science, however, narrowed with the introduction of a "new history" coming out of the social movements of the 1960s and 1970s, that merged quantitative methods with historical analysis and sought to recontextualize the past "from the bottom up" instead of the "top down." The "new" quantitative social history focused on creating and proving—or disproving—historical hypotheses, such as whether rapid economic and social mobility in America was a myth. The "new" qualitative social history, best associated with the French historians who published the journal, *Annales* (Tosh, 1991), promoted a history of ordinary people. This history "from the bottom up"—written about, for, and often by working people—remains one of the more exciting areas of current historical scholarship. By challenging the idea that only elites make history and by trying to both politicize history and make it accessible, radical historians drew many nonprofessionals into historical study (Floud, 1985).

History remains an important component of social science knowledge. Earlier landmark historical works, including those in social welfare such as Clarke Chambers's (1967) *Seedtime of Reform*, written about social welfare and social change in the 1920s; Allen Davis's (1967) *Spearheads for Reform*, an investigation of the social settlement house movement of the early 1900s; Jacob Fisher's (1980) *The Response of Social Work to the Depression*, an excellent book on the radical movement in social work during the 1930s; Roy Lubove's (1975) *The Professional Altruist*, a classic work on the emergence of the social work profession; and Frances Fox Piven and Richard Cloward's (1971) *Regulating the Poor*, an award-winning book on the social control aspects of social welfare, have significantly contributed to a better understanding of the predecessors of today's social movements. But the importance of historical research to social work is much more integral, its relevance to the formation of public life and its challenge of the context of global privatization much greater, than simply gaining a better knowledge of the past.

After all, in a private world focused on individual growth and economic progress, history is seen mostly as a nuisance, perhaps even a loadstone. *"That's history." "You're history."* These are contemporary phrases meant to marginalize an understanding of history. But it is the very objection to the past that should inform us, should tell us that historical and collective memory runs counter to the dominant trends and norms of the contemporary private world. Historical perspectives and research are important to social work because they inherently provide a longitudinal analysis of change over time in the lives of activists and organizations, for example, and a comparative analysis of social problems and solutions. History forces people to juxtapose efforts in the past with those in the present. It is also essential to the project of countering global privatization and rebuilding public life, because it inherently contextualizes and collectivizes issues. Historical analysis is fundamental to social change because it is a critical part of a broader contextualization that informs the understanding of contemporary social life. History provides social workers with a collective memory, one that ties the roots of past oppression to the struggles and victories of the past. As Sheila Johansson (1976) writes:

> It is not surprising that most women feel that their sex does not have an interesting or significant past. However, like minority groups, women cannot afford to lack a consciousness of a collective identity, one which necessarily involves a shared awareness of the past. Without this, a social group suffers from a kind of collective amnesia, which makes it vulnerable to the impositions of dubious stereotypes, as well as limiting prejudices about what is right and proper for it to do or not to do. (p. 8)

The new social welfare history discloses the politics and process of expanding public life and achieving social change (Chambers, 1992; Chambers, 1986; Reisch, 1988; Leahore & Cates, 1985; Vandenberg-Daves, 1992). Instead of narrowly defining the public good as a product handed down from social policymakers through social service programs, historical analysis demonstrates that it is a highly politicized process of ongoing struggle. It is a process that includes a multitude of participants and voices. As discussed in the second chapter, historical analysis reveals the existence of "multiple publics" and the struggle in the past and present for group inclusion in determining and affecting the public good. It is the multiple histories of individuals and groups of people that enrich understanding of who makes and who participates in public life. Janet Finn (1994) argues that because "an understanding of power demands an appreciation of history . . . [social work] . . . research needs to be contextualized in terms of the current sociopolitical environment in which it is conducted and the historical conditions that contributed to this situation" (p. 27).

A variety of important research opportunities can only be accomplished through historical analysis: histories of contemporary issues, problems, and policies; histories of social agencies, communities, social movements, and organizations; social biographies of social workers and other social activists; intellectual histories of social change theories and leaders; economic histories of communities or cities; and histories of social work practice interventions such as community organization or individual counseling. Like its quantitative cousins, the possibilities for historical research are unlimited.

Sources for historical research include secondary studies (that is, histories written by noncontemporaneous sources) and primary sources, which may include agency records; personal letters; public library materials; records in state, county, or local historical societies; newspaper articles; and records in local, state, federal, university, and private archives. In addition, newspaper files, ephemera, and records in the possession of individuals can also be consulted. Oral history, as with the ethnographic interviews, is an invaluable tool for more recent social history. Secondary sources can include biographies, previously written histories, novels, and so forth. Historical research is a valuable entrée in the cafeteria of research methods available to social activists.

Action Research

Because of their academic training, many social workers find it difficult to employ the principles of action research. This discomfort is based on the ways in which action research differs from the more traditional methodologies. First, the major scientific credo of objectivity is absent from action research. As such, action researchers are unconcerned with approaching a research problem free from values, prejudices, or preconceived ideas. Nor do they emphasize finding universal truths, discovering behavioral patterns among people, scientifically presenting data to their peers, or contributing to a body of scientific knowledge. Unless it advances social change through an organizational strategy, action researchers are indifferent toward widely distributing their research. Hence, the purpose of action research is to promote an agenda of social change or build an organization by developing and executing winning strategies (Bobo, Kendall, & Max, 1991).

On a more personal level, action research contains the possibility to save lives. For example, in May 1974 several children drowned in a rainstorm on the west side of San Antonio. After leaders for Communities Organized for Public Service (COPS) were turned down on their request for immediate action on a long-delayed, drainage project, they turned to research in the city archives. There, they found that the drainage projects desperately needed on the west and south sides of San Antonio had been authorized by bond elections several years before. However, the money had been diverted to projects on the north side of the city. Hundreds of COPS leaders filled the city hall, and four hours later the city staff had drawn up a plan for a $46.8 million bond issue to develop 15 new drainage projects. The bond issue successfully passed later that year. By 1994, those same inner-city communities were served by nearly $1 billion worth of new sewers, drainage systems, streets, sidewalks, libraries, literacy centers, clinics, and street lights (Rips, 1994). In short, action research is advocacy-based research in its purest form.

Action research is not the only form of advocacy-based research. Increasingly, there are new, activist models of research developing in response to the limits and contradictions of positivistic models of scientific objectivity. For example, Finn (1994) defines participatory research as grounded in:

> . . . an explicit stance and clearly articulated value base. It challenges positivist notions of scientific objectivity and value neutrality. Participatory researchers support a process of inquiry in which private problems become public questions. Participatory research links personal experience to political contexts through reflection and action. . . . Ideally, participatory research generates knowledge for action, contributes to organization building, and supports sustained efforts for social change. (p. 27)

The term "research" has come to be associated with certain characteristics of the social sciences. True (1989) defines research as "the process of studying in order to discover something" (p. 2). It is assumed within traditional, academic circles that scientific research must be divorced from social action if objectivity is to be retained. However, the reverse is true in action research. Namely, the linkage between social action and research is critical if this form of research is to remain true to the goal of social change. Given the limited resources of most progressive organizations, pure research is an unaffordable luxury. Moreover, research arms in most progressive organizations must pay their own way by directly contributing to the objectives of the organization. Hence, research is considered a waste of resources if it does not directly advance the goals of an organization or specifically serve the goal of social change.

Si Kahn (1991) lists four types of research generally done by progressive organizations: (1) survey research to find out what members think or feel about a particular issue, (2) research designed to enhance resources (e.g., fundraising efforts), (3) reconnaissance for building alliances and coalitions, and (4) tactical investigations that target landlords, welfare department officials, corporations, elected officials, and so forth. The following discussion breaks down tactical investigations, Kahn's fourth category, into (1) community power structure analysis, (2) corporate research, and (3) legislative or political power structure research. Also examined are key sources for locating useful information.

Community power structure analysis is concerned with identifying the locus of power in communities, which can take several forms, including economic power, political power, and social power. In addition, the power within a community can be either formal or informal. Although economic, political, and social power often overlap, they can also be discrete. For example, a particular church may wield social power; that is, the church may be a referent point in setting community norms. At the same time, it may not be an economic force. Conversely, an economic power in a community, such as a large corporation, may not wield social power.

Corporate research is useful in several ways. First, corporate research can help in the fight to stop corporations from polluting the environment, practicing employment discrimination, developing union-busting strategies, threatening plant closures, or attempting to extract all-too-generous community concessions (e.g., exemptions from property taxes, financial incentives for relocating or continuing to operate within communities, and so forth). As such, research can expose how the political and economic power of corporations directly affects communities, social problems, and social policies. Second, corporate research can assess the strength of a corporation in order to find chinks in its armor. These weaknesses can later be used to neutralize or defeat the power corporations hold over communities. More specifically, these strategies ultimately undermine the public good through the excessive power and preferential treatment demanded by corporations.

Corporate research can be useful in helping local groups receive a fair hearing. For example, research done by Association of Community Organizations for Reform Now (ACORN) in 1993 found that the level of homeowner insurance in thirteen Midwest cities was substantially lower than in high-income and white neighborhoods (Allen, 1993). In fact, almost 50 percent of houses in Chicago's low-income neighborhoods were not covered by homeowners' insurance. Moreover, ACORN's research revealed that in thirteen Midwestern cities, homeowners in low-income neighborhoods paid $10.41 per thousand dollars of coverage versus $5.25 per thousand in upper-income, urban areas and $3.79 in upper-income suburbs (Allen, 1993).

Legislative research can be beneficial in several ways, also. First, it can help track legislative bills. Notifying citizens of impending legislation or helping them track bills already introduced is a key function of legislative research. This role is critical since bills can go through multiple revisions—sometimes dramatically changing the intent of the bill—before passage. Such legislation is the essence of social policy, and legislative research seeks to directly affect social policy before and after it becomes law. Second, legislative research can be used to uncover potentially damaging information on elected officials. Finding "dirt" by either discovering direct evidence of criminal misconduct or even casting aspersions as to motives in opposing organizations or legislative bills can help neutralize political opponents.

Legislative research can take on other forms, including research on government agencies. For example, Gail Cincotta of the National People's Action group discovered that the insurance fund that backs FHA home mortgages was insolvent (Harney, 1992). In 1990 it had a net worth of −$2.7 billion, a precipitous drop of $5.3 billion from just one year earlier. According to Cincotta, this drop was due to the fact that since 1988, the foreclosure rate on FHA homes averaged 90,000 a year, at an estimated annual cost of $5.3 billion.

Despite different emphases, all three forms of action research have a common objective: They are concerned with exposing sources of power and discovering ways to influence or neutralize that power. In addition, these three forms of research are action-oriented in that their primary goal is to further progressive efforts and build organizations. The major difference between community power structure analysis, corporate research, and legislative research is their unit of analysis.

Finding Information. As Katz (1980) notes, the preponderance of information needed for action research is readily available: "the very complexity of the modern technological society compels the power structure to produce a continuous flow of data on almost every aspect of human endeavor. It is safe to assume that the information you need to investigate any segment of society is available somewhere in some form" (p. 2). Barry Greever (1972) lists two basic rules for acquiring information: (1) you can always find the information you need, and (2) it is your right to have that information.

Information on the power structure in a community can be gleaned from a variety of sources. For example, local maps and street directories are useful in analyzing upscale neighborhoods where the rich and powerful live. Local histories in public libraries or county museums can help identify local families who have been or still are powerful. While some of these families may have lost fortunes or moved away, others will have retained power through property ownership, seats on boards of directors, especially banks, or simply by virtue of being the historical gentry of a town (Lamb, 1952). Publications of local chambers of commerce and data tracks from the U.S. Census Bureau can also help shed light on the nature of community power.

Other important sources of information are found in courthouse records, including grantee and grantor indexes showing the purchase of real estate, tax assessor's records, court records indicating who has been sued and for what, and voting records (Bobo, Kendall, & Max, 1991). In addition, newspaper morgues often list topics by subject, name, or issue. Valuable information can be found by interviewing community people, especially older residents who have a larger historical view of the community. Finally, considerable information can be collected from interviews with business competitors or enemies of the established power structure.

Much of the information needed for corporate research is easily found in larger public libraries. These sources include various registries of *Who's Who*; professional directories, such as the *Martindale and Hubbell Law Directory*; bankers' registries; social registers and blue books; *Standard and Poor's Register of Executives and Directors*; and assorted Moody's manuals, including the series on transportation, public utilities, banking and finance, municipality and government, industrials, international business, and the Over the Counter register (smaller corporations with stock not traded on the stock exchange). In addition, Dunn and Bradstreet have several useful publications, including the *Reference Book of Corporate Management*, the *Million Dollar Directory*, and the *Middle Market Directory*. The "yellow pages" of directories is *Kline's Guide to American Directories*, which lists more than 5,000 other directories. One of the more important sources of information on corporations is the Securities and Exchange Commission (SEC). As a government agency, the SEC requires corporations to file an annual report that includes detailed information on corporate finances and ownership (Bobo, Kendall, & Max, 1991).

Two final tools for corporate research are newspaper indexes and databases. Many large newspapers, including the *New York Times*, *The Wall Street Journal*, and the *Washington Post* have indexes that are available at most large libraries. Other indexes include *Business Periodical Index*, *Funk and Scott's Index of Corporations and Industries*, and the *National Newspaper Index*. Databases, some of which are on-line and can be accessed by modem, are a growth industry. These databases such as Nexus, Dialog, Orbit, and MCI Mail, among others, can contain information culled from thousands of sources (Bobo, Kendall, & Max, 1991).

Sources for research on elected officials are found in a variety of places. First, each candidate running for political office must have a political committee. Contributions greater than a fixed sum must be recorded in state or federal disclosure forms filed by the election committee. Campaign disclosure forms list individual and corporate donors, their addresses, and the amounts they contributed. In addition, campaign contributions by Political Action Committees (PACs) are also recorded. These disclosure forms are open to the public and are available through the appropriate federal, state, county, or local agency responsible for monitoring campaigns. Occasionally, these forms may be available on-line.

Astute researchers can cross reference campaign disclosure forms with lists of paid lobbyists (also on file with the designated public agencies). Researchers can thus examine legislation proposed by elected officials and cross reference it to campaign donations by PACs and major individual and corporate donors. By using the investigative sources listed above, researchers can identify legislators' previous involvement with boards of directors, corporations represented by their former law firms, and property and stocks still held by legislators or members of their family. This information can help researchers find potential conflicts of interest and determine whether a pattern exists in bills spoken for or introduced by a particular legislator. The full financial disclosure required of most elected officials is an important tool in developing a comprehensive profile on political candidates and elected officials.

With the exception of the richest legislators, the enormous financial cost of running a political campaign has led to a frenzied search for large and stable contributors. This is especially true for U.S. House of Representatives candidates who, because they run for reelection every two years, must create a "war chest" for future campaigns even before the current one is exhausted. In effect, the electoral system has boosted the power of deep-pocketed PACs and corporate contributors, made legislators fiscally vulnerable, and undermined the power of constituents who lack wealth. Furthermore, the expense of participating in the electoral system has made legislators increasingly susceptible to bribery, the misappropriation of campaign funds, and other financial misdealings. Even if researchers fail to discover any patently illegal activity, they may find potential conflicts of interest, preferential treatment of large contributors, and undue influence of lobbyists. At the least, this discovery can cast a pall over legislators, thereby putting them on the defensive. It may also cause elected officials to distance themselves—at least temporarily—from the special interests they represent.

Local legislative research is often more difficult to undertake than national research. For example, factors such as political patronage jobs, religious or ethnic loyalties, local business interests, and police politics and corruption can play a prominent role in shaping local politics. In many places, the political machines like Tammany Hall are alive and well. Corruption or favoritism on this level may not be as easily discovered, since it can take highly camouflaged forms. For example, patronage jobs may not be awarded to traditional political operatives, but to members of a legislator's church or fellowship group. City contracts may be given to distant relatives or business partners of family members. In some measure, the distance needed in the deceit depends on the political comfort of those in power. In the end, the critical issue involved in corporate and legislative research is not simply catching offenders breaking the law or committing an unethical act. Instead, the key issue is, how through the law and within accepted corporate and governmental culture, those in power are able to maneuver without fear of reproach, and how corporations are able to influence policy and policymakers disproportionately to support their vision of a conservative public good.

All of the research designs discussed above (and methodologies that were not mentioned) are clearly useful in social change activities. In the end, the distinguishing feature of sound social work research is a strong empirical base—even action research must have a solid grounding in facts—coupled with a strong social commitment and social change agenda.

CONCLUSION

This chapter has examined the relationship between social work research, public life, and social change. As part of that examination, the chapter has explored the role of research within the social work profession. Several points have emerged from this examination. First, social work's overemphasis on quantitative methodology has led to the segregation of social action research from the mainstream of social work research. The effect of this exclusion has been the conferral of a second-class citizenship on research driven by social and political goals. Second, by devolving the onus for social change onto social action research, more mainstream social work research has been permitted to continue merrily on its way, unhampered by any real responsibility for social change. While social action research is tolerated because of its usefulness to the profession—especially its public relation function—it is neither highly valued nor highly rewarded within the corridors of social work research.

This chapter has also examined several critiques of social work research, especially those involving the innate conflict between qualitative and quantitative methodologies. While compelling, these critiques miss an essential point—namely, that the methodology employed in social research is less important than its ultimate goal. Hence, debates around appropriate social work research methodologies are diversionary since they often focus on the means without dealing with the ends. Discussions around narrow methodological arguments blur the important distinction between socially useful and socially irrelevant research that should be at the core of any meaningful examination of social work research. Consequently, ongoing debates about which methodologies are more apropos to social work research are not only unfortunate diversions, they are real obstacles in addressing the most important question: What is the ultimate aim of social work research?

All social research, including social work research, is both political and ideological. Its political nature is shaped by the choice of research topics or those not chosen, the questions asked or not asked, and the scope and funding of the research. Instead of denying the political character of research, social workers can use it as a framework for unifying the profession around the promotion of the public good. Moreover, accepting the inherent politicization of research implies that all social work research, including micro and mezzo, should be designed around its potential for advancing the social good. Several principles must guide a more politicized view of social work research: (1) an emphasis on the connection between individual problems and the political economy (politicizing the personal), (2) holding all research accountable to the best interests of the community it serves, (3) ensuring that research findings are comprehensible and accessible to lay people, and (4) designing social work research to give a voice to the voiceless by focusing on empowerment and by incorporating communities directly into the research process.

Social work has an historic commitment to promote the public good. Beginning with the social surveys of the early 1900s, social workers have used research as a clarion call to awaken public consciousness. To fulfill their obligation toward the public good, social work researchers must reengage in the public arena around issues of social policy. In order to accomplish this goal, the rules of academia, where most social work research occurs, must be changed. Instead of evaluating research solely by the patina of its methodology, other criteria must be employed, including its social utility and its impact on public policy. In effect, a balance must be reached between methodological astuteness and social commitment. We must encourage this balance in both our profession and in the schools where we work and study.

The following chapter argues that both the state and social policy are critical to the development of a progressive common good. While there is considerable disagreement over what constitutes the public good, social workers can nevertheless play a key role in the contemporary context by helping to advance progressive and social change-oriented visions for enhancing public life.

chapter **5**

Social Policy: The Ideology and Politics of the Public Good

This chapter addresses the need for the state to rediscover and establish standards for maintaining the public good. As such, the chapter examines the implications of competing definitions of the common good and shows how these definitions have molded public policy. Also addressed is the importance of the global economy in shaping domestic policy. In addition, the authors investigate the contributions that can be made by the social work profession in promoting the public good. Lastly, this chapter examines some of the skills needed in social policy analysis.

Social policy is an important component of a politicized social work practice, especially because politicized social work practice links all practice to a macro contextualization, thereby interweaving individuals, families, groups, and communities with collectivities, programs, and a vibrant public debate about social problems. Social policy, then, is inextricably linked to social work practice, and vice versa. Simply put, social policy informs social work practice. Conversely, the struggle for just social policies should be informed by a social work practice that is directly in touch with the "reality on the ground." Attempts to separate social work practice and social policy produce a social policy that is both out of synchronization with the needs of the poor and others, and a social work practice that lacks a political linkage to the public sector and the larger society. In both cases, the potential impact of social work intervention is compromised.

Social policy is important to social work practice because it addresses the role of the state in the allocation of resources and in the planning and implementation of social services. For social workers, linking the struggle over social policy to the need for the state to assume a more active and progressive role in domestic policy is essential to contextualizing social work practice within a broader framework. Understanding policy not only contextualizes practice within a larger framework, it also politicizes social work practice. Indeed, the understanding of social policy illustrates contemporary competing notions of a public good and the idea that such conceptions are fluid and highly politicized. Social policy, like public life in general, is the product of political ideology and social struggle. In the current context, social workers are forced to employ policy knowledge and practice skills to link clients to collectivities and challenge the neoconservative conception of the public good emanating from global privatization and public figures opposed to the social justice mission of social work. Progressive social policy and the creation of a state focused on egalitarian goals and democratic process remain essential building blocks in the design of a progressive public good.

COMPETING DEFINITIONS OF THE PUBLIC GOOD

The uneasy relationship between the public good and the welfare state has long been a knotty issue in American political economy. Gosta Esping-Andersen (1990) argues that workers traditionally depend on cash transactions for their welfare. According to Esping-Andersen (1990), social rights in a welfare state entail "decommodification," or granting citizens alternative means of survival to the marketplace. Decommodification also refers to the degree to which the distribution of goods, resources, or opportunities is detached from marketplace participation. The provision of welfare benefits does not, then, automatically lead to decommodification unless it significantly releases people from their dependence on the marketplace to meet basic needs. Esping-Andersen (1990) claims that citizens in a highly decommodified welfare state can freely choose to forego work under conditions that they consider necessary for reasons of health, family, age, or even educational self-improvement. Unlike many developed Western European nations, the U.S. welfare state was designed to minimize decommodification to ensure maximum labor market participation.

Esping-Andersen's ideas on decommodification are opposed to the very fabric of American social thinking. Specifically, American social thinking has always held the private marketplace in high regard, and as such, maintained that it was the optimal place for meeting people's social, cultural, and economic needs. The idea of the public good in American social thought was always linked to individual productivity within the marketplace. In that sense, the common good is the common economy, a place where everyone (at least theoretically) pulls their own economic weight. This ideology is grounded in the classical economic belief that without the spur of poverty, most rational people will choose leisure over work (Murray, 1984). Using threats of poverty and destitution as guiding principles in U.S. social policy has not only arrested any possible discourse on decommodification, it has also created a welfare state in which the only acceptable form of assistance is one that guarantees nonworking recipients fewer benefits than the prevailing wage.

The belief in the economic value of "insecurity" has also played a key role in the development of American social policy. Specifically, conservative economists have argued that economic insecurity forms an important building block of entrepreneurial energy. Simply put, the belief is that unless people are *compelled* to work, they will choose leisure activities over work. Conversely, providing economic security for large numbers of people through welfare programs leads to diminished ambition and fosters an unhealthy dependence on the state, one that can become intergenerational. Conservative economists implicitly argue that self-realization only occurs through marketplace participation. If so, welfare state programs actually harm rather than help the most vulnerable members of society. The belief in the social utility of economic insecurity has undergirded recent welfare reform initiatives calling for a maximum time limit on welfare entitlements. In short, the decommodification strategies advocated by Esping-Anderson are viewed by conservative policymakers as tearing at the very fabric of American economic existence. Given current conservative domination of political discourse, it is little wonder that tension between marketplace participation and welfare entitlement has played such a key role in defining American social welfare policy (Pierson, 1990).

Policy analysts such as Fred Block et al. (1987) have commented on the "meanness" of more recent welfare initiatives. Others (e.g., Karger & Stoesz, 1994) have noted that public policy is moving away from universal benefits (that is, benefits extended to the entire population) to more residual views (means-tested benefits) of social welfare. Indeed, for more than 20 years the federal government has been slowly shedding its responsibility for the public good. Much of the shift in government policy has been driven by an ideologically determined view of the public good. Hence, any analysis of the state and the common good must be based on whose definition of the common good is being examined. In a pluralistic society, ideas about the common good vary based largely on one's position in the social order. The definition of the common good is therefore grounded in the ideological continuum that makes up American political economy.

The Liberal Hegemony and the Public Good, 1935–1980

From the middle 1930s until the middle 1970s, the dominant concept of the public good—at least domestically—was predominantly liberal. Although moving in fits and spurts, the general direction of federal policy from the 1930s to the middle 1970s was to assume greater amounts of responsibility for the public good. This policy direction was led by liberal officials and pushed by liberal/left, grassroots efforts. Within this progressive framework, the common good implied that government had a major role in meeting the basic needs of citizens, especially those unable to fend for themselves.

This nascent American liberalism reached fruition with the passage of the first and most important wave of social welfare programs—the Social Security Act of 1935. Although motivated by a sense of the public good, the Social Security Act was also a political turning point for liberalism. Harry Hopkins (1936), a social worker, the head of the Federal Emergency Relief Administration, a confidant of President Roosevelt, a coarchitect of the New Deal, and a consummate political operative, had developed a calculus for American liberalism: "tax, tax; spend, spend; elect, elect." This liberal approach was elegant in its simplicity: The government would tax the upper middle class and the rich, thereby securing the necessary revenues to fund social programs for workers and the poor. It was a calculus that would dominate social policy for close to 50 years. (It was also a calculus that left out the role of social movements in pushing liberals to address the needs of the oppressed.) In fact, the momentum created by this approach was so strong that by 1975, social welfare spending had eclipsed military spending to become the single largest federal budget item (Karger & Stoesz, 1994). By 1980, social welfare programs accounted for 57 percent of all federal expenditures (Gilbert, Specht, & Terrell, 1993).

By the 1950s, the welfare state had become an important component of the American social landscape, and politicians sought to expand its benefits to more constituents. Focusing on the expansion of middle class programs, such as Federal Housing Authority (FHA) home mortgages, federally insured student loans, Medicare, and veterans' pensions, liberal policymakers could secure the political loyalty of a middle class that directly benefited from these programs. Even conservative politicians of the 1950s understood voters' support for the middle-class welfare state. Given this enthusiasm for the middle-class welfare state, it is not surprising that the largest post-World War II expansion of social welfare spending occurred under Richard Nixon, a Republican president. Nixon understood that a Republican president could not get elected without the working-class vote. He also understood the importance of securing that vote by expanding social benefits to the white middle class.

Scratching through its thin veneer, the liberal orientation to the public good loses some of its luster. The hallmark of American liberalism—the Social Security Act of 1935—was essentially a self-financing, social insurance program that rewarded working people. The public assistance programs—which contained less political capital and were therefore a better measure of public compassion—were rigorously means-tested, skimpy in their benefits, and designed to be operated by the less-than-generous states. Thus, while Social Security benefits were indexed to the cost-of-living (COLA) in the mid-1970s, public assistance benefits had so deteriorated that the Aid to Families with Dependent Children (AFDC) program lost 33 percent of its value from 1975 to 1992 (Karger & Stoesz, 1994). Conversely, the enactment of Social Security COLAs saw the poverty rate for the elderly halved from 1960 (25 percent) to 1980 (12.2 percent) (Karger & Stoesz, 1994). From the end of World War II until the War on Poverty, benefits under the public assistance portion of the Social Security Act consumed less than 1 percent of the Gross Domestic Product (GDP). In that same period, social insurance expenditures accounted for more than 8.5 percent of the GDP (Stoesz, 1996). This discrepancy was maintained during the liberal stewardship of domestic policy.

The expansion of means-tested social welfare programs occurred in its most focused form during Lyndon Johnson's Great Society and War on Poverty programs of the 1960s. The second wave of twentieth century social policy initiatives occurred in an era that came to represent the halcyon days of liberal influence in social welfare policy. Borne out of a concern with the seemingly intractable poverty in Appalachia, the public's awareness of poverty was heightened by the civil rights movement in the South and the publication of socialist Michael Harrington's (1962) book, *The Other America*. The urban riots of the middle 1960s underscored the urgency of federal action. In response to these challenges, some of the best minds of the period created aggressive social programs that promised a poverty-free America and a community-based system of social welfare. To realize these objectives, the Johnson administration developed a range of programs (e.g., Food Stamps, Head Start, the Model Cities Program, Job Corps, the Elementary and Secondary Education Act, and Medicaid) to provide relief and mobilize community resources. Common to these programs was a belief in the importance of a liberal conception of the public good. Specifically, social planners believed that government and the welfare state could be used to ensure at least a partial redistribution of social, economic, and political resources. It was also this top-down planning approach that eventually led to the public's disillusionment with aggressive social policies.

The second wave of social welfare initiatives also foreshadowed a second wave of reactions. (The first wave of reaction came in the late 1940s when public assistance programs were aggressively stigmatized. See Karger & Stoesz, 1994). Taking the offensive, conservatives argued that liberal planners had few successes to point to. Although poverty rates were halved from 1960 (25 percent) to 1970 (12.5 percent), this change was due, in part, to the doubling of AFDC rolls. Social problems, such as drug addiction, crime, teenage pregnancy, child abuse, and mental illness, continued to rise during the Great Society (Karger & Stoesz, 1994). America's flirtation with Johnson's bold social welfare initiatives ended with the election of Richard Nixon in 1968.

With Richard Nixon's election in 1968, the American welfare state took a contradictory turn. On one hand, the brief social experiments of the War on Poverty were eviscerated as Nixon terminated, diminished, or reassigned innovative programs to mainstream federal bureaucracies. On the other hand, Nixon understood that the key to reelection lay in building a wide base of support. Accordingly, he used the social insurance structure to reform public assistance by introducing several new social programs, including Supplemental Security Income (SSI), the Comprehensive Employment and Training Act (CETA), the Community Development Block Grant Program (CDBG), and the Rehabilitation Act (Jansson, 1988). Nixon even proposed an ill-fated guaranteed annual income for all poor families. In the end, the established social programs—Social Security, Medicare, Medicaid, AFDC, and Food Stamps—expanded dramatically under Nixon (DiNitto & Dye, 1987). Nixon's ambivalence toward social welfare was followed by two inconsequential presidencies, Ford and Carter, leaving many liberals with a sense that the most effective method for promoting the public good was incremental.

Beginning in the 1970s, the liberal goals of full employment, national health care, and a guaranteed annual income were being replaced by a neoconservative agenda that argued that high unemployment was good for the economy, that health care should remain in the private marketplace, and that competitive income structures were critical to productivity. Conservative economists argued that income inequality was socially desirable since social policies that promote equality encourage coercion, limit individual freedom, and damage the economy (Walker, 1990).

Throughout the 1960s, liberals argued for advancing the common good by promoting an ever-expanding economy and the growth of universal, non-means-tested social welfare and health programs. This goal was shared by virtually every social welfare scholar writing in the late 1960s and early 1970s (Wilensky & Lebeaux,

1965; Abramovitz, 1986). However, by the middle 1970s the goal of traditional liberals such as Senator Ted Kennedy, the late Tip O'Neill, George McGovern, and others to build a welfare state like those of Northern Europe was replaced by an incremental approach that narrowly focused on consolidating and fine-tuning the programs of the Social Security Act.

The Left and the Welfare State

The battle lines for the 1980s and beyond were drawn by the late 1970s: Traditional liberals who had vigorously promoted the common good through the expansion of the welfare state hunkered down and tried to cut their losses. Conservatives concentrated on attacking social programs. By the middle 1980s the Left was conspicuous by its silence.

The Reagan presidency marked a turning point in the historically uneasy relationship between the Left and traditional liberals. Before the 1980s, leftist social thought conflicted with liberal ideology in several important respects. First, many Marxians viewed the capitalist welfare state as being unable to address the common good. For these radicals, welfare state programs diverted attention from the structural problems of poverty toward those individuals experiencing poverty. Radicals saw the major problem as exploitation and the social injustice endemic to capitalism. While the compassion reflected in welfare programs was laudatory, it did little to address the structural causes of poverty. Hence, the welfare state was viewed as a palliative that provided just enough help to discourage revolution, but not enough to make a real difference in the lives of the poor (Piven & Cloward, 1971). While the Left believed that social welfare was better than nothing, and an improvement over private charity programs, it was definitely not enough and not primarily in the interests of those it was supposed to serve. Radicals argued that the common good could only be advanced by redistributing resources, not by charity (George & Wilding, 1976).

Despite their skepticism of welfare statism, many radicals in the United States and elsewhere were unprepared for the conservative juggernaut of the 1980s. Put on the defensive by a international shift to the Right, the American Left became a defender of the welfare state (Block et al., 1987; Harrington, 1984; Katz, 1986) within a few short years. Hence, the left-wing opprobrium once reserved for liberals was now focused on conservatives. The assertions of popular New Right thinkers provided ample ammunition for attack. For example, Martin Anderson's (1980) conclusion that the War on Poverty had been won except for a few mopping up operations, George Gilder's (1981) observation that to escape destitution the poor needed only the spur of their own poverty, and Charles Murray's (1984) recommendation to scrap the entire welfare and income support structure for working-aged persons all pushed public discourse and social struggle to a time reminiscent of the 1880s.

As the public debate shifted rightward, and the most damaging political epithet to call an opponent became "liberal," liberals moved right and the Left was forced to defend social welfare policy as a critical basis for a progressive public good. In defending the welfare state, the Left had inadvertently forfeited the opportunity to develop innovative welfare proposals in the face of bold and aggressive conservative proposals. Aligning itself with the remnants of traditional Democratic liberals, the Left moderated its criticism of welfare state programs, viewing them as working class victories not simply mechanisms of social control (Piven & Cloward, 1982; Gough, 1979). But, this stance weakened the Left's ability to formulate salient proposals on issues such as the so-called "underclass," regressive tax policies, the failure of welfare programs to diminish poverty rates, and the creation of alternatives to centralized public programs and spending priorities. In short, the Left found its creativity hampered by its newly formed defense of the social welfare state.

The Left's reconceptualization of the welfare state contained the seeds of an important shift in strategy. In progressive periods, such as the middle 1930s and 1960s, the Left could be a gadfly of the welfare state, pushing it farther along the path of equality and democracy. During these periods, the Left could push discussions on the common good and social policy toward increased inclusion and equality. In conservative periods, such as the 1980s and 1990s when the threat to prior gains and social life is great, the role of the Left takes on a more popular front strategy, which includes the creation of alliances with a wide range of progressive political forces. In effect, the Left turned away from sharpening class differences and turned toward trying to rebuild the important class, racial, and cultural bridges that had been weakened by the global economy and the dominance of neoconservative philosophy. The building of such progressive alliances between liberals and the Left, and the concomitant reformulation of a truly common good, remains essential to countering global privatization and restoring the public and the social in an increasingly private world.

Neoliberalism

By the late 1970s, the liberal view that the welfare state could advance the public good had all but disappeared. What remained of traditional liberalism was replaced by a neoliberalism that was more cautious of government, less antagonistic toward big business, and more skeptical of the value of universal entitlements. Traditional liberals and social democrats viewed government as the best institution for bringing social justice to millions of Americans who fail to participate in society because of obstacles such as racism, poverty, sexism, age, or disability. However, the defeat of Jimmy Carter—who embodied the transition from liberalism to neoliberalism—and the inauguration of a Republican Senate in 1980 forced many traditional Democrats to reevaluate their liberal leanings. While neoliberalism attracted a small following in the early 1980s, the landslide defeat of traditional liberal Walter Mondale touched the nerve of a Democratic Party fearful of losing its more conservative constituents (Peters, 1983).

In the late 1980s, a cadre of prominent mainstream Democrats including Paul Tsongas, Richard Gephardt, Sam Nunn, and Bill Bradley, to name a few, established the Democratic Leadership Council (DLC). In part, their goal was to wrest control of the Democratic Party away from traditional liberals who were so easily exploited by the Republican Party, and to create a new Democratic Party that was more at-tuned to the beliefs of the traditional core of voters and less antagonistic to corporate interests. In 1989, the DLC released *The New Orleans Declaration: A Democratic Agenda for the 1990s* (DLC, 1989). This agenda promised that Democratic Party politics would shift toward a middle ground that combined a corporatist economic analysis with a so-called "Democratic compassion." Two of the founders of the DLC were Bill Clinton and Al Gore. In fact, Bill Clinton chaired the DLC just before announcing his candidacy for president (Stoesz, 1996).

Neoliberals were skeptical of traditional liberalism, including its support of expensive social programs and its emphasis on governmental regulation. They were also more forgiving than traditional liberals of the antisocial behavior of large corporations. Not coincidentally, neoliberals were opposed to economic protectionism. Adherents of *realpolitik*, neoliberals viewed New Deal philosophy (with the exception of Social Security) as too expensive and too antiquated to address the current mood of voters and the new global realities. To reestablish the credibility of the Democratic Party, neoliberals distanced themselves from the large-scale governmental welfare programs associated with Democrats since the New Deal. Like their neoconservative counterparts, neoliberals called for a reliance on personal responsibility, work, and thrift as an alternative to governmental programs. Accordingly, neoliberal welfare proposals emphasized labor market participation (workfare), personal responsibility (time-limited welfare benefits), meeting family obligations (child support enforcement), and frugality in governmental spending (reinventing government). In place of comprehensive welfare reform proposals, neoliberals argued for reducing governmental spending while encouraging businesses to assume more responsibility for the welfare of the population. For Secretary of Labor Robert Reich (1983), a former Harvard professor and advisor to the Democratic Leadership Conference (DLC), a postliberal formulation meant substituting social welfare entitlements for investments in human capital. Public spending was consequently divided into good and bad categories: bad being consumption, such as unproductive expenditures in welfare and price supports, and good being investments in human capital, such as expenditures in education, research, and job training.

Neoliberalism altered the traditional liberal concept of the common good. Instead of viewing the best interests of large corporations as antithetical to the best interests of society, neoliberals argued for free trade, less regulation of corporate activity, and a more laissez-faire approach to social problems. Moreover, longtime Democratic Party supporters such as labor unions were viewed with skepticism. For example, when labor unions fought to stop NAFTA, Clinton continued to endorse it, despite labor's threats to oppose his reelection in 1996. The same was true for the GATT agreement. In both instances, Clinton was firmly aligned with conservative Democrats and Republicans. Traditional liberal Democrats therefore found themselves alone, bereft of support from the first Democratic White House in fourteen years. Even longtime Democratic allies such as the Rainbow Coalition and the minority caucuses were treated with skepticism. Refusing to bow to the pressures of the minority caucus, Clinton continued to back the death penalty component of his

1994 crime bill. The new shapers of the common good systematically excluded key parts of the old liberal coalition.

The neoliberal view of the common good reflects a kind of postmodern perspective. For neoliberals, the common good is elusive, and the form it takes is fluid and situational. Definitions of the common good change as the social order evolves and new power relationships emerge. Accordingly, neoliberals do not define the common good as tethered to industrial era norms and allegiances, but to a postindustrial society composed of new opportunities and new institutional shapes and forms. The state, then, is either good or bad depending upon the circumstances. Neoliberalism is therefore less of a political philosophy than a mode of pragmatic operation and can be characterized more as a political strategy and a technology (used in its broadest sense) than a well-defined ideology with a firm view on the common good and public life. This feature is both its strength and its weakness. Specifically, the strength of neoliberals lies in their ability to compromise and thereby accomplish things. The weakness is that when faced with an ideological critique (such as the Republicans' Contract with America), neoliberals are incapable of formulating a cogent ideological response. When Reagan argued for staying the course in the early 1980s, voters knew exactly what he meant even if they disagreed with him. When Clinton argued for staying the course in 1994, the public was uncertain as to what the course was. Substituting pragmatism for a progressive ideology has its price.

Accustomed to controlling the moral high ground in the debate over the public good, liberals were overwhelmed by aggressive, neoconservative policymakers, planners, philosophers, and ideologues. By the late 1970s, the public discourse on the common good came to be dominated by conservative perspectives.

Neoconservatives and the Common Good

The traditional conservative movement experienced a factionalization similar to that sustained by liberals. Old-style conservatives such as Barry Goldwater, who were more concerned with foreign policy than with domestic issues, were replaced by a new breed of neoconservatives such as Dick Armey, Newt Gingrich, Phil Gramm, and others, who were involved equally in domestic and foreign policy. With aplomb, neoconservatives cleverly manipulated the traditional American distrust of government. They raged against governmental intrusion in the marketplace, while simultaneously attempting to use the authority of government to advance their social objectives in the areas of antiwelfare planks, sexual abstinence, school prayers, abortion, and antigay rights proposals. Neoconservatives cleverly promoted a dual attitude toward the role of government. Mimicking their conservative predecessors in demanding a laissez-faire approach to economics, they steadfastly refused to translate that orientation to social affairs. Instead, neoconservatives argued for social conformity and a level of governmental intrusion into private affairs that would have made most traditional conservatives gag. In contrast to the traditional conservative skepticism about blending religion and politics—a division that the constitutional architects were careful to implement—neoconservatives unashamedly and opportunistically embraced the rising tide of fundamentalist religion. In doing so, they were partially successful in rewriting the spirit, if not its letter, of the American constitution. As a measure of their success, this cobbled-together coalition of economic conservatives, right-wing Christian ideologues, and opportunistic politicians had by the early 1990s virtually decimated what remained of Republican liberalism—those Republicans who were conservative on economic and defense concerns but relatively liberal on domestic issues. In effect, traditional Republicans went the way of traditional Democrats—both became an endangered species.

The neoconservative view of the common good differs dramatically from liberal and radical views. For liberals, the state represents either the best vehicle for achieving the common good, or at least, is an ally in promoting social change. For the contemporary Left, the state and social programs are a central site of social struggle, an arena for public debate and a lever to push capital into—at the least—becoming more socially responsible. For leftists, the public good is dialectical in that it is revealed in social struggle, a different conception from the liberal approach to the public good as a product, like programs and services, to be delivered to the people. In contrast, neoconservatives view the state—and, by implication, welfare state programs—as the cause rather than the solution to social problems. Neoconservatives argue that the very existence of the state is antithetical to the common good since it interferes with the maximization of individual self-interest. Hence, the neoconservative posture toward the state is predominantly adversarial, except when it uses the state to further its social agenda. In theory, neoconservatives see the primary role of government as protecting property and property owners. On the surface, the best state is a minimalist one that does not interfere with individual self-interest or the market economy. Beneath the surface, however, the neoconservative state is activist by virtue of its involvement in myriad social issues such as school prayer, abortion, sexual orientation, and drug testing.

Opportunity in the neoconservative paradigm is based on one's relationship to the marketplace, and legitimate rewards can only occur through marketplace participation. In contrast to the liberal emphasis on mutual self-interest, interdependence, and social equity, neoconservatives argue that the highest form of social good is realized through the maximization of self-interest. In the neoconservative view, the best society is one where everyone actively pursues their own good. Through a leap of faith (what Adam Smith called the "invisible hand"), the maximization of self-interest can be transformed into a mutual good. In that sense, neoconservatives occupy opposite ends of the philosophical continuum from liberals and radicals. The 1980s and the early 1990s saw the replacement of liberal philosophy with neoconservative dogma.

Neoconservative Social Policy

A half-century after the passage of the Social Security Act, the consensus on social policy became increasingly subject to redefinition. Even some traditional liberals became ambivalent about the ability of social programs to affect the common good.

This reappraisal came about partly as a result of the chronic economic problems of the 1970s, including stagflation (the combination of recession and high inflation), high levels of unemployment, a mounting federal debt, and the failure of welfare advocates to demonstrate the effectiveness of social programs in combating social disorganization. Neoconservative griping about wasteful welfare programs—so easily dismissed only a decade earlier—had by the early 1980s turned into the dominant critique, replete with a policy agenda.

Ronald Reagan's election brought the nascent welfare crisis to a head. Appealing to the public in his crusade to cut welfare programs, Reagan argued that government was the cause rather than the solution to social and economic problems. As the neoconservative-inspired, antiwelfare sentiment quickly spread, liberals were overwhelmed. Journalist Gregg Easterbrook (1986) wrote that "Neoconservative thinking has not only claimed the presidency; it has spread throughout our political and intellectual life and stands poised to become the dominant strain in American public policy" (p. 65).

The neoconservative agenda for social policy in the 1980s was fourfold: (1) end the liberal hegemony in social policy, (2) reroute public policy through the private sector, (3) preclude the possibility of a resurgence in social programs, and (4) stop costly social programs that allegedly lessen the profits and global competitiveness of corporations. During the 1980s, progressive advocates faced a steady stream of antiwelfare social legislation. Moreover, the Reagan administration sought to cripple social programs by using multiple strategies such as tax policy and federal budget deficits. The tax cuts of 1981 assured the Treasury Department of less revenue and the resulting federal budget deficits precluded the possibility of growth in social programs (Glazer, 1984). Even conservative economist Kevin Phillips (1990) admitted that, "Low-income families, especially the working poor, lost appreciably more by cuts in government services than they gained in tax reduction" (p. 87). Moreover, a study of AFDC families in Georgia found that 79 percent fell below the poverty level as a result of Reagan-inspired cuts, compared with 70 percent before 1981 (Wodarski et al., 1986).

By the early 1990s, neoconservatives had effectively prohibited the future growth of the welfare state. However, despite these victories, neoconservatives were unable to construct a programmatic alternative to the welfare state, all the more surprising given the enormous power they enjoyed during the early part of the 1980s. It is also surprising given the number of voluntary agencies, independent practitioners, employee benefit programs, commercial human service providers, and philosophers that the Right employed to construct an alternative vision of welfare. Had the neoconservatives of the 1980s not invested their political and economic capital in reckless foreign adventures in Nicaragua and El Salvador, or other scandals such as Irangate and the deregulation of industries like the savings and loan associations, they might have reshaped the American welfare state in a manner consistent with their vision.

After a decade of hammering away at social programs, neoconservatives had accomplished relatively little. By the early 1990s, the American welfare state remained intact, if a little battleworn. Despite the right-wing rhetoric, no major social programs were dismantled in either the Reagan or Bush terms. Moreover, costs for social insurance and entitlement programs such as Social Security, Medicare, and Medicaid continued to soar (Karger & Stoesz, 1994). In the end, neoconservatives had underestimated three important variables: (1) the resiliency of the American welfare state, (2) the continued support—however ambivalent—it enjoyed among the middle class, and (3) the difficulty of translating rhetoric into viable reform proposals. In the end, the Reagan and Bush administrations' most enduring legacy was not its contribution to social policy, but the $4.5 trillion federal debt left in the wake of fast and loose tax policies coupled with increased military spending.

Despite the Right's failure to reshape the welfare state in the 1980s, frustrated and fearful American voters seemed ready to give them a second chance in 1994. This time, neoconservatives had learned from their past mistakes. Instead of toying with incremental policies, the Right proposed bold, new welfare reform initiatives. No longer would AFDC policies be tinkered with; instead, they would be shifted back to the states in the form of a block grant. Even the formerly liberal House of Representatives passed welfare reform legislation that contained a two-year cap on benefits, something considered unthinkable just five years earlier.

Invoking the rallying cry of "states' rights," the current neoconservative strategy is based on the view that state officials should have the right to shape their welfare programs—presumably in punitive and highly restrictive ways—in the way they think best. Bowing to pressure, the Clinton administration, in granting AFDC program waivers, tacitly accepted the neoconservative vision of welfare reform by allowing these less visible reforms to take place on the state level. This action allowed states like Virginia, Michigan, and Texas to implement lifetime welfare caps and other restrictive AFDC policies. The creation of welfare reform by waivers, which allowed Washington to wash its hands of direct responsibility for punitive welfare policies, permitted the Clinton administration to maintain its liberal veneer while at the same time accommodating neoconservative forces. In effect, if far-ranging welfare policy could not be made on the national level, then it would be made on the state level. Knowing that most state governments would strangle welfare programs in ways never permitted given the spotlight in Washington, neoconservatives had won a victory that was unimaginable even during the height of the Reagan presidency.

Communitarianism: A Different Way?

As the political center dramatically eroded in the early 1990s—resulting in a marked drift to the Right—a lacuna emerged in American political life. Groups that were once considered fringe elements—for example, the Christian fundamentalist Right—were now in mainstream positions of power. At the same time, there was a uneasy sense among certain intellectuals and political leaders that the moral and social fabric of America was deteriorating along with its political center.

One such group are the communitarians, a loose group of intellectuals that propose a "third way." According to Peter Steinfels (1992), "communitarians essentially staked out political territory somewhere between the liberal advocates of the welfare state and civil liberties entrenched in one corner, and conservative devotees of laissez-faire and traditional values on the other" (p. B16). Communitarians generally agree with liberals on issues of individual rights, equality, and democratic change. They argue, however, that none of these values can be preserved unless America's basic communities and institutions (e.g., families, schools, neighborhoods, unions, local governments, religious institutions, and ethnic groups) succeed in rebuilding individual character and promoting the virtues of citizenship (Etzioni, 1993).

Amitai Etzioni (1995), a leading communitarian spokesperson, argues that communitarians are concerned with the social preconditions that enable individuals to maintain their psychological integrity, civility, and ability to reason. Etzioni (1995) argues that when community—social webs carrying moral values—deteriorates, the individual's psychological state is endangered. Communitarians also firmly believe in balancing rights with responsibilities. For Etzioni, strong rights entail strong responsibilities.

Communitarians are concerned with rebuilding communities. For them, radical individualism is responsible for the breakdown of society. In addition, they also advocate for strong, two-parent families (although they do acknowledge that some single parent families succeed), which is viewed as the main conduit for socialization and good citizenship. For communitarians, the family is the place where each new generation acquires its moral anchor.

Communitarians attempt to balance conservatism with liberalism. On the one hand, communitarians, like traditional conservatives, fault liberals for consistently citing economic and political forces as the causes of poverty, drug abuse, crime, and urban problems, while neglecting the importance of personal responsibility and the forces that have historically nurtured it. On the other hand, communitarians blame conservatives for deifying the marketplace, viewing the pursuit of self-interest as the answer to social problems, and simply ignoring the corrosive effects of the market and the subsequent economic pressures placed on family life and community spirit. Although priding themselves on being tough-minded, bold, and challenging, communitarians take no group position on either abortion or gay rights (Pollitt, 1994).

On the surface, some communitarians appear more conservative than traditional liberals. They argue for adolescent curfews, work requirements for welfare, family values, "drug free" zones, more emphasis on public safety, less access to legal redress for criminals, and the need for government to create more obstacles to divorce in terms of assuring child support. Communitarians also reject the idea that America is so divided over basic values that teaching moral education is impossible. In effect, they argue that moral education and character building should be taught all the way from kindergarten to college. While communitarians advocate the protection of basic rights, they also call for "sensible limits on freedom," which include road sobriety checkpoints and mandatory drug testing for those in public jobs. Echoing antifederal government sentiment, communitarians call for shifting power out of Washington and into the private sector and smaller government. Lest communitarians sound too conservative, they also advocate European-style child benefits, extended paid and unpaid parental leaves, and flexible working hours. Communitarians also call for national service and an end to private gun ownership.

Communitarians contend that terms like *liberal* and *conservative* are out of date. Etzioni (Benedetto, 1992) argues that, "When it comes to freedom of speech, enforcement of law, public safety, the family and schools, we find it better to talk about authoritarians who want to impose their moral solution on everybody, libertarians who oppose any voice other than that of the individual, and communitarians who want new moral standards reached through consensus" (p. 13A). There is some evidence of the bridging effects of communitarianism. For example, in the early 1990s communitarians developed a plank and asked interested parties to sign it. Among the signers were a variety of both Republicans and Democrats, including Democrats Daniel P. Moynihan and Al Gore and Republicans David Durenberger and Jack Kemp.

The various conceptions of the public good embodied in liberal, left, neoliberal, conservative, neoconservative, and communitarian philosophies are rooted in an ideological orientation to society and in a vision of the state's proper role in social affairs. Much of the rapidly changing nature of social policy is also attributable to the shifting economic realities of the 1990s, especially the effects of the global economy on all levels of society. Since social philosophy and economics are inseparable components of the social dynamic, the role of the contemporary welfare state can be understood best through a political economy perspective. It is to this point that we will now turn.

THE POLITICAL ECONOMY OF THE 1990s

The concept of the public good is driven by political forces. It is also largely lodged within the political economy of the modern welfare state. The public good is therefore shaped by myriad economic forces, including the demands imposed by the global economy. This reality has not escaped the gaze of community organizers, such the as Industrial Areas Foundation's (IAF) Ernesto Cortes, Jr. (1993), who maintains "The forces affecting our cities originate from changes in the national and world economies. Dealing with these forces will require some of the major shifts in economic policy. . . ." (p. 16). It is therefore important to examine how the global economy relates to and shapes social policy.

The Global Economy

The global economy is marked by contradictory trends. Close to 75 percent of the world's population live in poorer nations, most in the Southern Hemisphere. Life expectancy, child mortality, and educational attainment have all improved markedly in the past three decades. Yet, while incomes and consumption rose in developing nations by almost 70 percent between 1965 and 1985, almost one billion people in the developing world live in poverty, struggling to live on incomes of less than $400 a year. Although parts of the world's economy improved in the 1980s, especially in South and East Asia, other countries in Latin America and in most of Sub-Saharan

Africa (a population of 510 million) saw their real per capita incomes, living standards, and investments slip throughout the 1980s. Millions of Latin Americans now experience lower standards of living than in the 1970s, and most Sub-Saharan Africans saw their living standards fall to levels not seen since the late 1960s (The World Bank, 1990).

The impact of the global economy can be illustrated by comparing growth rates in Western and Asian economies. Between 1965–1980, South Korea's average annual growth rate in manufacturing was 18.7 percent; for Japan it was 9.4 percent; and for Singapore, 13.2 percent. In that same period, the manufacturing growth rate in the United States was 2.5 percent; in France, 5.2 percent; in Germany, 3.3 percent; and in the United Kingdom, 0.5 percent (The World Bank, 1990). Perhaps the most striking example of the expansion of Asian economies is evident in the growth of the Gross Domestic Product (GDP). While the GDP of the United States grew by slightly over five times between 1970 and 1991 (from $1 trillion to $5.6 trillion), Korea's GDP in that same period rose by a whopping 35 times (from $8 billion to $282 billion); for Singapore it rose almost 22 times (from $1.8 billion to $40 billion); and for Hong Kong it increased almost 20 times (from $3.4 billion to $67.5 billion) (The World Bank, 1993). The growth in exports shows similar trends. From 1980–1988, exports from Korea and Hong Kong rose 14.7 percent and 12.3 percent respectively; in that same period, exports rose by only 1.2 percent in the United States and 3.1 percent in the United Kingdom (The World Bank, 1990). Moreover, from 1965–1980, the gross domestic investment in Korea was 15.9 percent; in Singapore it was 13.3 percent; and in Japan, 6.7 percent. In contrast, the gross domestic investment in the United States was 2.6 percent; in Germany, 1.7 percent; in France, 3.9 percent; and in the United Kingdom, 0.6 percent (The World Bank, 1990).

The operative terms in global capitalism are "flexibility" and "competitiveness." This competitiveness consists of several strategies, including corporate downsizing, reducing labor costs, and increasing market shares through corporate takeovers. The reduction of labor costs is realized by using an extensive and inexpensive pool of global labor that can produce virtually everything: data processing, legal and engineering services, research and development, and basic production. Tied to lowering labor costs is the cutting of social costs and social wage supports. Barnet (1994) estimates that about one-third of American workers are at risk of losing their jobs to the growing productivity of low-wage workers in China, India, Mexico, and elsewhere. Two interrelated features of the global economy shape the structure, function, and direction of modern welfare states. These features include the actual trends in the global economy and the adoption of policies believed necessary to ensure economic survival.

The Global Economy and the Neoconservative Public Good

One of the most striking trends in the global economy is the inequality it fosters. For example, the average chief executive officer (CEO) in the United States is paid 149 times the average worker's salary. Moreover, the world's 358 billionaires have a net worth of $760 billion, equal to the bottom 45 percent of the world's population.

As technology wipes out or downgrades various kinds of routine jobs, "superstar" jobs (e.g., CEOs with multimillion dollar salaries, medical specialists, superstar lawyers, high-visibility entertainers, and sports heroes, etc.) have risen dramatically, although they continue to make up only a minuscule part of the labor force (Barnet, 1994). This "overfeeding" exists in an economy where 18 percent of full-time American workers earn poverty-level wages; where the number of children born into poverty since 1970 rose by 50 percent; where 22 percent of all children grow up poor; and where 50 percent of black children are born into a family living below the poverty line. While the wages of low-wage workers fell by 15 percent between the late 1970s and the early 1990s, the real earnings of high-end occupations like doctors and corporate executives rose by 50 percent or more (Barnet, 1994). Even the solidly middle class are affected by the instability resulting from the global economy. From 1991 to 1994, giant corporations such as IBM, AT&T, GM, Sears Roebuck and GTE announced layoffs totaling 324,650. This "payroll trimming" appears to be a permanent feature of corporate life in America (Barnet, 1994). The promise that the postindustrial job-creating machines of the early 1980s (e.g., financial houses, insurance companies, and real estate firms) would take care of workers was never realized. In 1992, the 4.9 million nonsupervisory workers in these industries were earning $10.14 per hour, less than the average production worker and considerably less than is required to raise a middle-class family in financial market centers like Manhattan, Los Angeles, or San Francisco. The 1.1 million bank tellers and clerks earned $8.19 an hour, while the back-office employees made an average yearly wage of $28,000. Middle managers also saw their earnings fall, as the median earnings of the two million American men between 45 and 54 with four years of college fell in constant dollars from $55,000 in 1972 to $42,000 in 1992 (Barnet, 1994). This inequality has occurred while the number of unionized workers in private industry has fallen to less than 12 percent of the workforce—less than the number unionized in 1936 (Barnet, 1994).

Instead of grappling with the root cause of the economic malaise—the stateless corporation that has little allegiance to a national economy—conservative economists have, instead, devised ways to enhance further the power of these corporations. In the 1980s, neoconservative economists outlined the requirements for success in the new global community: (1) a laissez-faire economic approach emphasizing free trade and markets, no tariffs, and a commitment to the free movement of capital; (2) dramatic reductions in corporate and progressive income taxes; (3) a decrease in governmental regulations and in the power of regulatory agencies; (4) privatizing the economy by selling off publicly owned industries, utilities, and transportation systems; (5) reducing the role of government in the marketplace, including slashing or eliminating public employment programs; and (6) decreasing welfare benefits, including major cuts in entitlement programs (Rabushka & Hanke, 1989). These neoconservative economic and social prescriptions have important consequences for the concept of the common good. Specifically, they call for redefining the public good downward, thereby allowing corporations to exercise more freedom in flexing their competitive muscles. In essence, neoconservative economists simply revised the old conservative adage: "What's good for business is good for the public good."

The downward economic trends experienced by most Western nations since the 1970s have precipitated a crisis in developed welfare economies. To survive in the competitive global economy, corporations and governments are compelled to increase efficiency, which can lead to economic restructuring, including plant shutdowns and major industrial reorganization. For its part, government is forced by its adherence to neoconservative economic logic to bolster the position of domestic industries by freeing up investment capital through freezing or lowering corporate and/or personal tax rates. For example, the percentage of total revenues received by the U.S. federal government from income, profit, and capital gains taxes decreased from 56.6 percent in 1980 to 50.7 percent in 1991 (The World Bank, 1993). This subsequent revenue loss led to staggering levels of governmental debt, a reduction in welfare services, a deterioration of the public infrastructure, and myriad social and economic problems. Moreover, the situation is aggravated as governmental cuts are met by increased demands for public services resulting from global-based changes. As a result, the huge governmental debts incurred by most Western nations make broad, new, fiscal-based social welfare programs almost inconceivable in the near future, despite the emerging social problems. In this way, Western governments assume the economic and social costs of the global economy. Government therefore recommodifies public services and welfare state functions by redefining the idea of public utilities through shifting more human needs into the private marketplace. This governmental load-shedding includes physical and mental health, housing, and food. Trouble looms as social injustice inevitably breeds either social disorder or repression.

Labor policy is another factor in the global economy. Multinational corporations demand a loose labor market—low wages and high levels of unemployment—in order to bring down or stabilize wage rates. As part of this strategy, corporations argue for loosening labor market controls while curbing the power of unions. This corporate strategy results in diminished levels of employee security as the strength and numbers of trade unions decline. In addition, shifting centers of production abroad also requires a transformation in the nature of jobs created domestically, including the development of a large secondary labor market (Friedrich, 1990). Thus, instead of achieving economic self-sufficiency, many workers in the burgeoning service sector remain eligible for basic welfare benefits because of low wages. Moreover, the need to compete in the global economy and continue to maximize profits compels corporations to downsize their operations. To cut costs further, corporations may opt to replace full-time employees with less expensive part-time workers who may be ineligible for normal employment perks such as health and pension benefits. Taken together, these conditions provide fertile ground for a growing legion of low-wage workers in the secondary and tertiary labor sectors.

The creation of a large class of working and unemployed poor poses serious threats for an already overextended welfare state. Because low-paid and marginal workers have few of the traditional employment perks and protections accorded a stable workforce, they require more social welfare benefits, including various forms of income support. With few retirement benefits and insufficient incomes to create their own retirement plan, this group will likely consume high levels of welfare benefits when they retire. By allowing corporations to create an unstable labor force, government agrees to strain its present resources while mortgaging its future. Despite increasing pressure for services, many Western governments continue to arrest or reduce their welfare programs (Glennester & Midgley, 1991).

The global economy has also led to the increased privatization of the economy, including social welfare services. In its simplest form, the privatization of welfare services involves shifting governmental welfare activities into private hands and into the marketplace. In that sense, privatization can be viewed from two perspectives. First, privatization is simply another mechanism for conducting public business. Second, privatization is a theory of political and administrative economy committed to reducing governmental responsibility for the provision of social welfare services to the population (Gummer, 1988; Carol, 1987). Politically and administratively, privatization has become a fashionable alternative to the liberal social policies of some advanced industrial countries, especially the United States and Britain (LeGrand & Robinson, 1985).

The effects of the global economy on the public good are complex. First, the global economy has fostered the scaling back or dismantling of state institutions. Second, the immersion into the global marketplace has led to substituting the advancement of the private good for that of the public good. It has also fostered the privatization of social life on several different levels, including the receipt of social welfare benefits, lowered governmental assistance to communities, and the reframing of discourse away from public to private problems and solutions. Third, the push toward competitiveness in the global economy has hastened the move toward an overwhelmingly residual form of social welfare that is means-tested, sparse in its benefits, and highly stigmatized.

Perhaps the most important question facing late twentieth-century policymakers is how to move a society from an industrial era comprehension of social policy to a progressive, postmodern formulation of the public good. The answer to this knotty question centers around the important role of the state in a postindustrial society.

Social Policy, the State, and the Corporate Good

The federal government has played a mixed and often contradictory role in advancing the public good. On the one hand, federal initiatives in social programs helped halve the overall poverty rate from 25 percent in 1960 to 12 percent in 1970. On the other hand, the state has exacerbated class and racial differences by its preferential treatment of social insurance over poverty programs. Fearing direct involvement in the marketplace, the state has attempted to manage existing opportunities, such as affirmative action policies, rather than focusing its efforts on enlarging the general pool of opportunities. The state has therefore created more, rather than less, social instability.

Social divisions exacerbated by myopic federal strategies also include policies focused on urban and city locales, which lead to geographic discrimination, and like global capitalism itself, uneven development. As a partial result of federal policies, millions of Americans migrated to the Sun Belt states of the South and the West in the 1970s and early 1980s. From 1975 to 1985, the South and the West accounted for 85 percent of the nation's population growth (Kasarda, 1988). For example, from 1970 to 1984, the population of Phoenix increased by almost 48 percent; San Diego and Houston grew by close to 38 percent. On the other hand, St. Louis, Detroit, and Cleveland lost almost 30 percent of their population. Those left behind tended to be the elderly and people of color. Accordingly, the nonwhite populations of northeastern cities rose from 33 to 42 percent between 1970 and 1985 (Kasarda, 1988).

The flight of working-class families and capital from older urban areas devastated whole cities and neighborhoods. Throughout this ordeal, the federal government did surprisingly little to help Northeastern and Midwestern cities in crisis. Instead, federal policy aided the new Sun Belt urban centers substantially by deregulating financial institutions. This move would later haunt taxpayers who in the early 1990s were forced to bail out the savings and loan industry (S&L) to the tune of $300–$500 billion. By deregulating the S&L industry, the Reagan administration had created an enormous development program that favored the Sun Belt states at the expense of the Rust Bowl states. By the time the S&L scandal reached a head in the early 1990s, the majority of financial institutions in conservatorship were in the Sun Belt. In the end, thirty-seven states financed the debt of the remaining thirteen, with the largest beneficiaries being Texas, Arkansas, Florida, California, New Mexico, Louisiana, and Arizona. Ironically, this massive bailout would cost the Frost Belt states $123 billion at a time when they were trying to rebuild their battered economies (Hill, 1990). Once again, the private corporate good was antithetical to the public good.

While federal policy punished poor, inner-city residents through slashing social programs and urban subsidies, it was extravagant in its help to the rich. The tax cuts of 1981 helped to nourish an "overclass" that needed little help. Corporations and lenders made billions as overpriced mergers, shaky real estate deals, and creative debt instruments substituted for industrial policy. The new economic heroes of the 1980s were not industrialists, but fast-talking capital barons who made quick fortunes by creating, managing, and leveraging debt. Not coincidentally, many of these Wall Street "traders" ended up in prison, although not before bilking clients out of billions of dollars. Throughout the 1980s, social policy was interchangeable with corporate policy. Moreover, the transfer of income to the rich came on the backs of the poor through social welfare cuts and on the backs of the middle class through cuts in basic services and programs. For the Reaganauts, the common good was the corporate good. This perspective only exacerbated the omnipresent divisions in American society between the rich and the poor, the whites and people of color, and between the North and the South.

These policies did not exist in a vacuum but were part of the ideological politics driving America. Policy options implemented by the state are chosen from a menu, many of whose entries are limited by the political discourse of the dominant ideologies. Consequently, by the beginning of the 1990s, the debt was coming due and with interest: Shaky financial institutions cost taxpayers billions of dollars, the infrastructure of older Northeastern and Midwestern cities continued to deteriorate, homelessness rose to somewhere between 1–3 million, the so-called underclass grew and became a prominent part of urban landscapes, race relations worsened as poor people of all colors fought for the few remaining well-paying jobs in the manufacturing sector, and the drug trade flourished as the breakdown of community life and the despondency of the poor increased. The social costs of the "corporate good" had a high price tag for American society. No wonder there is great skepticism about the salience of a public or common good in a neoconservative context of global privatization.

SKILLS IMPLICATIONS: SOCIAL POLICY AS SOCIAL WORK PRACTICE

Thinking too deeply about the weight, complexity, and harshness of contemporary American social policy can lead to an undefinable melancholy. Lest we allow ourselves to sink into this funk, there *are* alternatives for building a more just social order. However, the exercise of these alternatives requires the development of concrete skills. One area that lends itself to this skill development is social policy.

Social policy skills can be divided into two specific yet interrelated categories: policy analysis and policy activism. The aims are often overlapping, and the skills required for each are not discrete. The major difference between them is one of focus. While the attention of the policy analyst is focused on systematically analyzing a social policy, the activist is concerned with how to use that policy to achieve a specific organizational or social justice goal. Policy analysis and policy activism are both key components of the social change process.

Policy Analysis

Policy analysis is concerned with the systematic investigation of a social policy or a set of policies. Analysts are employed in a variety of settings, including federal, state, and local governments; think tanks on both the Left and the Right; universities; and in larger social agencies. The goals of policy analysis can range from pure research to information provided to legislators to advocacy research.

Policy analysis involves three interrelated areas: (1) determining whether a policy should be passed or enacted, (2) implementing the policy, and (3) evaluating whether the policy has efficiently and effectively accomplished its designated goals. As such, policy analysis skills can be broken down into the following three areas:

1. *The determination of whether a policy or legislative bill should be enacted or passed.* To determine adequately whether a policy or bill should be passed may involve skills related to using and developing policy frameworks, which are a set of systematic questions around which a policy or

bill is analyzed. The function of this framework is to ascertain whether a bill or policy is both viable and congruent with the values, mission, or goals of government, organizations, or agencies. Among other things, a well-constructed policy framework looks at the values and ideology inherent in a policy, its political and administrative feasibility, its effectiveness and efficiency, and how it compares to alternative policies and bills. Several policy analysts have developed useful frameworks, including David Gil (1981), Neil Gilbert and Harry Specht (1993), and Howard Karger and David Stoesz (1994).

2. *How a policy or legislative bill is implemented is as crucial as the original decision to enact it.* This is especially true since there is inevitably a gap between a policy or bill and its implementation (DiNitto, 1991). Apart from helping to judge whether a policy or bill should be enacted, policy analysts may also be called upon to help design the implementation of a policy or to evaluate whether that implementation was successful. Diana DiNitto (1991) argues that successful implementation requires the following: active communication, adequate resources, supportive attitudes on the part of personnel charged with carrying out the policy, and the bureaucratic character of the institution where the policy or bill will be lodged. Hence, policy analysts must have skills in developing effective means of communication, assessing the adequacy of resources, creating positive relationships to build support for a policy or bill, and understanding bureaucratic structures, especially in terms of how those structures are changed.

3. *Evaluating or understanding the consequences of a policy is an important aspect of policy analysis and the policy process in general.* Evaluation is guided by a simple question: "Does the policy work?" The answer to this question requires other questions, such as, "For whom does the policy work? Are people receiving the benefits they are expected to get? Is the policy or bill using resources efficiently? How effective is the policy? Do the benefits to society exceed the costs of the policy or bill?"

Specific skills in policy evaluation can take many forms, including formal evaluations, which use scientific methods and empirical data to systematically evaluate policy outcomes. Site visits and public hearings are yet other ways to examine policy outcomes. In short, evaluators must have a wide range of skills from which to draw when evaluating a policy or bill.

Skills in Policy Activism

Policy activism requires a somewhat different set of skills. While the policy activist may also be a researcher, he or she is primarily focused on the advocacy aspects of social policy. Hence, while activists may be expected to have skills in policy determination, implementation, and evaluation, they are also expected to have advocacy skills. Clearly, the skills expected of the policy activist overlap with those of the community organizer. For the purposes of this chapter, we will look only at those skills that relate to political advocacy and the policy process.

1. *Lobbying is an important skill in the process of political advocacy.* In short, lobbying is the persuasive presentation of an issue designed to influence decisionmakers (Haynes & Mickelson, 1991). This process of persuasion can take many forms, including face-to-face lobbying, letter writing, telephoning, and testifying in front of legislative committees and community or agency groups.

2. *Testifying is another important skill for policy activists.* This activity may entail giving testimony in front of various legislative committees or groups, or organizing the testimony of others. Testimony can involve the use of scenarios to make a point, or it can attempt to persuade those in power through the use of data both current and projected. The process of testifying can also be enhanced by incorporating clients or other beneficiaries of the policy or bill in the proceedings (Haynes & Mickelson, 1991). A variation of testimony involves using the policy activist as an expert witness regarding the ramifications of a particular policy or bill under consideration.

3. *Another necessary skill is bureaucratic or legislative monitoring* (Haynes & Mickelson, 1991). Specifically, this skill requires the activist to have intimate knowledge of the political and bureaucratic process. The policy activist must be able to track legislation and/or monitor the implementation of a policy or bill in the appropriate legislative or bureaucratic setting.

4. *The policy process also requires the activist to have skills in the careful manipulation of the media.* This area involves the preparation of press releases, the orchestration of press conferences, and the cultivation of media contacts.

While there are clearly differences in the skills expected of policy analysts and policy activists, they do share a central core of skills. First, both must be astute analysts of political agendas and the political process. Equally important, they must possess "ideological competency," that is, the skill to be able to identify the political orientation and objectives of policy makers and policy. Both the analyst and the activist must also be able to determine what is feasible and desirable. Second, both must have mastered the art of written and verbal communication. Documentation is the currency of the policy realm, and writing is the currency of documentation. In short, the skill of articulation is a major component in the policy process.

Alvin Schorr (1985) has argued that the differentiation between policy and practice is false. For Schorr, practitioners are policymakers in important clinical and organizational contexts, including their ability to manipulate agency settings, thereby helping clients to receive necessary services. The actual delivery of social services—where the rubber hits the road in social work—is critical in the analysis of social welfare policy (Martin, 1990). The skills discussed above are important and not difficult for most social workers to master. The question is not one of ability, but of will. As long as the responsibility for social change rests squarely on the shoulders of macro practice, micro-level social work practitioners will find little incentive to learn important policy skills. Only by contextualizing social work practice and by putting macro practice at its base will social change be truly integrated into social work.

CONCLUSION

The consequences of the global economy—perhaps even more importantly, the response of policymakers to it—has led to a shrinking tax base, accelerated joblessness, mounting insecurity in the workplace, increased poverty, and a climate in which the glaring disparity between the highly publicized super-rich and the growing legions of the poor (and *nouveau* poor) rarely receives the public limelight. Gone are the days when American corporations promised their workers job security, good wages, and generous benefits in return for industrial peace. Also gone are the days when U.S. corporate growth was an avenue for the poor to enter the mainstream of American society. In its place are stateless corporations who disavow any special relationship to the United States or its people. Policies designed to promote the competitiveness of American corporations have resulted in even more tax hardship for the middle class. For example, the General Accounting Office reported that in 1993 more than 40 percent of corporations with assets over $250 million doing business in the United States paid either no income taxes or taxes less than $100,000. In the 1950s, corporations operating in the United States paid 23 percent of all federal income taxes; by 1991 it was down to 9.2 percent. This shift occurred as the share of corporate taxes paid on the state and local levels stayed at the same level as in 1965 (Barnet, 1994). Not surprisingly, this tax shortfall is picked up by a middle class whose real wages have been flat since the 1970s.

Good economic news such as the increased production of durable goods, lower unemployment, and low rates of inflation only exacerbate the rage felt by the middle class since this progress rarely translates into their paychecks. Instead, what is good for the American economy is no longer synonymous with what is best for the American worker. The buoyancy of the American economy does not filter down either to the middle class or to the poor who are, in fact, increasingly insulated from the effects of economic growth. The rage felt by a middle class barely treading water takes on many forms, including the tax revolts that have been commonplace since the late 1970s.

Because the ownership of the media is concentrated in the hands of fewer and fewer megacorporations, there is little incentive to highlight the power of corporations over the daily life of Americans (Barnet, 1994). Even if the media decided to target large, multinational corporations as causing economic despair, these institutions seem beyond the reach of ordinary citizens. Most Americans feel powerless to change the institutions that hold their economic life in check. The more overwhelmed they feel, the more corporate power grows (Barnet, 1994). To ventilate their frustration, many voters replace elected officials or political parties like musical chairs. With each new election comes a new expectation for change. As hopes are quickly dashed, voter discontent grows almost immediately. Former Senator Robert Dole surmised that American politicians are only popular before and just after they take office.

Because of America's outrageously expensive electoral process, political parties are forced to turn to large corporate givers or political action committees (PACs) for funding. Hedging their bets, these contributors often give to both political parties.

Beholding to large corporations or well-funded PACs, neither the Democratic nor Republican parties have adopted comprehensive policies to curb the growing power of multinational corporations. Hence, the economic system is shielded by the political system, and the status quo is assured regardless of which party assumes power. A prime example of the magnitude of corporate power is illustrated by the death of health care reform. Without reaching far into their deep pockets, the medical-industrial complex convinced the American people that an overly expensive health care system that excluded almost 40 million people (and inadequately covered millions more) was not in need of reform (Karger & Stoesz, 1994).

The federal government has demonstrated an antagonistic attitude toward community life for at least two decades. On the one hand, the United States defunded urban and social programs and then built the largest prison system in the world to address mounting social disorder and fear of disorder. On the other hand, the laissez-faire attitude of the state is reflected in the dearth of progressive, community-based legislation passed since the 1970s. This "load-shedding" is also evident in government's failure to react positively to the increasing deterioration of America's inner cities. The retreat of the state from progressive social policy through shedding its responsibility to the public (either through downsizing or lethargy) is ultimately a retreat from social responsibility. In addition, the deleterious effects of the global economy on large groups of Americans requires a redefinition of government's role in a postindustrial society. If greater prosperity is to commence, government must take an active role in redirecting fiscal and social resources downward toward those who lack opportunity.

If progressive change is to occur, the state must stop from shirking its role as a key player in the promotion of the public good. In the end, the state is the only viable source for the large-scale funding required to rebuild America's deteriorated infrastructure, especially its poor urban and rural communities. While the work of nonprofit organizations such as housing coalitions, food banks, and antihunger projects is valuable, nonprofits lack the capital and power necessary to engineer changes on a massive scale. Although these organizations deliver needed services and function as important beacons of compassion for a middle class grown insensitive to the plight of the poor, they are no substitute for proactive and aggressive state policy. Furthermore, the state cannot reassert its role in the pursuit of the common good by choosing passivity over action. The cynicism of voters—at least as reflected in the low voter turnout rates—will not be reversed until the state establishes itself as a moral institution reflecting the general will of all its citizens. Ideally, when the will of the people and the common good collide—as in proposals for middle- and upper-class tax cuts that will invariably come on the backs of the poor—the state must resolve to function as the arbiter of a common good that transcends political expediency. Realistically, this goal will require vigorous activism on the part of the powerless, struggling around issues and pressuring the state to be more inclusive and responsive to the needs of ordinary citizens as well as the most powerful.

The stature of the state is not enhanced by pandering to the pecuniary interests of voters, but by establishing long-term, national goals, even when they mean short-term discomfort for the middle class. Otherwise, the cynicism of voters is heightened as middle-class tax bonuses are seen as "politics as usual." Beneath the cynicism of voters is a desire for the state to assume a moral leadership that transcends narrow self-interests. In that sense, voters want the state to construct a kind of moral road map built on integrity and fair play.

The advancement of the public good is dependent upon redefining the responsibility of the state to address social need. It is also dependent on reasserting the role of the state and the public sector in fostering social change, empowerment, and democracy. As part of this redefinition, the state must be viewed as the funder for decentralized, community-based programs. One of the most important components in resurrecting the state's responsibility for community life is the creation of a comprehensive and progressive idea of the common good. Building on the lessons of the new social movements (discussed in chapter 2), this newly minted idea of a truly public good must address the myriad features of human existence, including its economic, democratic, cultural, social, and spiritual dimensions. This mission will take a leap of faith for many progressives—including many social workers—who have shied away from developing and promoting an ideological framework that is inclusive. The challenge facing social workers, then, is to help construct and support a counterframework to the one employed by neoconservatives. Such a social justice framework must incorporate, among other themes, social responsibility, delight in multiculturalism, and an egalitarian vision of a new political economy. As discussed earlier, this new "human needs" framework must also encompass the right to basic necessities (e.g., food, clothing, shelter, educational opportunities) as well as personal autonomy, freedom, self-determination, and self-expression.

In advancing the public good, social workers must be actively involved in developing social policies that promote the increased interaction between the divided segments of an egalitarian-oriented society. The formation of a collective social entity should be promoted in which groups understand both their interdependence and shared social responsibility toward each other. Moreover, economic and social integration are important components in enhancing the common good because they close the gap between the classes. Meeting the challenge of structural integration will be crucial if the increasing tensions between social classes and cultural groups exacerbated by the global economy are to be relieved. Public policy must reinforce social integration. All socioeconomic groups should be encouraged, through economic incentives or appeals to altruism, to fulfill in meaningful ways their social obligation toward those less fortunate. The rich must pay more taxes, but simply paying taxes does not equal social responsibility or good citizenship. The civic-mindedness of both the poor and the better-off, along with a sense of mutual social responsibility, is essential to the democratic restructuring of a free society, which must begin with the progressive social commitment and action of those who already hold most of the power, wealth, and advantage. This result is not likely to occur without social struggle from below. The public good is a concept given short shrift in a society increasingly concerned with the promotion of economic privilege and individual good. The next chapter will examine how the idea of a public good can become the basis for reconceptualizing macro social work practice.

chapter **6**

Macro Practice: Putting Social Change and Public Life Back into Social Work Practice

This chapter explores the broad role of macro practice in social work, including its intellectual development. In addition, the chapter examines community organization and analyzes some of its limitations both within and outside the social work profession. This examination suggests the need to redefine macro practice to make it more congruent with the changing political economy of the 1990s. This reconceptualization has, at its roots, the promotion of public activism and a redefinition of the public good, one that incorporates both the needs of the poor and the middle class within the calculus of macro practice and social change. Finally, this chapter examines core skills needed in redefining macro practice, including critical consciousness, political social work, coalition building, fundraising, administrative skills, technology, and cultural competence.

For the careful reader, an emphasis on community organization and macro practice may seem to contradict the book's earlier call for an integrated practice model of social work. We agree with Ruth Parsons et al. (1994), that integrated practice "is not simply a multimethod approach. It is both a perspective and an approach to practice" (pp. xx). This book advances a perspective and approach called "critical contextualization." Using critical contextualization as a foundation, a contextualized and politicized social work practice can occur at multiple levels of intervention and with multiple methods. Social workers use what interventions are needed, depending upon the degree of general or specialized skills required. Given this approach, the base of critical contextualization must integrate various practice methods.

This chapter also focuses on macro practice because social work education and the practice community have marginalized community organization in the past two decades. Calls for an integrated empowerment practice often end up excluding or subordinating macro-level knowledge, theories, perspectives, and skills. The em-

117

phasis here is to make macro practice an integral part of a social work practice committed to social change and the rebuilding of public life.

If social work is to play a role in remedying social problems, all social work practice, irrespective of the level or method of intervention, must be concerned with creating a public good and countering the trend toward a highly segregated private life. Because macro practice is primarily concerned with the *social* world and is a principal component for contextualizing and politicizing social work, it should be an integral part of all social work practice. The centrality of a macro practice orientation, with its emphasis on social and political action, critical consciousness, and building linkages with other groups, and its grounding in socially useful research, helps guide social work away from more narrow conceptualizations of practice. Community organization outside of social work is fundamentally about building public life through democratic, social change institutions. Community organization practice within social work—sometimes its traditional *de facto* arm of social change and at other times its administrative/management wing—needs to be reconceptualized for the 1990s and beyond as a critical component in a profession working for social change and a renewed public life. As such, refashioning macro social work practice to fit the changing *weltanschauung* of the contemporary world requires a reconsideration of the history, limits, and value of community organization within social work.

THE EBB AND FLOW OF MACRO PRACTICE IN SOCIAL WORK

The social work profession has an erratic tradition of nagging the conscience of America. In the early 1900s, social work reformers developed social surveys that targeted exploitative industries ranging from garment manufacturing to bookbinding and mining (Zimbalast, 1977). Widely disseminated in newspapers and magazines, these subjective studies helped provide the ammunition for important protective labor laws, including those related to child labor. Throughout the 1920s and 1930s, many social workers continued to argue for progressive changes in labor laws, maternal and child health services, an end to child labor, and social protections for the poor and unemployed (Trattner, 1974; Jansson, 1988). Much of this effort took the form of community organization.

However, by the 1940s, community organization was walking a tenuous line between being a servant of social service organizations through Community Chest fundraising and its roots as an advocate for the downtrodden (Lubove, 1969). While agency needs were not necessarily opposed to community needs, the question arose as to whose interests were foremost. By the 1940s, the community organization literature had begun to reflect this fluctuation between competing poles. In effect, strains existed between the administrative and agency coordination model of community organization, which was inherently nonpolitical and de-emphasized social change, and the social action model of community organization, which had its roots in the settlement house movement. For many social activists, the administrative model of community organization was too bureaucratic, "professional," and agency-minded. These activists believed that community organization had lost sight of the social change focus promoted by social work activists and philosophers such as Jane Addams, Lillian Wald, Mary Simkhovitch, and others.

The dominance of these two competing models within social work roughly corresponds to distinct historical periods. Paul Sundet (1981) observes that "community organization's history is not linear, but follows a sine curve of liberal-conservative flow in our society. Like most human service endeavors it is responsive to both sentiment and funding" (p. 9). Consequently, the preoccupation with managerial efficiency consistent with the corporate rationality of the 1920s and concerns about financing and coordinating agency services drew attention away from the social reform activities of the early 1900s (Austin & Betten, 1990b). By the 1920s, as Clarke Chambers (1967) pointed out, "The role of direct agitation was often left largely to voluntary reform associations, to politicians, to labor leaders. . . . Social workers were more often found now working in and through government, on the staffs of numerous commissions, committees, bureaus, and agencies, than as voices crying out in the wilderness" (p. 82). This led to what Roy Lubove (1969) called the "bureaucratic imperative" in community organization (p. 183). According to Lubove (1969):

> Federation[s] employed the rhetoric of the early community organization movement, but its intensive concern with the machinery and financing of social welfare diverted attention from cooperative democracy and the creative group life of the ordinary citizen to problems of agency administration and service. . . . Community organization had barely emerged as a cause before it had become a function absorbed into the administrative structure of social work. (p. 180)

The 1939 Lane Report was the first comprehensive examination of community organization in social work. This report developed a working definition of community organization, made recommendations concerning theoretical models and a skills base for practice, and established community organization as a subspecialty within social work (Lane, 1939). Although the Lane Report acknowledged that community organization tasks could be carried on outside the profession, it conservatively noted that the goal of community organization was to "bring about and maintain a progressively more effective adjustment between social welfare resources and social welfare needs" (Lane, 1939, p. 27). In effect, the Lane Report helped set the stage for the present conflict in community organization by promoting an adjustment and maintenance context for social welfare rather than a framework for challenging structural inequalities.

Missing from the Lane Report was the social vision embodied in the work of early social reformers like Jane Addams. While Addams and others struggled with understanding and advancing the larger public good, including issues of war and peace, social ethics, and the meaning of democracy (Addams, 1907; 1922; 1911), the Lane Report generally viewed the promotion of the public good as synonymous with the advancement of the social agency. The emphasis of early social reformers on the "big canvas" of the larger society was replaced by a narrower focus on the social agency. To be fair, many agency-based reformers saw the growth of social agencies as synonymous with the advancement of the public good, since they saw the social agency as being the primary institution for protecting the interests of the poor. This vision was especially true given the absence of widespread public welfare programs.

Although much of the community organization literature of the 1920s and 1930s focused on agency financing and coordination, there were also social activists and philosophers who continued to be influenced by John Dewey's concepts of democratic participation in community decision making (Austin & Betten, 1990b). Many theories of these activists were grounded in the concept of promoting the public good. One such reformer was Eduard Lindeman, a luminary in the social work field. Lindeman emphasized the importance of small local groups through which people could guide their destinies. A social philosopher, Lindeman was deeply concerned about the ability of people to engage in democratic community decision making. Specifically, his goals included economic security for all Americans, efficient government, effective public health services, the provision of constructive leisure activities, free education, freedom of expression, and the development of community-based democratic organizations (Konopka, 1958). For Lindeman, the primary goal of community work was the creation of "democratic forms of organization, or community-wide organization through which the entire community might express its thought and see that its will is done" (Konopka, 1958, p. 103). Lindeman was not alone. Other democratically inspired reformers concerned with the larger public good included Jesse Steiner, Bessie McClenahan, Walter Petit, and Joseph Hart, who argued that the organizer had the responsibility to educate the community to "stimulate individual responsibility for the common good" (Austin & Betten, 1990b, p. 26).

As noted earlier, by the late 1930s the agency-based model of community organization had eclipsed the social change-oriented perspective. Although written much later, Arthur Dunham's (1972) work generally reaffirmed the agency-based approach promoted by the Lane Report. Dunham placed community organization within the aegis of the public sector, the traditional voluntary private sector, social service agencies, and the United Way. His frame of reference was the profession's identification of community organization with agency coordination and federated fundraising. While Dunham broadened the role and skills base of community organization, he continued the narrowly defined, agency-based tradition that had marked earlier periods—specifically, the "community organizer" as administrator and fundraiser.

A rash of writers have tried to incorporate the two conflicting streams of community organization under one umbrella. For example, Murray Ross (1967) broadened community organization by defining it as the process through which a community identifies and prioritizes its needs and objectives. Through this process, the community develops the necessary confidence to find the resources required to deal with its needs and goals. Ross believed that community organization should lead to collaborative attitudes within the community. For Ross (1967), "the primary role of the professional worker in community organization is that of a guide who helps the community establish and find means of achieving its own goals" (p. 204). Like Dunham, Ross expanded the boundaries of community organization, but without specifically addressing the knotty issues involved in the larger conception of the public good addressed by early social work reformers.

In contrast to Dunham and Ross, and building on efforts in the 1960s, Charles Grosser (1976) tried to tie together the disparate strands of community organization by calling into question social work's aversion to political conflict. Grosser's larger categories for community organization included the roles of broker, advocate, and activist. The primary difference between Grosser and earlier writers was his emphasis on the activist category. Grosser (1976) also expanded the boundaries of macro practice by proposing seven spheres of activity for the community organizer: (1) urban community development, (2) ombudsman services, (3) nonviolent direct action, (4) expertise and consultation, (5) objectivity and research, (6) publicity, and (7) fundraising.

Ralph Kramer and Harry Specht (1983) acknowledged the inherent differences between the two orientations when they defined the basic approaches to community organization as grassroots community development and social planning. While the community development approach is designed to help disenfranchised people mobilize and take action, the social planning approach is intended to coordinate or change the practices of community agencies. The rationale for the latter approach is that many poor people are legally and structurally bound to social agencies that control and guide their behavior.

Jack Rothman's model, originally developed in 1968, became a benchmark in the field of community organization. Modified again by Jack Rothman and John Tropman in 1987, this model implicitly acknowledges the problems in constructing an inclusive model of macro practice. In attempting to construct a taxonomy for community practice, Rothman and Tropman (1987) divide community organization into three ideal types: locality development, social planning, and social action.

The locality development approach emphasizes process goals, the coming together of all citizens to build or strengthen community. Sometimes called *community development*, this model emphasizes economic and social progress. Specifically, a broad band of community residents are involved in determining their needs and solving their problems. Locality development also stresses self-help and views the power structure as partners in social change.

The social planning model, on the other hand, involves the use of technical processes of problem solving to remedy social problems such as delinquency, poor housing, and inadequate physical and mental health care. This model assumes that change in a complex world requires deliberate, rational planning. Expert planners are expected to guide changes through myriad bureaucratic barriers with the goal of establishing, arranging, and delivering services to those who need them. This model views the power structure as a sponsor of social change.

The last category, the social action model, seeks more fundamental institutional and policy changes than the previous two models. Similar to Alinsky-style organizing, it assumes the existence of a disenfranchised population that must be organized in order to make demands on the larger community. Viewing the power structure as an oppressor, this model is based largely on the grassroots organization of powerless groups to pressure the "haves" and the wider community for greater resources and for social, political, and economic justice. In altering the relations of power, the social action model focuses on direct action tactics that require the community organizer to be an activist.

Other writers (Netting, Kettner, & McMurtry, 1993) have tried to accommodate the conflicting orientations to community organization by adopting a larger framework and calling it macro practice. F. Ellen Netting, Peter Kettner and Steven McMurtry (1993) define the macro practice approach as "professionally directed intervention designed to bring about planned change in organizations and communities. . . . Macro-level activities engage the practitioner in organizational, community, and practice areas" (p. 3). Netting et al. reject the inherent divisions in community organization by developing a framework that incorporates community and organizational intervention. Daley and Netting (1994) broaden the diverse field of community organization to include policy analysts, program planners, administrators and evaluators, resource developers and allocators, and community organizers and developers working with geographically or issue-defined interest groups and communities.

The dissonant strands in the community organization literature in social work revolve around tensions such as: (1) the importance of representing social agencies as opposed to empowering communities and constituents, (2) the collaborative versus conflict model of community organization, (3) the emphasis on administration versus grassroots community organization, (4) the procurement of resources versus systemic resource redistribution, (5) the social worker as expert versus the social worker as grassroots community organizer, and (6) the social worker as social planner as opposed to grassroots community organizer.

Although it is easy to vilify agency-based community workers, an overall repudiation of their work is too simplistic. On the contrary, most attempted to do good work, but their agency-based orientation as professional managers and administrators rather than as political practitioners tied to communities hindered their effectiveness. Combined with the difficulties generally facing the social work profession, this position marginalized agency-based organizers both within and outside the profession.

Alinsky and the Industrial Areas Foundation

While social work academicians were busily engaged in debates over the proper goal of community organization, Saul Alinsky and the Industrial Areas Foundation (IAF) were busy refining their prototype for building community power, a model largely borrowed from the Congress of Industrial Organizations (CIO) and the Communist Party of the 1930s (Fisher, 1994).

Alinsky's organizing style was built around two basic principles: (1) the community is the most important unit for political activity in modern society, and

(2) citizen participation is the strength and salvation of America (Marston & Towers, 1993). In Alinsky's model, the community organizer is the catalyst for change, and his or her goal is to create democratic community-based organizations. Within that framework, neighborhood residents are empowered through learning basic political and organizing skills, which, in turn, brings them to the bargaining table (Boyte, 1981; Fisher, 1994). Hence, Alinsky's method was designed to create neighborhood "people's organizations" that build community power, discover indigenous leadership, provide training in democratic participation, and prove that ordinary people can beat city hall (Fisher, 1993). Moreover, Alinsky's style of organizing focused on conflict strategies, direct action politics, and a belief in the need to moor community organizing in the everyday lives and traditions of the poor and working class (Fisher, 1993).

Despite Alinsky's debt to early social work reformers, at least in public he showed contempt for the profession. In a typically overstated fashion, Alinsky argued that:

> They come to the people of the slums not to help them rebel and fight their way out of the muck . . . most social work does not even reach the submerged masses. Social work is largely a middle-class activity and guided by a middle-class psychology. In the rare instances where it reaches the slum dwellers it seeks to get them adjusted to their environment so they will live in hell and like it. A higher form of social treason would be difficult to conceive. (Quoted in Homan, 1994, p. 8)

Alinsky (1971) also disavowed any contribution of the social work profession to his method:

> Then there were those who had trained in schools of social work to become community organizers. Community Organization 101, 102 and 103. They had done "field work" and acquired even a specialized vocabulary. . . . Basically the difference between their goals and others is that they organize to get rid of four-legged rats . . . we . . . get on to removing two-legged rats. . . . One reason is that despite verbal denunciations of their past training there is a strong subconscious block against repudiating two or three years of life spent in this training as well as the financial cost of these courses. (pp. 67–68)

Alinsky's public antagonism toward social work likely involved two issues. First, according to Alinsky, social work had not lived up to its promise of working toward social change nor matched its rhetoric with action. Perhaps in his view, the social work profession talked a good game, but when the going got tough, social work practitioners could always retreat into agency-based practice and into an emphasis on middle-class professionalism. For example, when civil liberties (and social activists) were threatened in the McCarthy era of the 1950s, many social workers found protection in casework. When federal funds for progressive social programs became available in the middle 1960s, social workers rediscovered the virtues of social justice-oriented community organization. When those same funds evaporated in the late 1960s, the social work profession's interest in community organization followed suit. In short, Alinsky did not trust social work's commitment to social change. Second, Alinsky was a master of drama. As a consummate self-promoter, he enjoyed shocking his audience through hyperbole and overstatement.

Despite his public derision of the profession, Alinsky's work and ideas had much in common with the community organization practiced in social work. After all, social action community organization is generally the same, regardless of who practices it. While some strategies clearly work better in different contexts and significant differences exist between community organization groups and approaches, all efforts generally share fundamental principles and methods of social action community organizing. Alinsky's emphasis on the value of neighborhoods, self-determination, and the need to build democratically controlled community institutions shares much with the philosophy of early social work reformers such as Jane Addams, Lillian Wald, Mary Simkhovitch, Eduard Lindeman, Kenneth Pray, Joseph Hart, and others. In fact, the emphasis on building neighborhood and community power was a mainstay of the more progressive settlement houses of the early 1900s. Their approach, however, was almost always more "top down" and service delivery-oriented than Alinsky's.

Despite images of Alinsky-style "conflict" organizing, much of Alinsky's work—and certainly the more recent efforts of IAF—were not based on direct confrontation. In fact, Alinsky's tactics were generally grounded in John L. Lewis's (the leader of the United Mine Workers Union and the Congress of Industrial Organizations) brand of union organizing whereby a group uses threats of conflict largely to get a seat at the bargaining table. Most recent IAF activities pursue essentially moderate strategies that focus on building civic and public life while empowering the disenfranchised (Fisher, 1994).

Given the emphasis on conflict in Alinsky's methods, however, most social workers were uncomfortable with its wholesale adoption. Moreover, Alinsky's organizing style contained an implicit acceptance of the ends justifying the means. For example, Alinsky (1971) argued that "the concern with ethics increases with the number of means available and vice versa" (p. 32). This principle is at variance with social work's value base and the emphasis in some forms of community organization on process-oriented outcomes. Murray Ross (1967) and Kenneth Pray (1931), for example, insisted on the primacy of the "process" in community organizing. As with Rothman's model of locality development, both stressed the therapeutic value of bringing together different interest groups, the importance of promoting self-determination, and the process of reaching consensus (Mondros & Wilson, 1994). In the end, the tensions between Alinsky-style "community organizing" and "social action" community organization were based more on disagreements over tactics and style than on principles. Nevertheless, the Alinsky method stood in stark contrast to the depoliticized, agency- and administration-based brand of community organization that marked social work's history.

Community Organization and Professionalism

An issue that surfaces with relative frequency revolves around the supposed incompatibility between social work professionalism and social activism (Burghardt, 1982). This supposed conflict hinges on whether social work is viewed as a "consenting" (adapting to the status quo) or "dissenting" (involvement in social change) profession (Cooper, 1977; Souflee, 1977). A third view held by Bertha Reynolds (1961) is that professionalism can coexist comfortably alongside partisan political activity.

In analyzing two studies of social work activism, one done in 1968 and the other in 1984, Linda Cherrey Reeser and Irwin Epstein (1990) found that while social workers in 1968 seemed more committed to social change activities than social workers in 1984, they held less social-structural views about the causes of poverty and were not primarily interested in serving poor clients. Disapproving of direct conflict, social workers in 1968 were more likely than later social workers to be involved in institutional forms of activism than in direct action protest. While social workers in the 1980s were more apt to link structural causes to poverty and more likely to approve of protest for social workers, they were also more prone to engage in noncontroversial social change activities (e.g., lobbying, working for social work licensure, etc.). Moreover, social workers in 1984 did not regard the elimination of poverty as a priority of their profession (Reeser & Epstein, 1990). In short, both groups studied preferred to engage in noncontroversial change activities and work with a mixed clientele. Based on their study, Reeser and Epstein (1990) concluded that professionalism had little impact on social workers' commitment to social action. Wagner (1990) agrees that the "big chill" of the 1980s was overrated, and that social work activism has been traditionally exaggerated.

The development of community organization within social work is part of a historical cycle rooted in the ascendancy and decline of the agency-based versus the social justice model of community organization. During conservative periods, community organization practice tended to embrace the administrative and social planning model and focus on the needs of social agencies. During liberal periods, such as of the 1960s, community organization practice assumed a grassroots posture that emphasized social justice. The relationship of the social work profession to community organization has followed a similar trajectory. When federal money was available for social programs in the 1960s, the social work profession embraced grassroots community organization. This acceptance was illustrated by a massive growth in community organization tracks in schools of social work. As in earlier periods, social workers in the 1980s and 1990s chose to accommodate the neoconservatism of the past two decades by focusing on micro-level strategies.

To be effective and assume its rightful place in social change, macro practice must not be an optional track in social work that fluctuates with the political winds. Instead, it must become an integral part of a contextualized and politicized social work practice. The following section will develop this argument further by examining the criticisms of community organization both within and outside of social work.

CRITICISMS OF COMMUNITY ORGANIZATION

In the past twenty years, reports about the death of community organization have been more frequent than sightings of Elvis Presley. This is especially true for social workers who believe that if community organization is dead in social work, it must also be dead in the rest of society. For example, Paul Wilson (1981) stated: "Grassroots community organization has not grown. The social change efforts embarked upon almost two decades ago have not yielded dramatic positive results. The need for redefinition and renewed focus for community organization practice is evident" (p. 1).

Several writers have debated the limits of community organization. They argue that few significant victories have resulted from grassroots community organizing. Even well-known social work activist Richard Cloward (1994) questions the utility of community organizations: "neither collective nor charismatic leadership is requisite to mass protest among the poorer classes. They are capable of action without either. . . . Moreover, the means of collective protest are always available and do not depend on organization and leadership" (pp. 24–25). Conversely, Fisher and Kling (1987; 1991) argue that organization and leadership are essential to social change efforts, and that ideology—which shapes the direction and politics of the organization and leadership—is fundamental to organizational success. The critical point, however, is that both critiques underline the difficulty of organizing low-income communities.

The difficulty of politically mobilizing poor communities on national and state levels has contributed to their increasing marginalization. For example, the knowledge that the poor generally vote in low numbers has encouraged the Republican Party to subtract their needs from its political calculus. This trend is increasingly being adopted by the Democratic Party. When Jesse Jackson's Rainbow Coalition failed to deliver a significant nonwhite vote in the 1980s, conservative Democrats used this failure to justify diverting attention away from nonwhite concerns. When Bill Clinton ran for president in 1992, he was careful to appeal to a wide cross section of middle-class voters. Few planks in his program were specifically designed to entice voters from poor or nonwhite communities. Moreover, the bulk of the important gubernatorial and congressional seats taken by Republicans in the 1994 midterm election were won by a slim margin. Hence, a large poor and minority voter turnout might have significantly altered the results. Yet, instead of attempting to increase voter turnouts in poor communities, the Democratic Party is emulating the Republican strategy by more intensely chasing middle-class voters. This chase is occurring at the expense of addressing the issues of poor and minority communities.

Questions also arise as to the viability of community organization in the changing economic milieu of the 1990s. For example, community organization was clearly alive and well in the middle 1960s. The robustness of community organization in this period is attributable to several factors: the liberal social climate of the time; social movement activism; the widespread availability of federal monies owing in part to healthy tax revenues—in 1969 the federal government had a $3 billion surplus (Karger & Stoesz, 1994); a sense of economic security in the middle class resulting from expanding real incomes and low unemployment—about 2.8 percent in 1968 (Karger & Stoesz, 1994); the fiscally healthy state of most American cities; the existence of a buoyant national economy including a large trade surplus; and a growing restlessness among the poor. Many Americans believed that the country was rich, and the only thing needed was a more equitable redistribution of goods and opportunities.

Because of the relative health of the economy in the late 1960s, the federal, state, and local governments could ease social discontent by creating massive, new social programs (e.g., Johnson's Great Society), enhancing employment opportunities, especially in the public sector, and coopting indigenous leadership by providing jobs and tailor-made positions. This is not to suggest that community organizations merely had to ask for money or other resources. On the contrary, city governments were reluctant to open jobs to people of color (political patronage jobs lay at the core of voter loyalty to the Democratic Party), most states preferred to spend their money on capital improvements rather than social programs, and entrenched bureaucrats refused to concede power. The point, then, is that although community organizations frequently had to force open the doors of opportunity, there were often resources to be found on the other side.

By the 1990s this situation was reversed. Because of changes issuing from the global economy and the restructuring of the federal tax system, the federal government could no longer afford to support social change. In fact, faced with almost a $5 trillion debt in 1995—over 90 percent of the GNP in that year—some commentators judged the federal government to be essentially broke. Moreover, the massive shift of capital from the public to the private sector through tax cuts and other incentives left states and cities in even worse financial shape than the federal government. The infrastructure of urban areas declined rapidly as capital improvement funds, much of which was provided by the federal government, dried up. When federal urban aid was dramatically slashed under Reagan, fiscally strapped states were unable to rescue their cities. In fact, many states found their already meager resources frozen because of the balanced budget amendments they hastily passed in the late 1970s. This fiscal predicament was further aggravated by the Reagan administration's foisting of Medicaid costs—the fastest growing part of state budgets— onto states in the early 1980s. Accordingly, by the early 1990s many states found themselves with virtually no discretionary monies (Stoesz, 1996). By the late 1980s, most large urban areas could barely maintain core city services (e.g., transportation, public safety, fire fighting, and schools) let alone engage in reallocating public monies to design bold social programs. While community organizations could still force open doors in the 1990s, there was often scant booty to be found on the other side. As a result, community organizations have been forced to turn inward, adopting self-help strategies.

Despite its apparent privation, the federal government continues to retain the bulk of public resources. Its ability to borrow and to repay through tax increases is unparalleled in state and local sectors. In that sense, locally based community organizations may be trying to squeeze water from a rock by focusing their energies on cities and states rather than on the federal government. Because of their local focus, the tentacles of the thousands of community organizations in the United States rarely reach effectively into Washington where the bulk of public monies continues to be allocated.

Critics argue that the successes pointed to by community organizations, among them the Community Reinvestment Act (CRA) of the late 1970s, which prohibited banks from redlining mortgages in poor areas, has resulted in only modest social change. On a local level, slums continue to mushroom and their conditions worsen; the streets of the inner city grow more unsafe; and despite the CRA, banks continue to redline, albeit more discretely. Critics also charge that the populism encouraged by community organizations has failed to spawn highly visible national leaders who can galvanize poor communities. In short, after almost fifty years of Alinsky-style organizing, some critics argue the community organization movement has little presence on the national scene and few concrete successes to report. Cloward (1994) dramatically summarized the problem:

> . . . periods such as the 1940s and 1950s, or the 1970s and 1980s. . . . These are reactionary periods, full of menace. In such periods, there is little readiness of people to take to the streets. They instead endure fatalistically. . . . Nor are great victories possible. Organizing in these periods is therefore small-scale, and goals are limited to localistic objectives defined as winnable by small numbers of people. The main hope in these periods is to keep the ideal of mass mobilization alive. (p. 36)

Many of these criticisms are based more on hyperbole than fact. Indeed, community organizations can claim a moderately successful track record. The proliferation and persistence of community organizing efforts remains a hallmark of contemporary public life (Fisher, 1994). For example, consider the work of one of the more successful efforts, the Industrial Areas Foundation, first started by Saul Alinsky:

- By 1993, the Nehemiah Homes Project in Brooklyn and the Bronx, New York, was responsible for building more than 3,000 single-family homes for working families in formerly devastated neighborhoods. A similar Nehemiah program was started in Baltimore.

- In San Antonio, Texas, Communities Organized for Public Service (COPS) collaborated with the Metro Alliance (another IAF group), state and local government, and the business sector to create a $7 million jobs training program around high-skill jobs (primarily in health care) for low-income people. By mid-1994, 650 inner-city residents were enrolled in the first class of Project Quest, which guaranteed graduates high-skill jobs on completion of the program (Rips, 1994).

- Baltimore's Commonwealth is a scholarship fund in which the corporate community contributed $20 million—matched by funds from local universities—for high school graduates with good grades and good attendance. The BUILD organization in Baltimore contributed by bringing in additional government funds and by "sweat equity"—organizing the participation of families and local schools. Similarly, COPS, the Metro Alliance, and the business sector created the San Antonio Partnership, modeled on Baltimore's Commonwealth (Cortes, 1993). By mid-1994, 2,000 high school graduates in San Antonio had attended college through scholarships provided by the Partnership (Rips, 1994).

- Organized by the IAF, the Colonias project in South Texas is promised $250 million in state grants and low-interest loans (leveraging federal and local funds) to build water and sewerage systems along the Texas-Mexico border (Cortes, 1993).
- In 1993, Chicago's United Neighborhood Organization (UNO) set a five-year goal to naturalize 130,000 Latinos. By 1993, they had already helped almost 3,000 immigrants become citizens (Sundman, 1994).

While grassroots organizing has been a central feature of politics in the Western industrialized nations since the late 1960s, this phenomenon is not limited to the West. As Frank and Fuentes (1990) argue, community organizing efforts, with hundreds of millions of members, have proliferated on a global scale in the past twenty years, extending from Western nations to those in the South, and most recently, with mixed results, to the East.

Social movement organizations do more than provide a free space for public life and public citizenship by simply keeping the progressive spark alive. Such community organization efforts have been instrumental in helping to resist oppression and advance collective interests in neighborhoods of varied class, ethnic, and racial groups, and in communities organized around special interests (e.g., domestic violence, toxic waste dumping, or gay, lesbian and African-American identity politics). The achievements of grassroots-based efforts by feminists serve as good examples. These efforts range from social service work on domestic violence and rape counseling to legislative advocacy and increasing consciousness on issues of family violence, pay equity, gender discrimination, sexual harassment, and abortion rights. The gay and lesbian movement has also successfully employed community organization strategies ranging from AIDS-related service delivery work to combating homophobia. The movement has also had mixed results in advocacy efforts to pass gay and lesbian rights ordinances and defeat discriminatory antigay voter referendums. Community organization efforts have also been successful in increasing the public's consciousness regarding AIDS, resulting in increased funding, ensuring rights for the physically handicapped, including the recent passage of the Americans with Disabilities Act, and fostering other important social movements. Contrary to the assumption of some critics, community organization is neither dead nor ineffectual. In fact, it is very much alive, although its form has changed from a predominantly neighborhood-based movement to one that is both neighborhood and culturally based.

Buoyed by the successes of the past generation, community organization activists argue that current efforts produce a more participatory and humane public life. They revive civic culture at a grassroots level where people live their daily lives; they empower previously marginalized and powerless groups. Community organizations build community capacity to help meet community needs and advance progressive agendas (Paget, 1990). A recent Kettering Foundation report found that beneath the "troubled view of politics . . . [is] an American public that cares deeply about public life . . . , a foundation for building healthy democratic practices and new traditions of public participation in politics" (Harwood, 1991). Alain Touraine (1985), Alberto Melucci (1989), Joan Cocks (1989), Manuel Castells (1983), Immanuel Wallerstein (1990), and many other contemporary social critics see grassroots community organizations as potentially the most effective progressive balance to the elite domination of the "new world order."

Obviously, the advancement of the public good does not automatically come from enlightened politicians, although on occasion that happens. Change is more often a dialectical process. Therefore, the very act of encouraging the participation of the grassroots is critical. In a globalizing framework where nation states are under economic duress, and where the public sector is less likely or able to initiate social change, community activism is even more important. On the other hand, critics are correct: The strengths and successes of grassroots organizations should not be exaggerated. The historic focus of the community organization movement on the neighborhood and community alone has never been sufficient to enact mass and broad-based social change.

Social Work Education and Community Organization

Despite critiques about the effectiveness and potential of grassroots organizing, the primary question facing social work is the continued relevance of community organization to the profession. Critiques of the suitability of community organization for social work come from several different quarters. The most obvious opponents are conservative social workers who argue against incorporating social change into social work. These social workers believe that social justice has no place in social work since it displaces important curricular real estate that could be better used by social casework (Bardill, 1993). Some progressive social workers argue that social work skills are better utilized in coalition building (Rosenthal & Mizrahi, 1994) or organizational and administrative practice (McMurtry & Kettner, 1994) than in traditional community organization.

Arguments for social work's retention of a narrowly defined, old industrial model of community organization eventually face a stone wall of reality. For example, until the 1960s, many American schools of social work refused to accept grassroots community organization as a legitimate practice concentration. This trend was reversed in the 1960s, and social work students majoring in community organization rose from 85 in 1960 to 1,125 in 1969, or from 1.9 percent to more than 9 percent of full-time graduate enrollments. However, by 1989 the number of social work students concentrating in community organizing (and planning) had so significantly declined that they constituted only 1.8 percent of the student body (a total of 154 students nationwide) (Rivera & Erlich, 1992). A National Association of Social Workers study in 1983 showed that fewer than one in fifty respondents listed community organization as their primary form of practice. This finding corresponds to Karen

Haynes and Jim Mickelson's (1985) survey of 25 percent of all undergraduate social work bulletins, in which they found that only six out of 122 courses surveyed across the curricular areas of Human Behavior and Social Environment (HBSE), practice, research, and social policy contained titles or descriptions reflecting political content.

While calls for community power, social justice, and the redistribution of resources and political power are not a major feature of much of contemporary social work practice, it is premature to tender a death certificate for community organization. As argued earlier, grassroots organizing is indeed alive and well in small pockets in various schools of social work and in community organizations and training centers such as the IAF, the Midwest Academy, ACORN, the Organizing Training Center, the Center for Third World Organizing, Grassroots Leadership, and the thousands of community organizations that dot America's cities and rural areas, not to mention the millions of efforts worldwide (Fisher & Kling, 1993). What is true, however, is that social work has, for the most part, relinquished its claim to grassroots community organization. In place of politicized grassroots organizing is administration, program planning (Mohan, 1980), and organizational development (Monk & Newdom, 1976).

Myriad reasons exist for social work's wavering commitment to community organization. Clearly, society's hostility to the tactics and strategies of conflict-based community organization has discouraged many students from entering the field. Community organization is also at variance with the antipublic ethos of the past two decades, which stresses narcissistic pursuits, material self-indulgence, and self-aggrandizement. Also, when defined narrowly as neighborhood-based work, traditional community organization does not reflect the shift in social change efforts to more culturally based politics transcending geographic communities. To be fair, other reasons also account for the lack of interest in a narrowly defined, neighborhood-based model of community organization. First, there are few jobs in the field of community organization. As federal and state funding for social change organizations has dried up, so, too, has the range of jobs available in that field. Second , students assume that wages for grassroots organizers are usually too low to retain professionally trained social workers (Rosenthal & Mizrahi, 1994), although a recent study of community organizers in Chicago (O'Donnell, 1995) calculated that nondegreed organizers had a median income of $31,500, while those with graduate degrees earned $35,000 or above. Many students enter social work programs with considerable financial and other costs. Some students are employed full- or part-time while supporting a family. Others return to school through federally insured student loans. Upon graduation, these students can face a mountain of debt. Still other students may find it difficult to justify the costs of undergraduate or graduate education to secure a job that calls for little academic training. Third, human service agencies are generally reluctant to hire community organizers because of political risk and conservatism (Wenocur & Weisner, 1992). Fourth, there is, in social work, a tension between training to become an expert, a professional, and doing democratic, collaborative community organizing practice. Community organizing would be attractive work only to those social workers with a strong critical contextualization of the need for social change, a fundamental belief in the importance of democratic process, and a galvanizing social justice ideology to fan the flames of political commitment over time.

For these and other reasons, social workers must develop a macro model that complements the real world in which they practice. This macro practice model must also prepare students for the realities they will face in the field of social work. While focusing on social change, this new macro practice must build on the inherent strengths of the social work discipline, including problem solving, planning, resource mobilization, organizational analysis, and so forth. In addition, this practice method must be organized around the idea of promoting the public good through social change. This is not to suggest that a new form of macro practice should be fashioned that excludes community organization, advocacy, coalition building, organizing collectivities, or social action research. Instead, community organization must be expanded beyond a narrow conceptualization to include these and other elements of macro and micro practice that enable social workers to better contextualize, politicize, and connect macro practice to the empowerment of citizens, the rebuilding of public life, and the effecting of social change. The next sections will explore some contours of this practice method.

A MORE INCLUSIVE PRACTICE

A critical first step in promoting more effective social change efforts is making them more inclusive of other classes and cultural groups. A common assumption in traditional community organizing is that problems of financial insecurity, the lack of community attachment, and political disenfranchisement are somehow unique to the poor. To counter this assumption, the belief in the economic and social health of the middle class must be reexamined. Specifically, the conviction that the middle class is economically stable, politically franchised, socially sound, psychologically intact, and ensconced in strong and viable neighborhoods is rooted more in ideology than fact.

In contrast, most social indicators point in the opposite direction. For example, the real weekly wages of all American workers since 1973 have declined nearly 20 percent (West, 1992). Among high school graduates with no college, wages dropped almost $7,000 between 1980 and 1990 (Karger & Stoesz, 1994). Much of the middle class has remained solvent only because of the additional income generated by more spouses entering the workforce. However, much of this increase in family wages is consumed by the incidentals of workforce participation, including day-care costs, clothing needs, and transportation expenses. Without a significant increase in real wages, the economic boost generated by spousal employment will eventually dissipate through the effects of higher taxes—especially the steep rises in Social Security taxes—and inflation. So, while the employment of a second wage earner may buy time, it is not a long-term panacea for flat wages. The problem of stagnant wages is also exacerbated by the corporate downsizing that began in the 1980s, which has led to greater economic insecurity for United States workers. In the end, much of the American working class is separated from the poor by only a few paychecks.

The myth of the politically franchised middle class also warrants examination. Again, contrary to popular belief, the anecdotal evidence suggests that the middle class feel almost as alienated from the political system as the poor. For example, the emergence of well-funded Political Action Committees (PACs) has reduced the reliance of political parties on the financial largess of middle-class contributors. The substitution of special interest money for small-sum political contributions has resulted in a profound shift in the importance of deep-pocketed PACs over small-contribution voters. As the large political parties become increasingly dependent on PAC money, the loyalties of these parties shift even more from constituent interests to special interests. In short, politicians spend more time chasing PACs than voters. It is little wonder that average voters feel alienated from the very political system purported to represent them.

Another false belief is that the middle class live in affordable housing in stable neighborhoods. First, the average American family moves every seven years or less. Second, home ownership for the middle class has remained static since 1960, hovering around 67 percent (Karger & Stoesz, 1994). Third, the cost of middle-class housing has outstripped the rise in wages. Between 1967 and 1991, the median income for homeowners rose slightly (in constant 1989 dollars) from $28,011 to $32,320, while the median home price increased from $56,466 to $67,672. During that same period, the total annual cost of home ownership rose from $4,727 to $7,806. This increase is even sharper when viewed in noninflation-adjusted dollars. In 1970, the average, new single-family home sold for $23,400; by 1995 it cost $158,600. For existing single-family homes, prices increased from an average of $23,200 in 1970 to $137,500 in 1995 (Karger & Stoesz, 1994; United States Department of Housing and Urban Development, 1995).

In nations that boast the most comprehensive social welfare systems (e.g., the Scandinavian countries), social policy has limited social inequality and addressed the needs of all citizens, including the middle classes. The public good in these progressive nations has been defined to cross boundaries of race, ethnicity, and social class. This is not true in America where class and cultural divisions divide constituents and undermine organizers' ability to connect local concerns to national issues. As Jacqueline Mondros and Scott Wilson (1994) note:

> Local organizers work mostly with low-income and blue-collar communities on "bread and butter" issues, while state and national organizations tend to work with middle and professional classes on issues of national or international import. While it is clear that there are connections among the national issues of peace, environment, and feminism, and the local issues of housing, unemployment, and crime, organizers don't know how to make those connections understandable to their members. Innovations in this area will be essential if a broader social change agenda has a chance of realization. (p. 129)

Any new conception of macro practice must span the boundaries of class, race, gender, and ethnicity. A central project is to build greater solidarity between the poor and the middle class. Macro practice must therefore define public life in broad terms and in ways that incorporate the interests of the middle class and the poor into the social equation. This is not to suggest that social work should abandon its emphasis on the poor; on the contrary, adopting a broader conception of a progressive common good would more closely align the interests of the poor with many in the middle class. The zero-sum game that is currently informing social policy thinking—directing resources at one group must inevitably diminish another group—must be reexamined. In effect, the fracturing of public life into special interest camps should be replaced by a new conception that is based not only on the special cultures and traditions of people, but also on the view that society is like a collective lifeboat in which *all* people should have reserved seats. A fair society for the poor is in many ways a fair society for the middle class, and vice versa. If society is to meet the challenges of the global economy, it must develop a collective orientation in which the social world is viewed as an interdependent organism. The politics of division and self-interest only encourages the damaging and unbridled individualism inherent in neoconservative dogma.

Of course, it is inappropriate to tell those who do not have power or whose voices were not heard before, to be less divisive or aggressive in pursuit of their interests and voice. The old and new divisions in society are real and require respect. For example, while multiculturalism contains qualities that fragment society, it has also conveyed an understanding and appreciation of the differences that exist among diverse racial, religious, ethnic, gender, and other disenfranchised groups. It has helped these groups attain a voice in a "melting pot" that otherwise refuses to accept significant numbers of people. In short, the call for greater solidarity among progressive constituencies encourages a "voice" for those historically excluded from participating in defining a progressive public good.

Nevertheless, a robust model of macro practice should address not only the ways people are different, but also push them toward a common understanding of a progressive public good. This is not to suggest a rejection of cultural differences; the various ethnic, racial, cultural, and gender groups in American society have clear differences in terms of history, social orientation, and cultural characteristics. Oppression and empowerment for a young, poor African-American man are worlds apart from oppression and empowerment for a young, white, upper-middle-class woman. This difference must be understood and its lessons applied. Yet, a decade or more of emphasizing cultural, racial, and gender differences has not resulted in significant social progress. Although arguably society may better understand the cultural differences of African Americans and Hispanics, their poverty rates have continued to soar. Moreover, categorizing these groups by emphasizing their cultural uniqueness has made it easier for politicians to segregate them from the mainstream of society by encouraging a "them and us" attitude among the white middle class. Hence, it is important for social workers and social activists to help build solidarity across progressive constituencies by emphasizing the commonalities between the middle class, working class, and poor, and between those of diverse cultural orientations. For example, all people, whatever their ethnicity, social class, or gender, have the same basic needs for economic security, adequate and affordable health care, decent housing, educational opportunities, affordable and nutritious food, suitable clothing, good transportation, personal safety, and a sense of community connectedness. Studies of international social policy inform us that viable solutions to social problems must be universal in nature, in that they must apply equally to all classes if they are to enjoy widespread support. An old African proverb observes that "people do not build bridges for other people, but for themselves." In short, viable social changes in the 1990s must address the needs of a wide cross section of American society by crossing class, ethnic, racial, gender, and other lines.

The theme of the "community-as-a-whole" is, by no means, a novel concept in social work. In fact, it has informed the thinking of early social work reformers such as Jane Addams, Eduard Lindeman, Lillian Wald, and others. It also permeated much of the early literature on community organization. Like the current communitarians, progressive social philosophers and community organizers of the early 1900s argued that the community must stress both the rights *and* duties of its members. The democratic organizer was expected to release hidden resources in each individual and group (Austin & Betten, 1990b). The belief in a public good transcending class, culture, race, religion, ethnicity, and gender has an historical precedent in social work. Its seeds are found in the writings of the early reformers whose vision and courage helped shape the empowerment tradition in the social work profession (Simon, 1994). In that sense, some of the blueprint for social work's future can be found in the dog-eared pages of its past.

While not specifically a cross-class organization, the Third Ward Community Cloth Cooperative, a coalition representing "stakeholders" (that is, providers and consumers of services, such as children, families, community organizations, civic groups, schools, churches, businesses, and private and public agencies) in Houston's low-income Third Ward, has broadened the traditional definition of community organization. Its mission is to "identify, mobilize, unify, stabilize, create and co-ordinate resources to nurture and enhance the bodies, minds, and spirits of children and families" (Third Ward Community Cloth Cooperative, 1994). Using a broad definition of the common good in a relatively homogeneous community, the Cloth Cooperative has incorporated myriad facets of human existence through weaving a community cloth whose twelve threads include: social services, spirituality, children and families, comprehensive health, cultural arts, economic development/employment, education, housing/environment, mental health, political/legal empowerment, recreation, and safety and security (Third Ward Community Cloth Cooperative, 1994). While focused on the poor, this "cloth" has just as much relevance to middle-class people experiencing an erosion in the economic, social, and political center that has bound them to the fabric of society.

Developing a universal orientation to macro practice involves important challenges for the social work profession. How can social workers thread the concerns of the middle class into the social cloth of a progressive common good while still addressing the needs of the poor and oppressed people of color? Clearly, there will be a temptation to minimize the needs of the poor when creating a new, more universal social agenda. This challenge has particular saliency, since much of contemporary community organization in social work has focused on the middle class, including community-based efforts to help and work with middle-class women who are victims of rape and domestic violence; gay men and lesbian women experiencing discrimination; and people with disabilities fighting for their rights. Much of feminist organizing, for example, has been heavily criticized for being too focused on white, middle-class women while excluding poor women and women of color. At its best, one of the strengths of identity/cultural-based organizing is that it is transclass in nature. Diverse groups can easily take up the mantle of efforts like the Community Cloth or the politics of universal human needs postulated by Doyal and Gough (1991). Work like that of the Community Cloth underscores poet Maya Angelou's affirmation that if we have come this far with a politics of exclusion, think of how much further we can travel with a politics of inclusion.

Increasingly, social workers are challenged to heal social fractures. Contemporary history suggests that modern societies fracture along various fault lines, including ethnic, religious, racial, tribal, and geographic lines. The brutal lessons of Bosnia, Chechnya, Rwanda, Burundi, and Somalia illustrate that exploiting social fissures is far easier than repairing them. The effort needed to arrest this phenomenon is herculean, and the more society unravels, the harder it becomes to reweave its diverse social threads.

Housing patterns illustrate that cross-cultural and cross-racial interaction has not increased and that de facto segregation is alive and well in America. For example, 86 percent of white suburban Americans live in suburbs that are less than 1 percent black (West, 1992). Given this reality, the job of social workers is to respect diversity while simultaneously helping to repair the social fractures from almost thirty years of government failure. To accomplish this goal, social workers must work toward eliminating the dichotomy between the needs of the middle class and those of the poor and between varied cultural/identity groupings. In doing so, social workers should help reframe cultural diversity to include programs, policies, and ideologies that "universalize the particular" around the demand for basic human needs (Doyal & Gough, 1991) This reframing links the fate of the middle class to the poor, rather than pitting one class against the other. For this vision to be realized, both economic and social boats must rise together in a transclass alliance that strives toward solidarity and incorporation of the voices of all potentially progressive classes. Given the absence of economic security for most members of society, the acknowledgment of mutual transclass goals may not be all that difficult to achieve. Ultimately, the questions remain: To what end do we promote public life, and how do we develop a form of politicized social work practice that addresses these new challenges?

VISIONS OF SOCIAL AND POLITICAL CHANGE

Critical to public life and social change is an informed vision of social and political change. It is not enough simply to encourage public life, although that in and of itself has merit. Social change agents need to be committed to the democratic and discursive process of public life while at the same time offering leadership and knowledge about its possible direction and goals. This commitment is certainly essential if public efforts are to begin to tie class and culture in their praxis. As commentator Harry Boyte (1989) argues:

> Much of citizen activism of recent years, on both local and national levels, has addressed itself to fairly narrow issues. Activists have not often asked what their work "means" in a larger sense, where they are going in the long run, or how their particular efforts might add up to more than the particular or localized campaigns they engage in . . . like conventional politics, much of the grassroots activism has spoken a thin, sometimes cynical language of narrow interests and protest detached from any enlarged social and political vision. (p. 12)

There are no universal blueprints for social change. Each and every effort, each and every period and place in history, is unique—the product of different contexts and political opportunity structures. But the long-term commitment to a vision of social change characterizes the most successful efforts. Take, for example, the class-based, environmental work of the Gulf Coast Tenants Organization.

> Nine years old, the Gulf Coast Tenants Organization has been an innovator since its early beginnings. Our focus mission has been to assist community leaders develop a vision of the future with an abundance of jobs paying a living wage, decent affordable housing, health care, quality education, wholesome recreation and a healthy environment. Through bimonthly workshops, demonstrations, mass meetings, and public hearings we assist community leaders develop organizing skills to match the long range vision that they acquire.
>
> Gulf Coast Tenants became widely respected in the early eighties for its leaders who defended and expanded tenants' rights in publicly subsidized and privately owned rental housing. At the same time, we linked the need for expanding rather than ending the government's role in housing, health care, and other human needs to the need for a reduction of military spending and rampant militarism. By 1984 these connections were made in the "Houses Not Bombs" programs developed by Gulf Coast Tenants, and now the major work of many regional and national groups including the Southern organizing Committee for Economic and Social Justice and Jobs With Peace.
>
> Then, in 1985, the Gulf Coast Tenants tackled an additional issue—environmental preservation. Tenant leaders we developed in St. Charles Parish, in Harrison County and Jackson County, Mississippi demanded training to help them protect their counties from industrial and governmental poisoning. Just a few months after the disasters in Bhopal and Institute, West Virginia, a major explosion at Union Carbide's Taft facility in St. Charles Parish made it clear to our board, staff and leaders that we had to get involved to make a difference. In the following six years we had to

learn to teach a new discipline—environmental protection—and weave it into the real world where our leaders live, work, and play.

Since 1985 we have helped to expand the definition of environment to include housing, health care, jobs, and physical resource conservation, and have enjoyed many highly notable and highly visible organizing successes including two ten-day marches in 1988 and 1990. Our program has brought tremendous attention to the disproportionate poisoning of people of color in the United States, particularly African-Americans in "Cancer Alley" and the Deep South. Along with the work of groups like the Southwest Organizing Project, the Panos Institute, the Commission for Racial Justice of the United Church of Christ, our work has been integral to the development of the National People of Color Environmental Leadership Summit, to be held in October 1991.

In the United States, industrial and municipal poisons have been deposited disproportionately in communities where African-Americans, Native Americans, Hispanic-Americans, Asian-Americans, and poor Euro-Americans live. Thousands of communities are on the verge of extinction from chemical poisoning. We think that the worst examples are here in Louisiana's "Cancer Alley," a corridor along the Mississippi River between Baton Rouge and New Orleans.

Risk of death, injury, and genetic changes from poisoning is greater here than most places in the nation. The frequency of cancer in "Cancer Alley," the corridor between Baton Rouge and New Orleans, in some places is as high as 18 times the national average. Twenty-eight percent of the nation's petrochemical production occurs here. Along this short stretch of 75 miles along the Mississippi River there are 138 major petrochemical facilities that account for more than 1 billion pounds of industrial poisons dumped into the environment yearly. Industry leaders discount their poisons as a major factor in Louisiana's and the nation's declining health.

Leaders we trained have been fighting back, utilizing mass protests, law suits, media accounts that are unfavorable to poisoners, and the ballot. Increasingly, corporations respond to these empowerment struggles by purchasing the land and houses of people in these affected communities at giveaway prices in exchange for release from tort liability arising out of the poisoning. While this is an advancement from what we found six years ago, in "Cancer Alley" more than a century-old slave communities are being uprooted, and a culture that has helped keep African-Americans in this region healthy is threatened. Our children are sick from chemicals that we suspect severely alters behavior.

State and federal agencies responsible for protecting the environment look the other way as the poisoning continues. Some of our politicians are the best that money can buy. That is to say, in petrochemical and chemical waste industries PAC money has been the big factor in Louisiana elections for some time. And it is becoming a more important factor in Mississippi and Alabama.

Gulf Coast Tenants Organization has more than 15,000 members located in communities from Baton Rouge, Louisiana to Birmingham, Alabama, situated in 37 communities along the Louisiana, Mississippi, and Alabama gulf coasts. We are governed by a board of directors elected from the communities from which our leaders are trained. We have a staff of six paid professionals (four African-American women, one black and one white male) and 150 volunteers operating from offices in Baton Rouge, New Orleans, and Gulfport, Mississippi. Our annual budget is $250,000, raised from members, churches, individuals, and foundations. (Gulf Coast Tenants Organization, n.d.)

POLITICIZING SOCIAL WORK PRACTICE

To help develop a more inclusive social work practice and a more informed vision of social and political change among social workers who see themselves as social change agents, we must help create a more politicized social work education that addresses contemporary challenges. Much of social work education currently classifies practice in terms of micro (individual), mezzo (middle-range), and macro (large-scale) systems. While this division is useful in helping to categorize social work's large field of endeavor, it also hinders the inclusion of substantial content on social change. As discussed earlier, community organization practice is rarely covered in depth, since it remains hidden in macro courses that focus mainly on organizational change and administration, or it goes ignored in generalist courses that focus almost completely on individual and family therapy skills. The traditional continuum of micro, mezzo, and macro practice results in a scarcity of time devoted to community organization. What is needed, then, is a politicizing of social work practice that integrates macro practice theories, perspectives, and skills throughout the curriculum, and understands the importance of micro skills and perspectives to macro social work.

Harry Specht and Mark Courtney (1994) argue that the excessively individualistic, laissez-faire, and social Darwinist policies of the 1980s were reflected in social work education by an emphasis on psychotherapy, a rejection of public-sector employment, the enhanced attractiveness of private practice, and an emphasis on management and administration in the community organization sequence. In essence, much of social work practice in the 1980s was depoliticized, personalized, and decontextualized (Fisher et al., 1994). On the other hand, support for politicizing social work has come from several quarters (Abramovitz, 1993; Haynes & Mickelson, 1991; Rees, 1991; Withorn, 1984). These authors argue that social work is essentially political, since at its core it is concerned with power, ideology, and social justice. The political nature of social work was also familiar to past leaders in the profession such as Jane Addams, Jacob Fisher, and Bertha Reynolds, to name a few (Davis, 1967; Chambers, 1967; Wagner, 1990; Reynolds, 1961).

Stuart Rees (1991) defines political social work as simply being good social work—that is, focusing on power, learning skills from the micro through macro levels, and linking social policy to practice. Given Rees's definition, the goal of politicized social work is not to train clinicians, community organizers, administrators, or elected officials, but to educate politicized social workers who see power as central to understanding and addressing social problems and social needs (Fisher et al., 1994). Students interested in micro practice can learn politicized social work by working through questions such as how to link the personal to the political, how to integrate policy with practice, how to challenge the depoliticized pathologizing of clients, and how to seek client outcomes of empowerment and social change rather than stabilization and adjustment to inequitable social conditions. Adopting a politicized view of social work also avoids the bifurcation of social work practice and the concomitant isolation of macro methods (Fisher, 1995).

O'Donnell (1995) proposes that it is time to develop a community organization curriculum that builds on both micro and macro knowledge and skills. She proposes "macro" courses in administration and policy developments, "micro" courses in human behavior and empowering individuals and small groups, and "community" courses in community analysis, organizing, leadership development, community change strategies, and so forth. Relatedly, the University of Houston (1991) defines political social work in terms of multiple methods and arenas for social change:

> The Political Social Work (PSW) Concentration is designed for the student who sees social problems as fundamentally political, that is, about power and social change. PSW students seek primarily to empower communities and clients or to affect electoral politics and social policies in the struggle for social justice. In the three major areas of PSW—electoral politics, grassroots politics, and personal politics—students learn advanced skills in empowerment; multicultural practice; community organizing; lobbying, legislation, and campaigning; and collaborative interventions (such as feminist practice) with individual clients. Career opportunities, ranging from the local to the international, include settings such as the offices of elected officials, legislative entities of all types, community organizations, social action and advocacy efforts, community development projects, and clinical or direct service work with oppressed constituencies that proceeds from the primary understanding that the personal is political and vice versa. (n.p.)

Any framework for macro practice grounded in a broad conception of public life requires specific skills. It also demands a reconceptualization of the role of social workers in the macro practice area.

SKILLS IMPLICATIONS FOR POLITICIZED SOCIAL WORK

One challenge is to cull out what is useful from traditional community organization practice and integrate it within a new model of macro practice. Despite criticisms about the failure of neighborhood-based community organizations to effect broad-based national changes, they have achieved significant local victories. These victories have been won through hard work, discipline, foresight, and a well-developed method of organizing. Honed over the last fifty years, the strategies, tactics, and insights of community organizing are valuable assets to all groups and organizations seeking social change. Instead of dismissing the contributions of community organizing, social workers must glean components that will be useful in promoting broad-based social change. Since community organization has become the de facto social change/social justice component of social work education, it must figure prominently in the base of social work knowledge.

Effective politicized social work practice requires the development of both general and specific skills. As part of functioning as macro practitioners, social workers can also carve out a social change role that complements other aspects of their training, career goals, and financial needs. This role can include coalition building (bringing together diverse groups in an attempt to influence social change through legislation, policymaking, or direct action) (Rosenthal & Mizrahi, 1994), electoral social work (e.g., lobbying, campaigning for elected office, staffing legislative committees, and so forth) (Haynes & Mickelson, 1991), or administration, planning, and direct service work. Thus, instead of working solely as traditional community organizers, social workers can also carve out roles such as facilitators/ organizers. All of these roles can be used in the service of contextualizing, politicizing, and connecting the individual to public life and social change.

To help advance social change, social workers may be called upon to teach democracy and citizenship skills (a role that formed the core of early groupwork) (Pappell & Rothman, 1966; Roberts & Northen, 1976); facilitate training in empowerment; engage in planning, negotiations, conflict resolution, multiparty decision making, exchange, consensus building, leadership and resource development; and help develop multilevel systems for accountability. An important role for social workers may also involve the development of intergroup cooperation for social change and for reestablishing ties between people and social institutions.

The skills taught in macro practice courses must be reassessed, given the current challenges facing social workers, especially the massive cutbacks that are eviscerating prevention and social justice programs. To meet these challenges, social work education must train practitioners in more refined, precise, and specialized skills and knowledge. Although not exhaustive, the following discussion represents some additional core macro skill areas that should be required of social workers at all levels of practice.

Critical consciousness is an important skill in developing a politicized social work practice. It is also essential to the practice of critical contextualization discussed in chapter 3. Using Paolo Freire's (1970) work, Thomas Keefe (1980) defined critical consciousness as:

> . . . the capacity to make critical assessments of one's social and economic structure predicating its egalitarian reform in the democratic interest. With critical consciousness, the individual's position on the course of social

change shifts from that of object to that of subject. The individual ceases to be a passive object of social forces and begins to act on his or her social environment as a subject or initiator of change. (p. 385)

Critical consciousness entails the rejection of a rigid form of social work professionalism. Freire (1985) argues that "one cannot be a social worker and be like the educator who's a coldly neutral technician. To keep our options secret, to conceal them in the cobwebs of technique, or to disguise them by claiming neutrality does not constitute neutrality; quite the contrary, it helps maintain the status quo" (p. 29).

The clear implication for social workers guided by critical consciousness is their responsibility to focus interventive strategies on helping clients change their social environment. The members of the Gulf Coast Tenants Organization know well that their health is less a matter of personal behavior choices, such as eating fewer eggs and less fatty meat, than it is a question of cleaning up the polluted air, land, and water where they live. To help change these conditions, social work practitioners must be skilled in critical thinking and in understanding the context of power. Moreover, real empowerment is driven by two interrelated factors, often called *praxis*: the insight gained from critical thinking and the conversion of that insight into concrete action. Without being guided by critical thinking, social action risks becoming social nihilism. Critical thinking without social action is simply armchair philosophy. John Longres and Eileen McLeod (1980) summarize the equation: "The two must go hand in hand; action without reflection is as unjustifiable as reflection without action" (p. 268). Freire (1970) calls for combining reflection and action into a unified system where they dynamically interact to foster social change. In short, critical consciousness must become an integral part of all social work practice.

Political social work is based on the idea that electoral and legislative politics is integral to all social work practice. Karen Haynes and James Mickelson (1991) observe that:

> Social work practice, at both micro and macro levels, continually acts either in support of or in opposition to the major institutions, policies, and values of our society. As such, social work is inherently part of the political process in the broadest sense, in that it is concerned with issues of either social conservation or change. . . . Perhaps social work has not always explicitly recognized that any set of values, including those of "professionalization," entails a political position and, consequently, represents a position on the nature of the social order as a whole. (p. 19)

Haynes and Mickelson (1991) identify an electoral-oriented, political social work as including the skills of lobbying; coalition building; bureaucratic monitoring; organizing, targeting, and working with PACs; and political campaigning. In addition, political social work skills involve political advocacy (Mahaffey, 1982), the legislative process (understanding how bills are made and passed) (Dear & Patti,

1982), and skills in campaigning for political office (Kleinkauf, 1982). It is not enough for social workers simply to understand the legislative process, they must also master how to communicate this knowledge to clients, community groups, and social service organizations.

Social workers' knowledge of the political process is important in other ways. By demystifying the legislative process, social workers can help better focus the aspirations of their clients, organizations, and constituents. Understanding the legislative process by knowing the rules of the game and the players allows social workers to help build the confidence of individual, community, or social agency clients. Armed with knowledge of the legislative process, these groups or individuals may be less hesitant to challenge authority and less apt to withdraw from pressure when elected officials try to squash their objectives through procedural tactics.

Coalition building is based on the idea that local community organizations must broaden their power base by coalescing on issues of common concern—a central means for building unity out of diversity, bridging gaps between cultural groups and efforts by the poor, working, and middle class. The goal of coalitions is to increase an organization's impact on issues by joining forces and pooling resources with other organizations. In addition, coalitions can increase an organization's effectiveness through expanded collective action, while maintaining the strength of the organization and its leaders.

Coalitions can be created on the local, state, or national levels and involves galvanizing diverse groups while attempting to influence an external target. As such, coalescing also demands specific organizational skills, including the ability to translate to constituents the experiences shared by different kinds of people in different types of organizations.

The creation of coalitions can be especially useful in issues of resource procurement, political advocacy, organizational legitimation, responses to external threats, interorganizational exchange, and influence on social policy (Rosenthal & Mizrahi, 1994). Moreover, coalitions have been effective in a broad range of issues, including mental health advocacy, homelessness, economic development, health care reform, environmental issues, and in combatting racism, sexism, ageism, homophobia, and domestic violence. Coalitions have been used effectively by a wide range of organizations and constituent groups, including radicals, liberals, and neoconservatives.

Fundraising is an important issue for all organizations. Veteran community organizers Kim Bobo, Jackie Kendall, and Steve Max (1991) argue that "more than any other single factor, it [the funding base] determines how the organization works and what it does" (p. 43). According to Bobo et al., funding sources can be divided into two areas: government or foundation fundraising and grassroots fundraising.

Progressive organizations in the 1990s are increasingly unable to rely on external grants. First, federal grants to these organizations virtually evaporated by the late 1970s. Although private foundations take up some slack, most grants are meager and time-limited. As a result of the recession in the late 1980s and the Aramony scandal of 1992, United Way contributions have also been erratic. In most places, they are either stagnant or in decline (Karger & Stoesz, 1994). Given these factors, most progressive organizations face unstable external funding and are therefore forced to rely increasingly on member contributions.

The often neglected commitment to financial self-sufficiency became a fiscal reality for progressive organizations in the 1990s. This financial hardship will likely increase as the short-term prospects for external funding continue to erode with the neoconservative welfare-cutting agenda bringing new pressures on an already over-extended private and public sector. Consequently, social activists are faced with new challenges for developing alternative means of fundraising, including internal funding mechanisms. One strategy for coping with this problem has been the creation of organizational service arms, which provide a variety of benefits, such as consumer discounts, health services, and special banking and insurance privileges.

In response to economic pressures and the conservative context of the 1980s and 1990s, some community organizations have begun to operate more like businesses. For example, Helena Sundman (1994) reports that while Chicago's UNO has grown steadily, the source of its income has changed. According to Sundman (1994), "Gone is the reliance on small donations from churches and community members. Today, UNO operates less like a neighborhood group and more like a business" (p. 1). For example, in 1988 UNO held a fund-raising dinner with tickets costing from $35–$45. The dinner lost $440. In 1993, UNO's fourth fundraising banquet, this time held in the Chicago Hilton, raised $140,000. Tickets cost between $150–$200, well above the amount that most community people could afford. Moreover, in 1985, UNO earned all but $25,000 of its $250,000 budget from services it provided to affiliates and other neighborhood groups. By 1993, the organization's budget jumped to $876,000, with only 9 percent of the money coming from program services. The remaining money came from grants, contracts, and the annual dinner. While in many respects this funding shift represents a positive change, it may have also hurt the relationship of the organization to its grassroots constituents (Sundman, 1994). As the world becomes more private, we can expect to see issues of private fundraising increase in importance for community-based organizations.

Administrative skill is an important and often overlooked component in developing progressive organizations. If the key to progressive change in the 1990s is building a widespread consensus around a progressive public good, then achieving this goal requires the creation of effective and stable coalitions of progressive organizations. Accordingly, working toward the public good also requires social workers to develop administrative skills that include project management; staff supervision and training; organizational development; accounting, budgeting, and bookkeeping; program evaluation; social planning; and public relations.

Technology is an important tool for all progressive organizations in the 1990s, since mastering it fosters a more efficient grasp of information and issues. Until the early 1980s computer and telecommunications technologies were primarily used to enhance the power of large corporations, the government, and the military. Recently, however, these technologies have become more affordable and widespread and can now be used in the service of social action organizations. When used properly, the tools of the "information society" can help promote a more democratic society (Downing et al., 1991).

Technology and communications have become inextricably linked. Broadcast faxing, electronic mail, the Internet, and desktop publishing all allow organizations a measure of rapid and inexpensive communication that was unimaginable twenty years ago. Through Internet conferences and Bulletin Board Services (BBS), neighborhood organizations can link up with each other to share information, develop joint strategies, and even build coalitions. One example of this is Peacenet, an electronic mail and data communication service that serves a growing number of peace groups internationally (McCullough, 1991), but there are dozens of other comparable efforts of progressive computer users.

Computer technology can be used in a variety of ways to share, gather, apply, organize, store, manipulate, and analyze information whose dissemination can assist empowerment efforts at local, state, and national levels. McCullough (1991) notes that computer maps have been used to help community groups understand where and how city government money is spent, databases have been developed in response to the problems of elderly people evicted in Brooklyn, the New Jersey Self-Help Clearinghouse provides voice-phone access to an extensive database on self-help groups, and databases have even been used to help Central American political exiles fight deportation from the United States. Databases give activists the ability to link up with persons who share similar problems, to identify underrepresented communities in voter registration drives, to track legislative bills electronically, to download masses of government documentation and studies, and to track requests for governmental grants. In addition, databases can organize membership and donor records, and help keep track of detailed information on organizational contacts, such as birthdays, family members' names, interest areas, and so forth (Bobo, Kendall, & Max, 1991). To be at the forefront of social change, social workers must have a conceptual mastery of the form and function of technology. They must also understand how to manipulate technology in the service of the public good.

Cultural competence and skills in diversity are often the most overlooked aspect of social change. Felix Rivera and John Erlich (1992) ask:

> Why has community organization not been more successful in working with people of color? What happened to some of the cross-cultural efforts that appeared to be so productive in the 1960s and early 1970s? Traditionally, much of the writing on community organization attempts to be color-blind. Organizers work with specific strategies and tactics applied to different situations, but the methods that combine them rarely if ever change. (p. 5)

Addressing the racial and cultural characteristics of oppressed communities represents an important challenge for social workers, one that requires an integrated and flexible paradigm for social change when working with communities of color (Rivera & Erlich, 1992). Instead of engaging in a color-blind macro practice, social workers must address the racial, ethnic, and cultural uniqueness of people of color. This work includes understanding the impact of differences in kinship patterns, social systems, power and leadership networks, religion, and language (Rivera & Erlich, 1992). The process of empowerment must be tailored to the uniqueness of each community. Bridging culturally oriented practice with class consciousness remains one of the great challenge for social workers in the 1990s.

CONCLUSION

This chapter has explored the role of macro practice in social work. It has examined that part of macro practice that aligns itself with the goals of political, cultural, social, and economic change. This chapter has also provided an overview of the intellectual base that makes up community organization in social work and has critiqued the limitations of community organization both within and outside of social work. Finally, this chapter has attempted to examine macro practice in a way that would make it more congruent with the changing political economy of the 1990s, including the project of expanding public life and social change in a privatizing and globalizing context.

A reconceptualized model of macro practice in social work should include several components. First, it must be organized around an inclusive vision of a progressive common good that builds solidarities between the middle and working classes and the poor. The vision must therefore incorporate the needs of the poor and the growing needs of the middle class into a calculus for political, social, community, and economic enfranchisement. A refashioned macro practice must understand that segregating the interests of the poor from those of the middle class only furthers the social divisions encouraged by the economic elite. The tacit acceptance of these differences leads to a zero-sum game in which the middle class and poor believe their gains can only come at the expense of the other. In the end, both groups lose as they expend their collective energies battling each other for a dwindling pot of resources. The only winners in this game are those who have an interest in maintaining the status quo.

Hostility toward the poor is likely to increase given the widespread power of neoconservatives on local, state, and national levels. It is also likely that the political environment of the 1990s will be less tolerant but perhaps much more in need of the direct action tactics that marked 1960s-style social movements. Paradoxically, the same middle class that is now generally opposed to conflict-based tactics is also the most fertile ground for organizing, as their sense of powerlessness and anger grows in the face of a privatized world promoting individual and family isolation, financial insecurity, lowered levels of personal safety, polluted environments, and a consumerism that is rapidly dissolving accepted notions of social life.

The knowledge required for effectively practicing in this new social arena demands more comprehensive skills and theory base than is currently being taught in schools of social work. If social work is to regain its rightful place in social change, it must incorporate basic elements of community organization into a macro practice that can serve as a social action-oriented base for all social work, requiring the explicit politicization of social work practice. In effect, this politicization will necessitate developing core skills such as, but not limited to, critical consciousness, political social work, coalition building, fundraising, administration, technological proficiency, and cultural competence.

Community organization plays an important role in social work as a basis for rebuilding public life and for the social struggle around place, class, and identity. It is critical in forming social movements around organizations, communities, agencies, and identity issues. Community organization is also an important tool in contextualizing and politicizing social work and in linking it directly to rebuilding the public good. Moreover, community organization remains central to making social work "social," even if some of the best organizing is done outside of the profession. As community organization proliferates in and out of social work, it must go beyond identity politics to reconnect with class consciousness and political struggle. Accordingly, it must broaden its focus to incorporate a politicized macro practice that goes beyond traditional community organization.

The battle between a private world and a progressive public life is not only played out in policy, practice, and research, but also in the everyday world of agency life. Since most social workers are employed by public or private agencies, their most immediate locale for integrating social change with social work practice is the workplace. In some ways, it is also the most dangerous arena for the struggle. It is to this topic that we will now turn.

chapter **7**

Empowering the Social Service Workplace: Democracy and Organizational Change

This chapter investigates the role of democracy in the workplace. In particular, it looks at how the privatization of public life is transformed into the workplace relationships of social service agencies. Accordingly, this chapter is organized around how the current privatized notion of the public good shapes social agencies—their mission, focus, and organizational hierarchy. This chapter also examines how social workers are being deskilled through the adaptation of the industrial model of production to social agency life. Moreover, this chapter explores the two principal approaches that social workers can take to democratize workplace relationships: organizational reform, and the creation of alternative organizations. Finally, this chapter examines some of the skills necessary for democratizing the social service workplace.

ORGANIZATIONAL CHANGE AND THE PUBLIC GOOD

The economic, social, and political effects of the global economy, the federal government's retreat from its responsibility to enhance the well-being of low-income people and communities, the privatization of social services, and the devolution of community life and community institutions shape both the nature of social work and the very structure of social institutions. Paradoxically, the very institutions once perceived as buffering vulnerable populations from the economic dislocations of modern capitalism are now seen as obstacles—or even enemies—rather than supports (Fabricant & Burghardt, 1992). The Aid to Families with Dependent Children (AFDC) program is seen by many people not as a system designed to provide needed income supports, but as one grounded in social control and thus antitheti-

149

cal to the basic interests of the poor. Hence, instead of viewing AFDC as a bulwark against the caprice of the marketplace, many people, including much of the poor, view the public welfare system as populated with "busybodies" and rigid bureaucrats more concerned with removing people from the rolls than helping them maximize their benefits (Karger & Stoesz, 1994). On the other hand, others have come to see public assistance as expensive, ineffective programs that reinforce dependent behaviors and poor work habits. Child protection services (CPS), originally designed to assure communities that neglected and abused children would be protected, is now seen by many as an adversarial program that arbitrarily removes children from their natural parents (Costin, Karger, & Stoesz, 1996). The foster care system, created to provide out-of-home children with a homelike atmosphere, is viewed by some as a warehouse created by child welfare officials to expedite the removal of children from their parents. The Food Stamp program, which was designed to subsidize food prices and help ensure affordability for the poor, is now seen by some recipients as a stigmatized obstacle to be negotiated, and by many in the middle class as a wasteful dole. The list goes on and on. The very social welfare programs designed to protect the poor from the vicissitudes of a market economy are seen as a first-line oppressor by many recipients and a first-rate failure by the middle class.

Caught within the maze of this human service system, politically committed social workers often find themselves trapped between the implicit—and often repressive—goals of their agencies and the well-being of clients. Moreover, some social workers view themselves as victims of agency policies in much the same way as the clients they serve. Social workers often find themselves in a quandary when faced with flat incomes, little job mobility, high caseloads, and the mushrooming expectations fostered by the severe fiscal austerity measures adopted by state and local governments. On the one hand, many entered the profession to serve people. On the other hand, agency policies antagonistic to recipients and the abject working conditions experienced by increasing numbers of human service professionals in both the private and public arenas hinder the delivery of quality social services in all-too-many settings. Facing difficult choices, many social workers choose to quit the profession and seek work outside the human services. Some go into private practice. Others resign themselves to agency life only to accept their fate benignly. Still others resist in myriad ways.

While the social work literature rarely addresses the connection between the workplace conditions of social workers, the best interests of clients, larger issues of social policy, and the advancement of the public good, a clear relationship nevertheless exists between these factors. First, the treatment of frontline social workers and the conditions they labor under is directly transmitted to clients through a shortage of worker time, the structure of the worker/client relationship defined by agency policy, and the range of services social workers are permitted to explore with their clients. When clients are given a narrow range of service choices, or denied basic rights of access or grievance, the social service system suffers. When social workers are treated as "grist for the mill," that attitude is all-too-often deflected onto clients.

Social services function as a stabilizing influence in an economically volatile postindustrial economy. The economic turmoil in community life that marks the global economy dislocates high numbers of current and prospective workers. A large portion of the unemployed find jobs in industries paying wages that are inadequate to elevate working people above the poverty line without governmental assistance. In turn, income maintenance programs are expected to draw in the slack. When these programs are underfunded, poorly managed, and repressive in their orientation to clients, social instability grows and the common good is jeopardized. The fragile balance in the social order is tilted as life for the working poor becomes more difficult. Crime and antisocial behavior increase as the delicate cloth of society is further frayed.

As previously discussed, survival in the global economy on the one hand is akin to a massive tug of war between corporate needs for capital accumulation, economic growth, and a competitive position in the world economy. On the other hand are the social and human needs of the population. This tension migrates into social service agencies where the economic priorities of government result in agencies that are underfunded, understaffed, and have adversarial policies toward clients and workers. Fabricant and Burghardt (1992) summarize the dilemma: "At the local level, where programs are implemented, there is a dynamic interplay between the troubles in the larger political economy (the federal government and the private economy) and the breakdown in the delivery of social services" (p. 12).

Some social workers see the advancement of public life as occurring through confrontational politics on the local or national levels. Grassroots community organizations or national advocacy groups are viewed as playing a significant role in social change. Nevertheless, social service institutions also play a major role in social change. Masses of poor and disempowered people experience society firsthand through the institutions designed to serve or subjugate them, depending on one's perspective. The major contact for the 15 million poor people on AFDC is not with progressive political movements or reactionary politicians, but with intrusive and hierarchical public welfare agencies. These agencies come complete with intractable policies that ensure that clients will not meet anything beyond their rudimentary subsistence needs. For those living on or beyond the economic margins of society, political struggle on the community or national level is subordinate to the harsh daily struggle of surviving on meager resources that must be supplemented with legal or antisocial, illegal income. The growing legions of citizens requiring social and public assistance benefits, coupled with the parsimony of funds allocated to social welfare services, leads to the creation of an industrial model of social work and the deskilling of social workers.

Deindustrializing Social Work

This section is concerned with the consequences of the industrial model of production on the work life of social workers and the experiences of clients. Stated simply, when the industrial model of production, focused on efficiency and rationalization, is imported into the social services, it produces a detrimental effect upon the client, the worker, and the social agency.

Social Services, Funders, and the Industrial Model of Production.   Pressures for higher levels of efficiency have increased during the last twenty years. This pressure results from a combination of global economic factors, dwindling fiscal resources allocated to social welfare, the refusal of government to increase the tax base substantially, a staggering federal debt of close to $5 trillion, the stiff competition for resources between the social welfare industry and the military, and the conservative social climate of the past twenty years. In addition, growing numbers of social work positions, especially in health care, are marked by the same "downsizing" used by large manufacturing and service sectors in the United States.

The emphasis on system rationality and efficiency is evident in all areas of social work, including the fields of health, mental health, and public welfare. Greater rationality is especially evident in the health field where managed competition, designed to cut hospital and physician costs, has resulted in higher caseloads for social workers, fewer resources, and more time-limited interventions. Social workers in many managed care systems are limited in their professional role by profit-oriented managers charged with rationing service. Not surprisingly, social workers in medical settings often experience high stress levels as they realize that the urgency of discharge planning overrides the psychosocial and health needs of clients.

High levels of job dissatisfaction in both private and public social agencies complement the new fiscal austerity. Many social workers in these agencies are reporting problems in relation to severe "burnout" and low agency morale (Freudenberger, 1974; Cohen, 1992). This crisis is making its way into many social welfare agencies, especially child protective services. In asking the question, "If you take everything into consideration, how likely is it that you will make a genuine effort to find a new job with another employer next year?" researchers Srinika Jayaratne and Wayne Chess (1984) found that almost 45 percent of child welfare workers reported that they were very likely or somewhat likely to search out new employment. An internal review panel for New York City's Human Resources Administration found that in the first four months of 1986, New York City child protection workers had an annual turnover rate of 65 percent, including an agency attrition rate of 32 percent. This turnover rate occurred while the number of cases requiring investigation rose by 14 percent, and the number of cases requiring court proceedings rose by 48 percent (Grinker, 1987).

A 1987 study by Russell and Hornby found that annual turnover rates in direct service positions ranged from 15 to 23 percent nationally. In comparison, the turnover rate in the general economy is less than 2 percent. According to Russell and Hornby (1987), the major reasons for high turnover rates include large caseloads, standby duty, the high stress related to the job, insufficient salary and promotional opportunities, lack of agency and public support, inadequate training, and changes in the nature of job responsibilities. Shapiro (1974) noted that the most frequent reasons cited for leaving CPS included inadequate working conditions, low-quality supervision, and restrictive agency regulations and practices.

This dissatisfaction comes on the heels of social work's adoption of the industrial model of production, including various forms of scientific management (e.g., management by objectives, goal attainment scaling, etc.), and a plethora of designs used to evaluate and measure the use of worker time. In part, the development of these sophisticated evaluative technologies was a response of agencies to funders' demands for greater efficiency. Nevertheless, under the guise of efficiency, the length of time it takes a social worker to perform a task becomes more important than what is accomplished. Greater economic rationalization through increased technological monitoring is likely to continue in the future given the recent fiscal measures adopted by public and private social welfare agencies (Pecora & Austin, 1983; Karger, 1983).

It is important to examine the key characteristics of technology to better understand its relationship to the industrial model of production and the delivery of social services. First, technology is driven by the desire to cut costs, specifically the costs of labor. Savings and cost containment are realized through increasing the scale and intensity of production. In theory, this scheme results in higher productivity by increasing the quantity of goods produced—in human service organizations, the number of clients processed. The goal of technology is, thus, to create the most goods or process the largest number of people at the lowest possible cost.

While agency savings can also be achieved by cutting the number of clients served, legislative mandates require government to provide services to citizens at prescribed levels of need. Hence, unlike corporations, social agencies cannot directly control their level of production, and direct decisions about the actual productivity of a social agency are subordinated to federal and state legislation outside an agency's purview. In turn, federal and state policy is determined by past legislation. This Gordian knot came close to being untied in 1995 when the House of Representatives and the Senate proposed welfare reform legislation that devolved AFDC programs to the states. This reform legislation was to take the form of a block grant that encouraged experimentation by the states. In effect, the states would become free to restructure the missing component in the industrialization of social services: the ability to regulate directly the flow of clients entering the system. However, decreasing the flow of clients would also profoundly affect the stability of American society.

The goal of social welfare technology is to increase the number of clients processed while simultaneously cutting costs. To accomplish this goal, the industrial model of production requires standardized raw materials, clients and workers, to increase the efficiency of production. Clients and workers must therefore have attributes that are dependable, regardless of whether this is the case in reality; each party must have a prescribed notion of their role; and exceptions to the production process must be rejected. In short, the entire production process must be normative for the system to be rationalized.

The Deskilling of Social Workers. The values, philosophy, and culture of social work are in conflict with the goals of the industrial model of production. Specifically, social work places a high premium on human interaction, is labor-intensive, and incorporates a broad view of systemic interrelationships. In contrast, the industrial model of production molds the production process to fit the strengths of a particular technology. As a result, social service agencies often attempt to shape social work practice in ways that complement the organizational technology they are using. If a particular organizational technology is perceived as cost-effective, social workers are expected to adjust their practice to fit it. Since many organizational technologies contain their own evaluative criteria, certain forms of social work practice, especially macro practice, may be judged as ineffective if they fail to satisfy the evaluative criteria inherent in the technology.

For example, many social agencies are currently adopting technologies that measure how workers spend their time. Social workers who spend more total "contact time" (face-to-face interaction) with clients are rewarded. Conversely, social workers who spend less contact time with clients may be penalized. While this system measures client contact hours, it does not measure the effectiveness of a social worker's practice. For example, a social worker who views a client's problem as economic may spend many hours in collateral efforts trying to secure various forms of income maintenance services. Another social worker who wants to be "successful" will simply spend more face-to-face time with clients. To justify this expenditure of time, a predominantly economic problem will, by necessity, be transformed into a psychological one. While clients may remain unable to pay their rent, they will likely end up with deeper insight into the psychological causes of their problem. In fact, living on the streets may well give them more time to ponder the real meaning of life. The savvy practitioner looking to get ahead—or stay afloat—quickly learns to substitute quantity for quality—a mainstay of the industrial model of production.

Organizational technologies conform to the industrial production model in other important ways. As stated earlier, both industrial and social agency production demand standardization of the raw materials of production, both client and workers. When adapted to social services, the industrial model of production forces a nonroutinized type of work into a routinized and standardized format. An example of standardized raw materials is found in the Diagnostic and Statistical Manual of Mental Disorders (DSM). Using the DSM, client problems are diagnosed, catalogued, and treated. Medication is prescribed, and a diagnosis is offered based on the symptomology contained in the manual. This process occurs even when psychological symptoms are vague and overlapping. Symptoms that defy categorization are either dismissed, ignored, or placed in a "trash bin." Although Axis IV of the DSM deals with psychosocial and environmental problems, including support groups, the social environment, housing, economic issues, and so on, its implementation in diagnosis is generally limited. Tilting toward the psychological side, the DSM minimizes macro contextual factors. In effect, a routinized process of psychological diagnosis and treatment is initiated to treat what the DSM has defined as a problem. Conversely, if a particular kind of human misery is not catalogued in the DSM, the client may be denied help. The DSM is one illustration of the dominance of production over human need.

The mandate to increase efficiency and productivity has transformed the work of many social workers into simple routines. Social workers become transformed from competent professionals into machinelike components, possessing only rudimentary knowledge of their work environment. In the end, these social workers become "factors of production." The expropriation of skills removes social workers from the dignity and worth that accompanies meaningful work and completes their transformation into marketable and replaceable commodities (Gil, 1984). Social work practice thereby becomes more specialized, mechanized, and automatic. Moreover, a profession that devalues its members becomes obsolete. Unless social workers work more cheaply, gain new technological skills, or compete more effectively as private agents in the human services marketplace, many will be subordinated to inferior work roles. Fabricant and Burghardt (1992) found this subordination in their study of the contemporary proletarianization of public and nonprofit social work.

The deskilling cycle is complete when the trivialization of social work skills becomes a reality. At the core of this trivialization is a devaluation in the social worker's worth and the reduction of professional skills into mechanical operations. For example, many social workers in health settings spend the vast majority of their time helping clients fill out Medicaid and Supplemental Security Income (SSI) forms, arranging for AFDC payments, and completing other forms of paperwork. This clerical role is reinforced by the agency and often met by silence within the profession. This silence is not surprising since resistance to the industrial model is often punished by agency sanction. Clearly, the refusal to capitulate to the industrial model entails substantial risks.

Much of the organizational technology used in social service agencies was not designed by social work professionals, but by nonsocial work managers and external consultants. In part, this trend was nurtured because social workers failed to engage in serious research on the value of their interventions vis-à-vis client improvement. Had the profession engaged in the requisite fiscal analysis to determine the unit cost of service under different modes of delivery, it might have been able to help stem the rationing of service carried on by managed care agencies and overly cost-conscious managers. In effect, social work might have developed its own technologies. Instead, social workers neither engaged in comprehensive research on the value of their interventions nor on the cost of their services. As a result, the absence of data documenting social work effectiveness made the profession vulnerable to managers whose business it is to cut costs and services.

While the causes for the disempowerment of social workers are manifold, so, too, are its solutions. In general, however, social workers face two avenues for empowering the workplace: organizational reform, and the creation of alternative organizations.

ORGANIZATIONAL REFORM

Certain fundamental principles apply regardless of whether an organization is being reformed or a new organizational form is being developed. First, the idea of workplace productivity must be redefined. Mechanistic notions of productivity must be replaced by a view of production anchored in a human context. As such, new criterion for productivity must reflect the best interests of clients and workers. Alternative measures of productivity would evaluate social work interventions not in crude quantitative terms, but as a reflection of agency, worker, and client goals. This measurement requires developing new organizational technologies that define efficiency in human terms. At its base, this new criteria for measurement must be grounded in a progressive ideology that understands the role of work in modern life.

In addition, social service organizations must develop humane and democratic organizational forms. Hierarchical organizations that pit worker against administrator and give decision-making powers to an elite few must be replaced by more collegial work formats that allow for greater worker control. Effective workplace organization requires both cooperative and adversarial approaches to employee representation. Finally, social work organizational technologies must be participatory, flexible, and open to input by frontline workers, administrators, and clients. In short, criteria used to measure effectiveness should be determined by social work managers, practitioners, clients, and the public to which the agency and social worker are responsible.

Choices involving the use and development of organizational technology are inevitable given the demands for accountability placed on social services. However, with a humane and democratic vision, new forms of organizational technology can be a potent force in positively changing the face of social welfare services. It is, however, not enough simply to develop principles. Without political power, those recommendations—whatever their merit—will be dismissed. The next section explores unionization, one of several methods for reforming social agencies.

Unions and the Social Service Workplace

Many authors suggest ways of advancing democracy and workplace productivity (Ouchi, 1976; Peters & Waterman, 1984). W. Edwards Deming (1986) talked about Total Quality Management (TQM) as a means for promoting efficiency and effectiveness in both public and private workplaces. Most of these authors, however, have been relatively naïve about power. They believe that the new realities of globalization demand a cooperative, decentralized, "team" approach. Unions are seen as too confrontational and passé (Creech, 1994). What these authors fail to recognize is that all work is political, and as such, workplace models that promote democracy must recognize the political nature of work. Heckscher (1994) argues that "independent employee representation is essential to democracy in a modern economy" (p. 19). If power at the workplace is not roughly equal among the parties, workers will be ignored on critical issues.

The standardization of professional tools, the increasing pressure toward greater productivity, and a diminishing influence in policymaking are all cited as indications of a decline in the professional autonomy and status of social work (Tudiver, 1982; Wagner & Cohen, 1978; Fabricant & Burghardt, 1992). For many social workers, the dismantling of key human service programs over the past twenty years has resulted in more job insecurity, higher unemployment, a stagnation in real wages, and the occupational displacement of higher- with lower-degreed social service workers (Ratner, 1985). Moreover, inequities such as unilateral reductions in hours and arbitrary layoffs, unfair merit salary increases, favoritism in awarding promotions, the unfair distribution of salaries and salary increments, low pay, new workers hired at higher wages than veteran workers, massive disparities in income between frontline workers and administrators, and sexist and racist salary practices are all of central concern to social workers (Tambor, 1979).

In response to these organizational problems, social workers have used tactics ranging from consensus building to strikes. Consensus building can lead to significant organizational changes, and in the present conservative atmosphere, it is the approach most commonly used (Fisher, 1994). But this strategy remains only one of many. Often, the inherent power relations in social agencies block consensual change, and social workers find that workplace empowerment can only be achieved through the creation of a formal structure (Karger, 1988). These formal structures may vary from collaborative Deming-style TQM groups to conflict-oriented labor unions.

Many workers turn to unionization as a vehicle for defending professional autonomy and for improving working conditions. As the collective voice of workers, unions are built upon mutual support. Workers act together as agents of change based on their own interests and within their own work settings. By advocating for themselves, social workers can also be more effective in helping clients gain a greater measure of power and control over their lives (Sherman & Wenocur, 1983).

Unionized social workers are found in both the public and private sectors, and in institutions such as hospitals, schools, public welfare departments, voluntary agencies, state-run institutions, and mental health clinics. In contrast to unionized teachers and nurses, most social workers are not in exclusive bargaining units composed solely of one occupational group. In addition to professional social workers, social service bargaining units often represent service, support, and clerical workers.

Social workers join labor unions for a variety of reasons. Okafor (1985) maintains that overall, white-collar workers unionize to acquire greater job security, better pay and fringe benefits, better working conditions, and job dignity. Social workers may also join unions as a means of advocating for improved client services. Frustrated by fiscal cutbacks in social services, increased layers of administration, nonaccountable agencies, and insensitive state and federal governmental structures, many social workers turn to unions as an ally of last resort. Some social workers may also choose unionization as an expression of solidarity with nonprofessional, social service employees. Besides advocating for job security and other "bread and butter" issues, social workers in public sector unions may seek to expand the scope of bargaining to include agency-level decision making.

Collective bargaining is the mainstay of the union process. Specifically, collective bargaining refers to the formal face-to-face interaction between unionized employees and management for the purposes of developing a workplace contract. Ideally, both groups bring their workplace agendas to the bargaining table, and a compromise is hammered out. Bargaining is done in good faith with the legal rights of workers being guaranteed by provisions in the National Labor Relations Act. If these bargaining rights are abridged, workers can petition the National Labor Relations Board to address grievances related to the collective bargaining process. The glue that binds this process is the right of workers to strike if the bargaining process breaks down. In theory, both parties have a vested interest in a successful bargaining process—strikes hurt both union members and the companies or agencies with which they are bargaining. In a strict sense, collective bargaining is often a confrontational process.

Collective bargaining agreements can also address professional issues such as caseload size and benefits relating to educational concerns like tuition reimbursement, sabbatical and educational leaves, conference release time and reimbursements, payment for professional dues and subscriptions, and flexible hours of work. One union leader observed that: "To the professional—the teacher or caseworker—things like class size and caseload size become as important as the number of hours in a shift is to the blue collar worker" (Weitzman, 1975). In one organizing drive, for example, caseload size, career ladders and training, pay equity, and classification downgrading were the major issues. In a mental health clinic in the voluntary sector, safe working conditions, benefits for part-time workers, workloads, and participation in agency decision making were the primary focus of organizing efforts (Tambor, 1988).

Social workers are primarily unionized through the American Federation of State, County, and Municipal Employees (AFSCME) (55,000 social workers) and the Service Employees International Union (SEIU) (26,000 social workers), two of the fastest growing unions in the United States. Other unions that have social work members include the Communications Workers of America (CWA) and the American Federation of Government Employees (AFGE). All told, over 125,000 social workers are unionized (Shaffer, 1987). Despite a decline in the overall percentage of unionized workers in the labor force, the number of unionized social workers has either grown slightly or remained steady. In addition, while overall union membership has declined in the past decades (from a high of 34 percent in 1955 to 16.4 percent in 1991), unionization among professionals and public employees continues to increase (Farber & Kreuger, 1993). As Tambor (1988) puts it, social work unionization is occurring within this context of increased labor organizing among professionals. Despite the numbers of social workers in unions and the steady growth in unionization among professional and public employees, the impact of unionization and collective bargaining on service delivery has rarely been addressed in the professional literature or in the curricula of schools of social work (Shaffer, 1979; Tambor & Shaffer, 1985).

Anti-Unionism in Social Work. Despite the similarity of goals between some unions and social work (e.g., concerns with social justice and social welfare benefits), opposition to union organization is widespread in some sectors of the profession. Opponents of unionism maintain that: (1) unions cost employees money, (2) strike losses are never retrieved, (3) union members have little voice in union affairs and are often purposefully kept ignorant, (4) bureaucratic union hierarchies control the economic destiny of employees, (5) union corruption is rampant, (6) the consistent refusal of unions to increase productivity hinders organizational growth, (7) union "featherbedding" results in unneeded employees and unnecessary payroll expenses, (8) union membership campaigns foster conflict rather than collaboration, (9) the right of managers to strive for greater productivity is curtailed by union rules, and (10) unions have little consideration for the effects of increased wages on future employment, inflation, and tax increases (Laliberty & Christopher, 1986). Even some progressive critics point out problems in union democracy, labor's loss of moral authority, and a problematic union culture that has historically excluded women, people of color, and recent immigrants (Kallick, 1994).

The antiunion bias within social work is focused around issues of professionalism, bureaucracy, a form of social work "exceptionalism," and pragmatism. Apart from fears that clients are harmed by strikes, antiunionism centers around a concern that organized social workers will become like other workers, thereby subordinating professional concerns to union issues. Opponents fear that if social workers view themselves foremost as "workers," management views will follow suit.

A belief in the "exceptionalism" of social work underlies the general debate on professionalism. Specifically, this exceptionalism implies that tasks performed by social workers are more important than those performed by other workers—especially nonprofessionals. Assumptions about the exceptionalism of social work can lead to moral and ethical dilemmas. Moreover, a belief in the exceptionalism of social work has aided the market forces conspiring to keep social work salaries below those of other professions. For many social workers, the label of "worker" is more of a reality than the preceding "social."

A second concern of antiunion forces involves the issue of bureaucracy. Many social workers believe that all administrators are stridently opposed to unions, that union members will be compelled to strike, that they will have little voice in union affairs, that unions are only another layer of oppressive bureaucracy, and that unionization will cause a deterioration in the fabric of employer-employee relations. Many social workers employed in bureaucratic settings view unions as interfering with professional priorities and autonomy by introducing rules, regulations, and an administrative hierarchy that superimposes authority of office over authority of expertise (Lightman, 1982). For these social workers, unions are yet another bureaucratic structure and another hindrance to professional practice.

Finally, unions appear as anachronistic in the context of global privatization. Specifically, since social work and its clients are already under attack, why ally with an organizational form that is seen as part of the problem? Social work is also an inherently pragmatic profession. In conservative times, when funding is diminished, it shifts rightward or demands less conflict. The vast majority of the profession, often quite reluctantly, find ways to appear more conservative. The primary goal of social work is to serve the needs of clients in an environment that is usually hostile to social efforts, and in the best of times, is only modestly supportive. Social workers are reluctant to take up the mantle of unionization at a time when unions are under attack or in disrepute, at a time when labor relations are increasingly being defined as private affairs between employers and employees, and in an era where conservative discourse pushes debate about organizational development and productivity into consensus building rather than conflict-based models.

The Compatibility between Professional Social Work and Unionism.   While the research suggests that most unionized social workers see little conflict between professionalism and unionism, studies do hint at a bifurcated attitude regarding unions and professional associations (Alexander et al., 1980; Shaffer & Ahearn, 1982; Lightman, 1982; Kirzner, 1985). For example, Alexander et al. (1980) found that social workers clearly preferred a job-conscious or instrumental form of unionism over an approach that stressed professional or political concerns. A similar finding was reported by Lightman (1982). Unionized social workers appear to segregate their professional and workplace concerns by viewing unions as representing their workplace interests (e.g., pay, seniority, and job security issues) and professional associations as embodying their professional concerns (Alexander, 1980; Lightman, 1982). This important finding is not surprising since professional social work associations possess little actual clout in the workplace. For example, NASW has little power over social agencies except to censure them by publishing their name in the *NASW NEWS*. On the other hand, unions can pursue grievances through National Labor Relations Board hearings, law suits, and other avenues.

Although unionism and professional social work seem compatible, many social workers prefer them to be kept independent of each other, or to develop organizational forms that reflect a mutual compromise between the two. Indeed, traditional approaches to trade unionism often fail to address many of the professional concerns of social workers. Moreover, many union officials fail to appreciate that while bread-and-butter issues are important, social workers are also concerned with issues that impact upon their clients. Hence, unions must find ways to fuse business unionism with the professional concerns of social workers (Alexander, 1980). Conversely, professional organizations must understand that collective bargaining complements self-determination, a cherished social work value. In its purest form, collective bargaining is a mainstay of democracy, empowerment, and self-determination since it represents a meeting of minds rather than an administrative decision grounded in capricious rules and regulations. The focus on professional concerns and the underlying philosophy of collective bargaining can complement social work's emphasis on higher values. These are not very different from the issues that confront successful unions of professional teachers or nurses.

If social work associations are to support unionism, they must aid in eradicating common misconceptions about them. For example, most social work curricula have little content on collective bargaining and unionization, even for administrative-track students at the masters level. According to Shaffer (1979), "Most social workers have not been prepared by education or experience to deal effectively with union issues" (p. 84). Masi (1981) maintains that the "knowledge of . . . union problems, the subtleties and nuances of labor/management relationships, and the grievance procedure of the collective-bargaining agreement is essential in order for a social worker to function in the workplace" (p. 45). Given the growth of antiunionism in the 1980s and 1990s, social work curricula probably contain even less content on union issues than in the 1970s. Nevertheless, curricula should minimally contain content on collective bargaining, public sector labor laws, negotiations, impasse procedures, the scope of bargaining, unit determination, and the process of union certification. Social workers must understand that they are as vulnerable to unfair labor practices as other workers.

Given the contemporary context of global privatization, social work and public sector unions can provide essential forms of worker and client empowerment. In addition, unions can help in collective problem solving, fostering a public debate on social issues, and promoting class-aware groupings within a contemporary context that seeks to undermine this awareness. Bridging the gap between unionism and social change is the goal of several organizations, including Jobs with Justice. As Heckscher (1994) points out, while new approaches to unionization "are still in their infancy . . . the rich variety of innovations being tried today has the potential to restore an essential pillar of labor's strength: the sense among the wider public that employee organization contributes to the general good" (p. 29).

Toward a New Conception of Workplace Democracy

The current attack on unions is part of an overall attack on progressive institutions. Their reinstatement, while not popular because of the antiunion rhetoric that has dominated political discussions since the 1970s, is an act of rebuilding collective public life. However, in the current context of privatization, it is neither sufficient to understand the continued importance of unions nor appropriate to argue simply that unions are the answer to all problems in the social service workplace. Instead, as society shifts from an industrial to a postindustrial orientation, social work must alter its relations to various forms of organizations. On one level, traditional unions that are part of the industrial model are outdated—a response of workers to the industrial production model we argue against in this book. But as long as the industrial model persists throughout society—as it does in social work—then labor unions are a viable means for representing the collective interests of workers. To move to a more postindustrial and postmodern orientation would not do away with unions, as many have suggested, but, rather, would lead to building alternative forms of unionization. These new forms can be erected based on the persistent class and power relations inherent in all organizations—whether they are industrial or postindustrial in orientation. In both instances, unions remain a viable means of representing and defending social workers and their clients. Alternative unions should also reflect contemporary moves toward more postindustrial and postmodern forms of organization. They should build on collective power and class consciousness, but also reflect an emphasis on issues of workplace diversity, autonomy, quality of life, relationships, and democratic participation and control.

Heckscher (1994) argues that the old dualism between adversarial and cooperative models of worker organization must be reconsidered. Workers need both. They need strong, independent organizations that understand the strategic importance of confrontation, but workers also need to enhance their position in the workplace through tactics of "influence," including trustworthiness, flexibility, persuasion, and "responsible contribution to the success of employers" (p. 21). This approach is especially true for workers "with a 'professional' orientation, favoring the tactics of individual career-building over collective confrontation" (p. 22). These workers want a decentralized and participatory approach to employee representation that supports their professional goals beyond a specific workplace. One example, outside of the social work field, is the joint effort between the CWA (Communication Workers of America) and AT&T to bring union representatives into high levels of company planning as well as to encourage worker participation at the site of production.

Old stereotypes must be reconsidered in order to develop a more dynamic paradigm in public- and private-sector labor-management relations. One concept that bears reconsideration is the belief that rigid and hierarchical forms of administration are necessary to manage large social service organizations effectively. Although appearing efficient, hierarchical managerial forms carry a heavy burden. Managers in private industry are only now beginning to understand that shop-floor workers have a better grasp of the production process than office-bound supervisors. Some enlightened managers are relying on these workers to identify problems and discover more efficient production methods. These strategies were, most recently, promoted by W. Edwards Deming (1986) and captured under the organizational umbrella of TQM (Total Quality Management). In such systems, the new managerial role becomes one of facilitator, director, booster, and overseer. Adopting this new framework entails redefining traditional ideas of administrative-based power. Managers are no longer expected to be the undisputed authorities, with intimate knowledge of the entire production process. Although overall responsibility for production rests with management, input and decision making are shared with workers. The same system could be applied to the social service workplace. Acknowledging that social workers intimately understand the nature of their work, administrators could rely more heavily on line staff to develop and implement policy and to establish methods for evaluating the quality of social services. This system could help breathe new life into eroded notions of professional autonomy while allowing for more effective work with clients.

The "enlightened management" approach proposed by Deming and others clearly has merit. It bespeaks a new way of thinking and a new paradigm for viewing work. Moreover, these new management approaches criticize the old production systems as too rigid by focusing on quantity over quality. Workers, they argue, should not be expected to leave their minds at home when they come to work.

Overall, there are two basic orientations to the new management approaches: the TQM movement associated with Deming and the Socio-Technical Systems (STS) approach. Although similar, they exhibit slight differences. For example, Deming (1986) argues that 85 percent of production problems are systemic and caused by management. Only management can, therefore, decide how to solve these problems. The STS approach is based on the belief that attention must be paid to both the technical and social aspects of production. In effect, STS argues that if workers are able to interact in the course of their work and have their needs addressed, they will be happier and more productive. STS approaches are based on team production (that is, work groups), which gives more power and decision making to line workers. The STS system formed the basis of the much-publicized Volvo plant in Udvalla, Sweden, where teams of six to eight workers build complete cars (Richardson, 1992).

The interest in new management strategies and their effect on productivity has not escaped even the highest echelons of American government. In 1993, President Bill Clinton asked Secretary of Commerce Ron Brown and Secretary of Labor Robert Reich to convene a conference titled, "The Future of the American Workplace." This conference brought together leaders from business, labor, academia, and other sectors, as well as frontline workers, to discuss issues regarding the development of innovative workplaces. The meeting was designed as a day-long working session to highlight examples of successful organizational transformations, identify barriers to change, and help define public and private strategies for encouraging more companies and organizations to adopt participatory work practices. The publicly espoused goal of the conference was to accelerate the pace of workplace change in order to enhance the competitiveness of American business and thereby improve the skills and living standards of American workers.

The conference, "The Future of the American Workplace" (1993), argued that the most successful companies and organizations shared the following characteristics:

- A commitment to the continuous improvement of products, services, and cost reductions;
- Decentralized decision making, worker participation at all levels, and generally greater reliance on frontline workers;
- Productive worker-management relations based on the consideration of mutual interests and concerns, and worker participation at all levels;
- Managers who assume more leadership functions, including long-range planning, coaching, and facilitation;
- Ongoing training and retraining of all workers, including frontline employees;
- Wider information sharing between managers and workers;
- Flexible benefits and innovative compensation schemes, including profit-sharing, gain-sharing, and pay-for-performance systems; and
- A demonstrated commitment to a safe and healthful workplace.

Box 7.1 is based on the recommendations of the conference.

While participatory management schemes are gaining in popularity, some unions remain skeptical of these approaches because of their contradictions. Unions point out that TQM systems were originally developed by companies who wanted to keep out unions (Brecher & Costello, 1992). According to Steve Weingartner (1992), a union official, "Members' reactions [to quality approaches] ranged from

Box 7.1 The New American Workplace

EMPLOYEE EMPOWERED
Workers are empowered with the knowledge and skills on all facets of work processes and organizational goals and actively participate in organizational decision making.

MANAGEMENT CONTROLLED
Communication is mostly top-down and work is tightly controlled through management established procedures.

WORK TEAMS
Work is organized into self-managing units whose job boundaries cut across traditional organizational lines. Supervisors act as coaches and mentors. Workers are responsible for both production processes and organizational duties such as hiring and scheduling.

FUNCTIONAL DEPARTMENTS
Work is organized by functional departments with job boundaries well-defined. Jobs are designed with narrow scope and limited responsibility. Minimal cooperation between functions and departments.

EMPLOYEE-CENTERED WORKPLACE POLICIES
Workers are viewed as an asset. The organizational culture is supportive, flexible, and sensitive to the needs of workers. Diversity is valued. Organizations strive to create safe and healthy workplaces sensitive to worker family demands.

COST-FOCUSED WORKPLACE POLICIES
Impersonal organizational cultures focus on the cost side of employee issues. Conformance and uniformity are the norm, and sensitivity to issues outside the realm of the job is minimal.

CONTINUOUS INNOVATION/IMPROVEMENT
Innovation is market-driven and organizations continuously strive to improve the quality and timeliness of new products. Various departments collaborate on improving organizational service and establishing a system of concurrent innovation.

SEQUENTIAL INNOVATION
Services have long life cycles and innovation tends to occur infrequently. The process is slow and completed in stages as different elements of the development process are handled by separate departments and then "tossed over the wall" to the next.

CLIENT- AND EMPLOYEE-DRIVEN QUALITY
Quality and client needs are the major drivers of change. Quality is continuously measured by workers and results are fed back to all.

PROBLEM INSPECTION
Quality is the result of program evaluation done only after services have been delivered.

Box 7.1 (*continued*)

TOOLS FOR COMPETITIVENESS
Measurement tools used by workers are critical to gauging internal performance.

FLEXIBLE PRODUCTION PROCESSES
Leading-edge technology is implemented to complement the skills and knowledge of employees. Tightly integrated systems provide "real time" information to employees.

NEW WORKER SKILLS
Work requires creative thinking and self-motivation. Problem solving, decision making, business, financial, negotiations, and interpersonal skills are essential for employees.

WORKER/MANAGEMENT COOPERATION
Relationships are based on mutual interests and a cooperative approach to problem solving.

INNOVATIVE COMPENSATION PLANS
Pay increases based on skill attainment and/or performance. Systems reward worker contributions, such as teamwork and quality.

EXTERNAL PARTNERSHIPS
Alliances with consumers provide feedback/collaboration to increase quality and productivity. Networks of service providers encourage information sharing and co-innovation.

INTERNALLY DRIVEN PERFORMANCE STANDARDS
Managers track/record performance based on internal goals.

INFLEXIBLE, DESKILLING TECHNOLOGY
The technical system dominates the work. Inflexible systems produce products in high volumes. Workers are viewed as completing repetitive tasks following standard procedures.

TECHNICAL SKILLS ONLY
Labor intensive work requires the technical skills to get the job done, no knowledge of product or process outside the immediate task is necessary.

ADVERSARIAL WORKER/MANAGEMENT RELATIONS
A power/rights-based system.

SENIORITY-BASED COMPENSATION
Pay determined by rigid job classification rules that are based on tenure with the organization.

FEW ALLIANCES
Other social agencies are viewed as competitions. Client feedback is not sought. Agency information is closely held to maintain advantage.

enthusiasm to cynicism" (p. 71). Other union leaders were more critical. F. L. Hamer (1992) wrote:

> Though workers were uneasy [about GM's new management approach called "jointness"], our first responsibilities under jointness were promising. . . . We were responsible for getting the job done, but in spite of all that talk about cooperation, we didn't decide how much work would be done, or how fast we would have to work. . . . Jointness at GM is a cruel hoax. "Real partners" decide together how and where to invest in new plants and equipment, CEO salaries and perks, and the like. That's never been on the agenda at GM. All we've gotten from jointness is greater management control . . . speed-ups . . . skyrocketing injuries . . . increased worker competition . . . and worst of all, workers disciplining other workers. (p. 70)

Despite these criticisms, similar management approaches are being tried in social work. For example, public child welfare agencies are generally problematic places to work, with substandard working conditions only adding to the difficulties facing workers. According to Burton Cohen and Michael Austin (1994), these substandard conditions include neglected and unsafe physical plants, lack of clerical assistance, high caseloads, inadequate supervision, and excessive paperwork, regulations, and monitoring. In studying a Philadelphia public child welfare agency, Cohen and Austin (1992) found that almost half of all social work supervisors (46.8 percent) ranked the quality of their work life "poor." Over 81 percent of social workers in that agency ranked the quality of their work life from "fair" to "poor." Only 28 percent of social workers reported that they were satisfied with their jobs. In response, Cohen and Austin (1994) helped introduce a variation of TQM into the agency. The success of the experiment is not yet evident.

The current workplace malaise affecting social workers may be partly remedied by democratizing the worksite. As such, traditional and hierarchical forms of management must give way to new ideas about cooperation between frontline social workers and managers. The project of social change can take place within social work agencies as well as the larger society. New forms of employee-management relations should be based on a system of fair and equitable wages and respect for professional autonomy and judgment. Moreover, real cooperation is easier among equals; true cooperation rarely occurs when there are two or more unequal classes. More often than not, hierarchical workplace relations lead to subservience and compliance rather than commitment and cooperation. Cooperation among equals is one way to ensure long-term stability in employee-management relations.

Administrators must also be willing to accept the benefits of workplace democracy—either through unionization, participatory management schemes, or a combination of both—if they are to establish a new framework for employee-management relations. Unions or other organizational forms can contribute to the stability of democratic societies by helping to focus worker grievances on appropriate targets. Although democratic organizational forms may add slightly to the costs of agency operations, they also lower fixed costs by helping to reduce job turnover and heighten worker satisfaction, by ensuring the use of professional management practices rather than arbitrary decision making, and by improving information about worker preferences (Kwasi, 1983; Freedman & Medoff, 1984). With mutual respect and cooperation on both sides—themes central to new workplace conceptualizations—democratic organization can help provide an efficient and stable labor force that possesses the collective power and organization to address the worker and client needs often ignored by agencies and bureaucracies.

A new model of labor relations should be predicated upon mutual understanding, cooperation, and examining the concept of the "culture of worklife" (Gortner et al., 1987; Ouchi, 1976). However, while participatory control systems promise to enhance the quality of work life for social workers, they are not a substitute for the protection offered by unions nor are they a substitute for a comprehensive system of employee-management relations. Moreover, participatory work schemes fail to obviate a key workplace problem; namely, while employees may participate more at the worksite, both profits and the central core of decision making remain with management. One alternative to reforming agencies is the creation of new and alternative forms of social agencies, which would incorporate at their roots principles such as self-determination, democracy, flexibility, a progressive view of productivity, and an emphasis on quality over quantity. It is to this idea that we will now turn.

ALTERNATIVE ORGANIZATIONAL FORMS

Social workers have long sought to gain more control over and transform the workplace. To this end, unionization is a key strategy. There is also a tradition in social work of seeking progressive change by getting out from under rigid and hierarchical social agencies. One of the more common avenues for achieving autonomy and workplace freedom has been private practice.

For many progressive social workers, private practice is seen as one of the more disturbing tendencies in the profession. For one, private practice reinforces the larger social trend toward the privatization of society, including the delivery of social services. Private practice is often viewed as oppositional to social change efforts because it lacks a direct connection with the communities served by public or nonprofit agencies, and because it represents the distancing of the social work profession from poor individuals who cannot afford to pay private fees. For progressive social workers, private practice symbolizes the abandonment of the poor in favor of a middle class capable of paying high fees that are then often funneled through private healthcare insurance, an institution that excludes many of the poor. For other social workers, it represents a dual system of social services: The poor are served by inexperienced social workers in understaffed and underfunded public agencies, while the middle class are treated by experienced social workers able to limit their caseload size and thereby provide higher quality services. Despite the political problems inherent in private practice, it is important to examine why so many social workers find it an irresistible alternative to the confines of traditional agency work.

Apart from the obvious reasons for entering private practice—an increase in wages and status—private practitioners are perceived as having more professional autonomy than social workers fettered to the personnel policies of traditional agencies. The image of private practice is based on freedom, opportunity, and few regulations. In a study of private and agency-based social workers, Srinika Jayaratne and his associates (1988) found that "whereas 55 percent of the private practitioners report a high level of congruence between their expectations and their activities, only 18.3 percent of the agency practitioners do so" (p. 329). Moreover, private practice allows professionals to specialize in activities in which they excel instead of being forced to conform to the organizational requirements of private and public agencies. Jayaratne et al. (1988) reported that 66.5 percent of private practitioners felt they were able to do those things in which they excelled, compared to only 22.9 percent of agency practitioners. It is not surprising, then, that social workers—who are usually female and underpaid—view private practice as a way to increase both their earnings and status (Jayaratne et al., 1988). Moreover, the decision by social workers to enter private practice involves more than just money and status. Jayaratne et al., (1991) reported that "Those in private practice reported fewer psychological and health strains, reported higher levels of performance, and in general, felt better about their life circumstances . . . than those in agency practice" (pp. 226–27).

The career choice to enter private practice may also involve personal and familial issues. For example, in contrast to the rigid time constraints imposed in agency settings, private practitioners have the freedom to determine when they will work, for how long, and under what circumstances. Agencies forced to operate with fewer resources are displacing more of their fiscal problems onto workers. Weekend and night work is becoming more frequent, as is forced overtime. The compensatory time offered by agencies may provide little consolation for workers who lose the opportunity to spend evenings or weekends with their families. Private practice is a seductive alternative for many individuals trying to balance family life with careers.

The rush toward private practice is reflective of the problems and workplace dilemmas faced by many social workers. First, social agency constraints on freedom and professional autonomy are problematic for social workers who have invested untold hours and dollars in professional training. Second, rigid agency rules that restrict time and make little allowance for the multiple responsibilities that characterize family life are seen by many social workers as obstacles to maintaining a healthy balance between work, family, and other interests. Third, the stress of large and increasingly difficult caseloads, coupled with the dearth of private and public agency resources, makes traditional social agency work less appealing for a growing number of social workers. While private practice may provide an escape hatch for some disenchanted social workers, current studies suggest that social work in smaller voluntary-sector organizations is not very different from the "proletarianized" work in large public agencies (Fabricant & Burghardt, 1992).

Public-sector unions are clearly an important part of the future of progressive social work. In addition, there are other options available, including worker-owned cooperatives and employee-owned organizations. Many of these alternative organizations can be constructed in ways that afford workers greater levels of freedom and flexibility while still maintaining strong ties to the community and a commitment to public life. In all cases, however, new progressive organizational forms must address the reasons why growing numbers of social workers are rushing toward private practice.

Lappé and Dubois (1994) illustrate one example of a worker-owned company:

> Five years ago, Florinda DeLeon was on welfare, a single parent bringing up three children by herself. Today, Florinda makes $6.50 an hour as a home health care worker. She loves her job. And with her company's revenues growing by 20 percent a year, Florinda boasts that, "I don't ever have to think about being back on a welfare line."
>
> Almost everywhere else, home health care workers suffer a precarious existence: no benefits, irregular hours, and tough working conditions. But Florinda DeLeon's life is different. Not only is she earning higher-than-average wages for her industry, she receives health benefits and a paid vacation as well. She gets top-notch training, and she's treated with respect by her company's owners.
>
> Why? Because she—along with 170 of her co-workers—*are* the company. Florinda works for Cooperative Home Care Associates (CHCA), founded in the Bronx in 1985. Florinda also recently completed a two-year term on the company's board of directors. "Being worker-owned means *we* decide what's best for us," she says proudly. (p. 73)

Worker ownership has been a buzzword among management gurus for almost three decades. However, the ownership to which they generally refer is psychological rather than legal. While psychological ownership may be an important concept in participatory management, it is just that—psychological. While psychological ownership may lead to more psychic income, it does not necessarily translate into higher real wages. Actual ownership, on the other hand, has the propensity to bring the discussion of workplace democracy to another level.

By 1990, more than eleven thousand companies were owned in whole or part by 12 million employees. These employees had accumulated $60 billion in stock (Lappé & Dubois, 1994). While that figure only represents 3 percent of the value of all stock, in four important industries—private hospital management, shipbuilding, construction, and steel manufacturing—workers own the majority of stock in companies that rank among the top ten. In addition, fifteen employee-owned companies now rank among America's four hundred largest firms (Lappé & Dubois, 1994). The most frequent vehicle for employee ownership has been Employee Stock Option Plans (ESOP). Through ESOPs, workers have gained ownership of at least 25 percent of many companies, including J. C. Penney, Kroger's, Avis, Coldwell Banker, and United Airlines (Lappé & Dubois, 1994). While companies that are wholly or partly owned by employees offer the possibility for important improvements in the quality of worklife, the size of these companies and the continued influence of CEOs and externally elected boards of directors often limit the gains that can be expected.

At the end of the organizational spectrum—and the model that may be the most relevant for social workers—is the employee cooperative. Within this organizational design, employees are full owners and control the daily life of the organization, including control of boards of directors. There are roughly one thousand employee cooperatives in the United States, although most have only a handful of workers (Lappé & Dubois, 1994).

While worker-owned, social service cooperatives cannot be expected to have the same impact as the large-scale organizing of social service workers, the recent trend toward privatizing social services and the push toward devolving welfare responsibilities to the states may ironically provide a window of opportunity for social workers to develop alternative and progressive forms of service delivery. Specifically, the current legislation to develop fixed, lifetime welfare entitlements, ranging from two to five years, will require states to pursue more aggressively intensive case management strategies. The potential failure of states to respond effectively to welfare reform will have dire consequences, including the creation of legions of former beneficiaries who are neither employable nor eligible for benefits. This situation would result in widespread domestic instability not seen since the turbulence of the middle 1960s.

Given the increased latitude of states to design and implement experimental social and income maintenance programs, at least some states may use this opportunity to find ways to develop more effective social services. Clearly, however, most states will use this opportunity only as a way to save money by curtailing services. Apart from the ideological preference for privatization, most welfare departments do not have appropriate administrative or personnel staffing to implement a comprehensive case management strategy. Consequently, states will be faced with two choices: to retool public welfare agencies to provide case management services— unlikely given the trend toward privatization—*or* to search out new agencies to subcontract for the provision of intensive case management services (that is, literacy, job training, and mental health services) for welfare recipients.

If for-profit organizations are awarded these contracts and allowed to fill the income maintenance gap, social services will continue to be detached from community control. On the other hand, social workers can respond positively to the coming challenge by not only unionizing to resist the changes but by forming new organizational modalities, including social service cooperatives, to provide the necessary income maintenance and social services required. These cooperative social agencies can be jointly run by social workers and community-based boards of directors. In short, cooperative, employee-owned, social service agencies can be developed to fuse professional interests with community concerns. Social work's response to the challenge will clearly require bold innovation, risk, inventiveness, discipline, and more than a modicum of skill.

SKILLS IMPLICATIONS FOR
ORGANIZATIONAL CHANGE

Key skills are required to either change an organization or create a new one. While a full accounting of the range of skills necessary to effect organizational change is beyond the scope of this book, the following skills are generally considered important.

One of the most important skills in organizational change is communication, which includes oral, written, and even nonverbal forms. Without developed communication skills, the social worker interested in change will likely find it hard to move an organization in a positive direction. If information is power in organizations, then its access and manipulation is a prerequisite for attaining power. Conversely, an employee's impact as an effective change agent is severely diminished without the ability to compose lucid informational flyers, statements, memos, reports, e-mail messages, or even conduct organizational meetings. Written and oral communication skills continue to be an important currency in the organizational realm.

A set of organizational requisites frequently overlooked is the area of financial and accounting skills. Although many schools of social work have administrative tracks, few offer specific courses in accounting and financial management, despite the fact that social workers with major administrative responsibilities will undoubtedly have to tackle an array of budgetary functions. Moreover, even frontline social workers who want to influence organizational change may be required to understand budgetary processes in order to counter administrative claims about the lack of funds for training, perks, developmental leaves, and so on. Social workers trying to ensure that unions are run democratically may also be required to understand accounting principles in order to ascertain where and how union dues are being spent. Finally, social workers wanting to develop alternative social service agencies will undoubtedly need to understand budgetary functions such as fiscal projections, budgeting for overhead and staff salaries, and basic tax and accounting laws. Without fiscal and budgetary knowledge, social workers are reduced to passive participants in the dance of organizational change and workplace democracy. As long as fiscal skills remain within the knowledge boundaries of a select few, the organizational impact of frontline social workers will be minimal.

Social workers involved in organizational change must also possess a rudimentary knowledge of labor laws and labor relations. Apart from understanding national labor laws, social workers should be familiar also with the labor laws in a given state, city, or municipality. Moreover, processes like collective bargaining, arbitration, local grievance procedures, the structure of a bargaining unit, the role of union stewards, union certification, and the authority of the National Labor Relations Board in determining union elections and grievance procedures must also be understood. Social workers need to understand how to expand the scope of bargaining to include agency-level policy and decision-making processes. Social workers should also understand how to use union structures to negotiate items such as caseload size; health insurance; salary scales related to training, experience, and job requirements; and standardization of promotional procedures. Social workers should also understand the legal ways to neutralize management opposition to unionization. Finally, social workers interested in organizational change should understand the structure, function, and the nature of a labor agreement signed between a bargaining unit and an employer (Tambor, 1988).

To effect organizational change, social workers should be acquainted with the concepts of planned change, including ways of assessing the economic, political, and organizational forces in the environment, the interests and politics of colleagues and the differential influence each may have on organizational change, and the ability to analyze the internal forces for change within the organization. In addition, skills in planned change encompass knowledge of the various tactics available to employees, and how to choose an appropriate strategy to meet worker goals. Finally, skills in planned change include preparing the organization for change, as well as initiating and institutionalizing change (Brager & Holloway, 1978).

Employees seeking to institute change may emerge as leaders within their own organizations. Hence, to be effective, they must possess leadership skills related to organizing and mobilizing fellow workers. They should also understand how to motivate workers, identify other potential leaders, and build organizations. Other important skills in organizational change include more generalized social work skills such as problem solving, mediation, and macro skills related to community organization like negotiation, community development, social action, and bargaining.

CONCLUSION

As the fiscal crisis of the state has deepened, social workers have lost control over their daily labor (Fabricant & Burghardt, 1992). Accepted tenets of practice such as autonomy, discretion, self-determination, and independent practice have given way to more constricted frameworks emphasizing productivity and accountability. Bureaucratization and individualization are increasingly used as cost containment measures to erode rather than expand the professionalization of social services. Moreover, attempts to increase worker and agency efficiency, often under the rubric of accountability, are being designed to reduce the costs of social services. Unfortunately, these accountability measures often operate at the expense of delivering high quality social services (Fabricant & Burghardt, 1992). It is within this context that workers are deskilled. However, while the forces promoting the deskilling of social workers are potent, they are neither immutable nor must they inevitably lead to the proletarianization of social work. Fabricant and Burghardt (1992) observe that, "In some respects, these roles are not predetermined by the larger social and economic forces affecting the state" (p. 30).

Clients and social workers have clearly suffered from the loss of workplace control. While some social workers choose to lament this dilemma in a solitary way, others have organized into collective bodies to gain greater workplace power. For the latter group, public-sector unions and other organizational forms function as important vehicles in their attempt to regain workplace autonomy, fair wages, and the provision of quality and accountable services to clients and communities. However, traditional unionization may not be enough. To democratize the workplace, social workers may have to combine strategies such as traditional unionism with more innovative approaches that link struggle, growth, and invention. The democratization of the workplace is, in many ways, a mirror of the democratization of society. Both instances require analysis, innovation, struggle, and determination.

chapter **8**

Conclusion

American society is in a period of profound social transition, if not upheaval. Newspapers are filled with daily accounts of senseless personal and property crimes, most of which are directed at helpless victims. Crimes that are not random are often gang-related drive-by shootings, executions, and other forms of warfare. These crimes take a heavy toll. The National Center for Health Statistics reported that the firearm death rate for adolescents aged 15–19 rose to 23 per 100,000, the highest in America's history. From 1985 to 1990, the firearm death rate for male black teenagers tripled, reaching 105.3 deaths per 100,000 (Stoesz, 1996). The seven people killed in the St. Valentine's Day Massacre of the 1930s, an event that shocked the nation, is paralleled almost every weekend in large urban areas.

Some critics argue that high levels of urban violence indicate that society's threshold for social deviance is being ratcheted dramatically upward (Moynihan, 1993). Others point to society's willingness to respond to the violence simply by incarcerating people, usually the poor and people of color. In fact, too many poor African-American men who survive an increasingly violent world often end up in the prison system. In the 1980s approximately one in four African-American males between the ages of 20 and 30 was either in prison, on parole, or involved in some other way as an offender in the criminal justice system. By 1995, the figure had jumped dramatically to one in three, most of whom were in trouble with the law over drugs. It is ironic that a society so ambivalent about helping its least privileged members is so enthusiastic about incarcerating them at a rate almost unprecedented among nations.

Part of the problem lies in the retreat from a more inclusive vision of the public good. Years after enacting affirmative action policies and civil rights legislation, racism is again on the rise. California's Proposition 187 sought to deny Fourteenth Amendment protection to immigrant residents. Proposed legislative changes in affirmative action policy, backed by much of the U.S. Congress, would have effectively turned back the clock on racial equality. Moreover, survivalist and right-wing groups proliferate in a climate of public discourse filled with violence, hate, and antisocial rhetoric. The increase in racial intolerance is attendant with the rise in classism, as the "haves" continue to systematically exclude the poor from the matrix of power. As the ranks of the disenfranchised grow, Americans of all ilk become more frightened and confused.

The forces leading to the attack on public life and the disconcerting sense that the public good is becoming more exclusive and restrictive operates in other ways. Low public-assistance benefits ensure that almost 30 million Americans will live day-to-day with little hope for improvement. In many places, public schools fail to provide an education that will make students competitive in a keen international marketplace. The lack of accessible and affordable health care for many poor and working-class families is causing an increase in preventable diseases and a rise in wholly unnecessary deaths (Karger & Stoesz, 1994).

It seems that Americans are increasingly dividing into hostile camps: black against white, male against female, gay and lesbian against straight, city against suburb, the Northeast against the Sun Belt, and a white overclass against an increasingly angry and fearful working class threatened by redundancy and the fear of tumbling into poverty. In addition, much of the middle and upper classes have become so cynical about government's ability to protect them, that they isolate themselves into barricaded neighborhoods that resemble miniature nation-states. Walled off by high fences, private roads, private schools, and private recreational areas, the affluent prefer to invest in private security services rather than in publicly sponsored law enforcement. This development is especially troubling since one of the few agreed-upon principles between liberals and conservatives is the government's responsibility to insure personal safety.

SOCIAL DISLOCATION, THE GLOBAL ECONOMY, AND THE PUBLIC GOOD

Many of today's social problems have been exacerbated, if not created, by the centralization of power inherent in the global marketplace. First, the global economy has led to a shrinking tax base, more joblessness, greater insecurity in the workplace, higher numbers of people in poverty, and a climate in which the disparities between the overclass and the poor are growing. Corporations that once yielded to union pressure and provided workers with decent wages, job security, and benefits are being replaced by stateless corporations that repudiate any long-term obligations to their own workforce, let alone to the United States or the common good of the people. The costs of this global economy are borne by the working poor and by a middle class whose real wages are at best stagnant. Whatever robustness exists in the American economy rarely filters down to the lower reaches of the working class, and much less to a growing class of ultrapoor who are insulated from the effects of economic growth. According to Marc Miringoff, director of Fordham's Institute for Innovation in Social Policy, "We really have to begin to reassess the notion that the gross domestic product—the overall growth of the society—necessarily is going to produce improvements in the quality of life. . . . Because if we look at this data, particularly over time . . . it's kind of like a crocodile's jaw opening—the two lines, one going up and one going down" (quoted in Landsberg, 1995, p. 1C).

Instead of developing social policies to tame the negative features of the global economy, for almost three decades federal and state governments have shown scant commitment to improving community life. For example, the Clinton administration's 1993 proposed $16.3 billion stimulus package contained several urban aid programs: $1 billion for a summer youth employment program, $15 million for a National Service program, $2.5 billion for an urban Community Development Block Grant, and $423 million to support urban housing. The plan was defeated because of defections within his own party and a filibuster by Senator Bob Dole. The 1994 Clinton budget was Draconian in its makeup. After adjusting for inflation, appropriations for low-income housing programs fell $856 million below fiscal 1994 levels. Job training for the homeless was reduced from $13 million to $5 million. Funding for severely distressed public housing was cut from $799 million to $500 million (Stoesz, 1996). The 1995 budget promises to be even more punitive towards the poor. Under the guise of fiscal austerity, governmental "load-shedding" has both aggravated and stimulated the deterioration of America's cities and public infrastructure.

The state's retreat from progressive social policy is a retreat from social responsibility. Contrary to neoconservative dogma, the demands of the global economy require government to be more, rather than less, active in social affairs and in redirecting fiscal and human resources. The guiding principle behind governmental action must be to advance an inclusive and egalitarian vision of the public good. In the final analysis, the state is the only institution that has the resources necessary to rebuild America's neglected social and public infrastructure. While grassroots groups and local public life are essential for pushing government to address problems, ensure services, and support—or at least not crush—progressive social change, the state remains invaluable for funding and legitimizing social change. Moreover, voter cynicism of the political system will not subside until the state reestablishes its moral authority as an institution capable of representing the will of all its citizens. It is difficult to have public citizenship in a context where the very idea of government is doubted and vilified. Without a legitimate public sector there are no public citizens, only private consumers. Beneath current voter cynicism is a genuine desire for the state to assume a moral leadership that transcends elite self-interest. To accomplish this goal, the state must have the courage to define an inclusive and egalitarian public good that transcends simple political expediency.

An important element in restoring public citizenship and government responsiveness to community life is the creation of a progressive view of the common good. The civil rights movement teaches us that such a vision must address the economic, democratic, cultural, social, and spiritual dimensions of human existence. Any egalitarian framework for the common good must encompass human need for both material security and individual autonomy, including the need for adequate nutrition, health, suitable clothing and shelter, access to educational opportunities, as well as the need for autonomy, freedom, self-determination, and self-expression (Doyal & Gough, 1991).

The concept of a public good has long been debated in American political life, albeit often with different terminology. Because of society's class, racial, gender, and cultural divisions, the question inevitably becomes "whose public good is to be advanced?" The underlying motif in the current political debate is no different. For example, Clinton's 1992 presidential campaign slogan was Putting People First, which called for shaping a neoliberal vision of the public good to aid those who do the work, pay the taxes, raise the kids, and play by the rules. (Notice, for example, which groups were left out of this equation: the poor, unemployed, and deviants who don't play by the rules.) To accomplish this public good, Clinton called for a series of reforms including putting able-bodied public-assistance recipients to work, curbing excessive CEO salaries, closing tax loopholes on foreign companies operating in the United States, ending tax incentives that reward American companies relocating abroad, attaching strong labor and environmental standards to NAFTA, and toughening the U.S. trade stance toward Japan and China (Judis & Lind, 1995). Well into the fourth year of the Clinton presidency, little of that agenda had been realized.

On the other hand, "New Republicans" such as Newt Gingrich, Richard Armey, Phil Gramm, and Bob Dole, have argued that the public good is best advanced by a primitive antistatism that was as anachronistic in the late 1800s as it is today. Contrary to the premises of the 1994 "Contract with America," further crippling the national government will do little to return power to individuals or forge a common consensus around national social policy. Nor will the Contract bring stability to an increasingly fragile family structure torn by market forces, regardless of whether these families are traditional, nuclear or nontraditional families—is equally reflective of our contemporary era. A further weakening of the federal government will only strengthen the stranglehold that large corporations, banks, Wall Street brokers, and foreign governments with large investments in the United States have over the country (Judis & Lind, 1995). Even more cynically, neoconservatives believe they can further their vision of the public good by instigating a "culture war" that exploits differences over abortion, school prayer, homosexuality, women's rights, and affirmative action. While these efforts mobilize conservative and right-wing forces and appear on the surface to increase the discourse regarding public life, they actually diminish civic life since the essence of the neoconservative position is essentially antisocial, antidemocratic, and antipublic. In contrast to neoconservative and neoliberal dogma, advancing public life requires a stronger, not a weaker, national government. Only a strong federal government pushed from the grassroots by progressive movements, organizations, and agencies can reduce the growing disparity between the economic classes. In the end, a just public good is incompatible with large disparities in wealth and power, nor can it coexist with discrimination of any kind. Public life is the arena for addressing and struggling over these inequities and inequalities, and the public sector is an important part of public life.

As noted in the Introduction, society is clearly in a state of upheaval. However, the answer lies not in stitching inequality and oppression back together again, nor in supporting the neoconservative vision of public life, but in discovering and addressing what causes the social fabric to fray and what promotes social change—never a simple project. However, it is more feasible in a society where public life is rich, where public discourse regarding social problems is expansive and open to diverse opinions, and where society is committed to the improvement of conditions for all its members, not just the rich and powerful.

GETTING BACK OUT IN PUBLIC

The social conflict we have described is occurring just as many professions, including social work, are busying themselves with narrow professional concerns. Physicians worry about a loss of income and professional control even as larger numbers of people are without any form of health care. Prosecutorial and defense attorneys spend massive amounts of money and valuable court time defending high visibility criminal cases, while innocent defendants receive heavy sentences as the result of forced plea bargains, and guilty defendants walk the streets to perpetrate more crimes. Social workers are also guilty of pursuing narrow self-interests, including spending large amounts of time, money, and energy on licensure and third party reimbursement for private practitioners. Like most professions, social work is deflecting its social justice mission onto narrower professional issues. This trend is unfortunately occurring just as the social work profession is being pressured from without and struggling from within to find its identity and its niche. For social workers, this diversion is particularly problematic since it is the only profession that has the historical mandate to protect the poor and vulnerable.

Like other professionals, social workers have sometimes fallen victim to the belief that social change and the public good can only be advanced through individual moral reformation or by profound psychological insight. This belief is based on the idea that real institutional change must be preceded by individual change. It is a message embedded in popular psychology and self-awareness movements from Esalen to biofeedback, from transpersonal psychology to Enneagram, and from crystal-gazing to organizational and religious gurus. The personal search for "truth and wisdom" has led some social workers away from the inescapable truth that public life can only be promoted by redesigning institutions and by rethinking strategies for changing them.

Social workers can play a major role in advancing public life and social change. More than other professions, social workers understand the relationship between the environmental and the psychological side of human existence, especially since a core tenet of the profession is that human beings exist on the boundary between the social and the psychological. Given that political life is an inextricable part of social life, all good social work is therefore political at heart. As Reisch (1995) puts it:

> We need to discard the notions that partisanship and conflict are incompatible with professionalism. Whether we like it or not, whether we relish

combat or shy away from it, we are engaged now in an ideological and political war with individuals and groups who see us as the enemy. We have to give ourselves permission to vilify our opponents as they vilify us—not by engaging in name-calling or character assassination but through the targeted use of facts and by appealing to the best instincts in people. We need to become responsible extremists in the cause of social justice in order to move the center of the political debate back towards the progressive end of the political spectrum. (p. 4)

The promotion of public activism and a vision of an inclusive and egalitarian public good are principles by which social work can be organized. To accomplish this goal, social work practice at all levels must be linked to the macro context. Once contextualized, the rigid boundaries between micro, mezzo, and macro social work practice become permeable. Social workers involved in advocacy, community organization, legislative activity, social planning, and social policy analysis are enhancing the individual good just as surely as micro level practitioners. Relatedly, direct service work with individuals contributes to the development of more effective citizens and public life. In that sense, the level at which social workers practice is incidental to working toward social change. All good social work practice promotes changes at multiple levels. All good social work is concerned with developing the capacities of people for public action. This book has argued that contextualizing practice is one of the keys.

Getting out in public also means that social workers must advocate for social policies that provide increased interaction between the social classes and the diverse ethnic and racial groups that make up American society. Economic and social integration are necessary to further a progressive public good because they narrow the gap between social classes. Structural integration is also necessary if the tensions between social classes and cultural groups are to be reduced. However, structural integration must start from assisting the working class and the poor to wrest power and advantage from those who monopolize it. Real change cannot occur without social, political, and economic struggle.

A reconceptualized social work practice must be framed in a vision of public life, social change, and a progressive common good that unites oppressed classes and aggrieved groups. It must incorporate the needs of the disenfranchised and the middle class into a practical strategy for political action. Compromise and mediation are essential to any transclass alliance. We do not, however, wish to suggest that social workers should avoid or undermine social conflict. On the contrary, social conflict is an essential component in the development of a more inclusive and progressive public life. To be part of public life is to engage difference, even among allies. Lesbian activist Julia Penelope underscores the value of disagreement and criticism for building strong communities:

When we disagree, when we criticize other Lesbians, we're sharing ourselves and our own ideas and opinions. Disagreement isn't only a way of affirming ourselves; we also affirm the significance of the individuals we criticize. Arguing and disagreeing are our ways of paying attention to the ideas and beliefs of others. . . . Silence often signals indifference. What we don't find worth responding to, we ignore. (Quoted in Kitzinger & Perkins, 1993, p. 151)

As noted earlier, all good social work is concerned with developing capacities for public action and the willingness to engage in conflict. Dealing with differences in public is an important part of the process of social change and social action.

Macro practice must become an integral part of social work's attempt to rebuild public life and in its support for the struggle to form social movements around organizations, communities, agencies, and identity. But macro practice must go beyond a concern with community and identity politics to reconnect with class oppression and struggles concerning issues of political economy. To accomplish this goal, macro practice must be broadened to include, and go beyond, traditional community organization. Communities are part of the whole, the sites of primary service delivery and grassroots organizing. But the concept of getting out in public seeks to unite local efforts in both the larger social struggle of public life and the larger vision of a public good, a vision that includes—not excludes and fragments—social groups and social change efforts.

This project will require social workers to develop a comprehensive theory and skills base that changes how and what is presently being taught in most schools of social work, including the development of core skills in structural theory and analysis, ideological competence, critical consciousness, political social work, coalition building, fundraising, technological proficiency, and cultural competence and diversity. At the heart of these new skills is the explicit politicization of social work practice.

Social work research is also an important component of social change. To use research effectively, social workers must accept its political character and utilize it as a tool for advancing social change in a world hostile to it. Implicit in this formulation is the redesigning of social work research around five principles that help contextualize and politicize it: (1) politicizing the personal through connecting individual problems to the political economy, (2) evaluating research on its potential to further the public good, (3) making certain that research findings are understandable to lay people, (4) incorporating communities and individuals directly into the research process, and (5) advancing public life and social change by actively engaging in public discourse. This goal can only be accomplished by changing the rules of academic life and by evaluating research not solely on its methodological merit but also on its potential for affecting social change. A better balance must be reached between methodological concerns and social commitment.

Engagement in public action is not only played out on the larger canvas, but also in the everyday world of agency life. Because most social workers are employed by social agencies, the most immediate venue for integrating social change into social work practice is often the workplace. Much of the current organizational developments in human services center around implementing various cost containment measures designed to rationalize social services. Often, these fiscal measures erode social services and further the deskilling of social workers. Not surprisingly, clients suffer from a reduction in benefits and from the loss of workplace control by social workers. To regain control over their working environment, social workers will have to devise strategies that win more power for them and their clients while democratizing the workplace. This may require social workers to combine traditional unionism with more innovative approaches encompassing struggle, growth, and invention.

Curiously, we now conclude this book about contemporary changes and the future prospects of social work with a turn to the past. This glance is necessary since those who seek to undermine the social justice objectives of social work want to divorce us from our history, to rewrite our past as if it were a horror from which we need now escape. Social history has become hotly contested political terrain. "Public memory is contested memory," argues Michael Berenbaum (1995), director of the U.S. Holocaust Research Institute. "How the decade of the '80s is remembered is contested memory; how the decade of the '60s is remembered is contested memory. Part of our political struggle in the United States is how these two decades are remembered" (p. E5). Part of the political struggle in social work is also how to remember its past. To be effective in the struggle for social justice, social workers must have one eye on the past and the other on the future. We must build a macro practice that is rooted in both the history of the profession and in the realities facing social workers today, clearly a daunting task.

The best traditions in social work encompass an historic commitment to enhance public life and social change. Just as the development of critical contextualization is an ongoing and dynamic process, the understanding of public life must reach back into the past in order to understand its prospects for the future. The collective historical memory of the social work profession reveals not only that the causes of social problems lie in institutionalized inequalities and social policies and in the conservative practices within the profession that reinforced them, but the fact that today we stand on the broad shoulders of the progressive social workers who preceded us. Such a realization can empower contemporary efforts. Consider the experience of social workers such as Jane Addams, founder of Hull House and Nobel Prize-winning peace activist; Mary van Kleeck, social researcher and activist; Bertha Reynolds, leading thinker and author in progressive social work; Helen Keller, human rights and socialist activist; and Jacob Fisher, editor of the former *Social Work Today* and an important social work union organizer in the 1930s, to name but a few. While these activists are acknowledged in history books, countless others have worked without public acclaim in cities and towns throughout the nation, helping clients and affecting social change. The very knowledge of their work informs how we contextualize practice, get out in public, engage in social change, and develop a progressive vision of the public good. It also offers connection, legitimacy, and support to current social workers involved in social change.

Social work has both an extensive historical experience to draw upon and a collective memory of social change and social justice upon which to build. Contextualizing the past means not always having to reinvent the wheel when responding to the latest attacks by political forces or demagogues. It also means grounding contemporary struggles in a knowledge and understanding of prior struggles, battles, debates, and the personal experiences of the forbears of the profession. The process of contextualizing social work practice includes remembering those people and groups upon which our work stands. We are not alone. Nor are we the first to confront and challenge difficult eras. Social change is a long and difficult process. One of the keys to public life is recognizing that a baton is passed to each of us. Building a collective memory of the past helps effect social change in the present. The larger project of rebuilding progressive public life and countering the pernicious aspects of our contemporary private world will take considerable energy and time. Because social change is not a short-term project but a life-long process, all progressive social work is invaluable and helps plant the seeds of social change.

We hope that students will not be daunted by the obstacles and tasks laid out in this book. Nor should students think they can do everything. On the one hand, this book offers a means for contextualizing social work, enhancing social change, and reforming social work education and practice. On the other hand, it is meant as a primer to help the process, not a bible that asks readers to live up to all its parts.

Social workers should be committed to the cause of social justice. Given that commitment, do what you can—help clients, foment social change, plant the seeds for more public action, and pass on your knowledge and skills. These acts rebuild public life and ultimately help clients, both now and in the future. But because progressive social change is a long-term project requiring the work of millions of people, know that your work cannot be all inclusive. No one really knows the exact formula for building highly effective social movements; they erupt out of the conditions of an era. One of those conditions, however, is the groundwork laid by organizations, neighborhoods, agencies, and social activists. Because you are not seeing dramatic results does not mean that your efforts won't bear fruit in the long run. Effective social change requires a coalescing of efforts and a broad, comprehensive view of a progressive public world. Work toward those ends, but don't be disempowered by them. Good social work is social change, which in turn, is essential to creating a just public society and a truly social world.

References

Abramovitz, M. (1993). Should all social workers be educated for social change? *Pro. Journal of Social Work Education*, (29), 6–11, 17–18.

—— . (1986). The privatization of the welfare state. *Social Work, 31*(July–August), 257–64.

Addams, J. (1922). *Peace and bread in a time of war*. New York: Macmillan.

—— . (1911). *Newer ideals of peace*. New York: Macmillan.

—— . (1907). *Democracy and social ethics*. New York: Macmillan.

Akins, R. E. (1985). Empowerment: Mastering independence of the older adult. *Aging Network News, 11*(5), 10–12.

Alexander, L. B. (1980). Professionalization and unionization: Compatible after all? *Social Work, 25*(6), 476–482.

Alexander, L. B., Lichtenberg, P., & Brunn, D. (1980). Social workers in unions: A survey. *Social Work, 25*(3), 216–223.

Alinsky, S. D. (1971). *Rules for radicals*. New York: Vintage/Random House.

Allen, J. (1993). Friends and neighbors: Knowledge and campaigning in London. In R. Fisher & J. Kling (Eds.), *Mobilizing the community* (pp. 223–245). Newbury Park, CA: Sage.

Allen, J. L. (1993). Big gap found in home insurance coverage. *Chicago Tribune*, (February 5), 12.

Alvarez, S. E. (1993). "Deepening" democracy: Popular movement networks, constitutional reform, and radical urban regimes in contemporary Brazil. In R. Fisher & J. Kling (Eds.), *Mobilizing the community* (pp. 191–219). Newbury Park, CA: Sage.

Amin, S. (1990). The social movements in the periphery. In S. Amin, et al. (Eds.), *Transforming the revolution: Social movements and the world-system* (pp. 80–105). New York: Monthly Review Press.

Amin, S., et al. (Eds.). (1990). *Transforming the revolution: Social movements and the world-system*. New York: Monthly Review Press.

Anderson, M. (1980). Welfare reform. In P. Duignan & A. Rabushka (Eds.), *The United States in the 1980s* (pp. 171–176). Stanford, CA: Hoover Institution.

Annis, S. (1987). Reorganization at the grassroots: Its origins and meaning. *Grassroots Development,* (11), 21–25.

Applied Research Center. (1993). Research for social action. Conference held at the University of California–Berkeley, July 16–18.

Aronowitz, S. (1973). *False promises.* New York: McGraw-Hill.

Atlas, J. (1995). The counter counterculture. *New York Times,* (February 12), 32–38, 54, 61–65.

Austin, D. M. (1976). Research and social work: Educational paradoxes and possibilities. *Journal of Social Service Research, 2*(4), 170–181.

Austin, M. J. (1990a). The intellectual origins roots of community organizing. In N. Betten & M. J. Austin (Eds.), *The roots of community organizing, 1917–1939* (pp. 16–31). Philadelphia: Temple University Press.

Austin, M. J., & Betten, N. (1990b). The roots of community organizing: An introduction. In N. Betten & M. J. Austin (Eds.), *The roots of community organizing, 1917–1939* (pp. 3–15). Philadelphia: Temple University Press.

Austin, M. J., & Lowe, J. I. (Eds.). (1994). *Controversial issues in communities and organizations* (pp. 86–97). Boston: Allyn & Bacon.

Bardill, D. (1993). Should all social workers be educated for social change? *Con. Journal of Social Work Education,* (29), 11–17.

Barnekov, T., Boyle, R., & Rich, D. (1989). *Privatism and urban policy in Britain and the United States.* New York: Oxford University Press.

Barnet, R. J. (1994). Lords of the global economy. *The Nation,* (December 19), 754–757.

Bell, D. (1993). *Communitarianism and its critics.* New York: Oxford University Press.

Bellah, R., et al. (1991). *The good society.* New York: Knopf.

Bellah, R., Madsen, R., Sullivan, W., Swidler, A., & Tipton, S. (1985). *Habits of the heart: Individualism and commitment in American life.* New York: Harper & Row.

Benedetto, R. (1992). A new approach to nation's problems. Interview with Amitai Etzioni. *USA Today,* (April 23), 13A.

Berenbaum, M. (1995). Quoted in G. Niebuhr, Whose memory lives when the last survivor dies? *New York Times,* (January 29), E5.

Berman, M. (1988). *All that is solid melts into air.* New York: Pantheon.

Block, F., Cloward, R., Ehrenreich, B., & Piven, F. F. (Eds.). (1987). *The mean season: The attack on the welfare state.* New York: Pantheon.

Bobo, K., Kendall, J., & Max, S. (1991). *Organize.* Washington, D.C.: Seven Locks Press.

Boddy, T. (1992). Underground and overhead: Building the analogous city. In Sorkin (1992), pp. 123–153.

Bookchin, M. (1987). *The rise of urbanization and the decline of citizenship.* San Francisco: Sierra Club Books.

Boyte, H. (1992). The pragmatic ends of popular politics. In C. Calhoun (Ed.), *Habermas and the public sphere.* Cambridge, MA: MIT Press.

——— . (1989). *Commonwealth: A return to citizen politics.* Chicago: Free Press.

——— . (1981). *The backyard revolution.* Philadelphia: Temple University Press.

Boyte, H., & Riessman, F. (Eds.). (1986). *The new populism: The politics of empowerment.* Philadelphia: Temple University Press.

Boyte, H., Booth, H., & Max, S. (1986). *Citizen action and the new American populism.* Philadelphia: Temple University Press.

Brager, G., & Holloway, S. (1978). *Changing human service organizations.* New York: The Free Press.

Brecher, J. (1993). Global village or global pillage. *The Nation,* (December 6), 685–688.

Brecher, J., & Costello, T. (1994). *Global village or global pillage: Economic reconstruction from the bottom up*. Boston: South End Press.

——— . (1992). A long history of controlling workers. *Labor Page*, (October/November), 72.

——— . [1990). *Building bridges: The emerging coalition of labor and community*. New York: Monthly Review Press.

Brecher, J., Childs, J., & Cutler, J. (Eds). (1993). *Global visions: Beyond the new world order*. Boston: South End Press.

Bronner, S. E. (1990). *Socialism unbound*. London: Routledge.

Burghardt, S. (1982). *The other side of organizing*. Rochester, VT: Schenkman Books.

Burghardt, S., & Fabricant, M. (1987). Radical social work. *Encyclopedia of social work* (18th ed., Vol. 2, pp. 455–462). Silver Spring, MD: NASW Press.

Capek, S., & Gilderbloom, J. (1992). *Community versus commodity*. New York: State University of New York Press.

Carley, M. (1981). *Social measurement and social indicators*. London: Allen & Unwin.

Carniol, B. (1992). Structural social work. *Journal of Progressive Human Services*, (3), 1–20.

——— . (1990). Social work and the labor movement. In B. Wharf (Ed.), *Social work and social change in Canada*. Toronto: McClelland & Stewart.

Carol, J. D. (1987). Public administration in the third century of the constitution: Supply side management, privatization, or public investment? *Public Administration Review*, (Jan/Feb), 76–82.

Carr, E. H. (1987). *What is history?* London: Penguin.

Castells, M. (1983). *The city and the grassroots*. Berkeley: University of California Press.

Chambers, C. A. (1992). "Uphill all the way": Reflections on the course and study of welfare history. *Social Service Review*, (December), 492–504.

——— . (1986). Toward a redefinition of social welfare history. *Journal of American History*, 73(September), 407–433.

——— . (1967). *Seedtime of reform: American social service and social action, 1918–1933*. Ann Arbor, MI: University of Michigan Press.

Chaney, D. (1994). *The cultural turn*. London: Routledge.

Cloward, R. (1994). Should charismatic leaders be recruited by grassroots organizations to promote social change? Yes. In M. J. Austin & J. I. Lowe (Eds.), *Controversial issues in communities and organizations* (pp. 23–27). Boston: Allyn & Bacon.

Coates, J. (1992). Ideology and education for social work practice. *Journal of Progressive Human Services, 3*(2), 15–30.

Cocks, J. (1989). *The oppositional imagination*. London: Routledge.

Cohen, B. (1994). Organizational learning and change in a public child welfare agency. *Administration in Social Work, 1*(18), 22–36.

——— . (1992). Quality of working life in a public child welfare agency. *Journal of Health and Human Resources Administration, 15*(2), 130–152.

Compton, B., & Galaway, B. (1994). *Social work processes*. Pacific Grove, CA: Brooks/Cole.

Cooper, S. (1977). Social work: A dissenting profession? *Social Work*, (22), 360–367.

Corbridge, S. (1991). Third world development. *Progress in Human Geography*, (15), 311–321.

Cortes, E. (1993). Politics of social capital. *The Texas Observer*, (January 29), 16–17.

Costin, L., Karger, H. J., & Stoesz, D. (1996). *The politics of child abuse in America*. New York: Oxford University Press.

Cox, E., & Parsons, R. (1994). *Empowerment oriented social work practice with the elderly*. Pacific Grove, CA: Brooks/Cole.

Cox, K. (1988). The politics of turf and the question of class. In J. Wolch, J. & M. Dear (Eds.), *Power of geography: How territory shapes social life* (pp. 61–90). New York: Routledge.

Crawford, M. (1992). The world in a shopping mall. In Sorkin (1992), pp. 31–30.

Creech, B. (1994). *The five pillars of TQM*. New York: Dutton.

Dalton, R., & Keuchler, M. (Eds.). (1990). *Challenging the political order: New social and political movements in western democracies*. New York: Oxford University Press.

Daley, J. M., & Netting, F. E. (1994). Is community organization dead and is the future organizational practice? No. In M. J. Austin & J. I. Lowe (Eds.), *Controversial issues in communities and organizations* (pp. 103–110). Boston: Allyn & Bacon.

Davis, A. (1967). *Spearheads for reform*. New York: Oxford University Press.

Davis, M. (1992). *City of quartz*. New York: Vintage.

de Tocqueville, A. (1969). *Democracy in America*. New York: Doubleday, Anchor Books.

Dear, R. B., & Patti, R. J. (1982). Legislative advocacy: Seven effective tactics. In M. Mahaffey & J. W. Hanks (Eds.), *Practical politics: Social work and social responsibility* (pp. 99–117). Silver Spring, MD: NASW Press.

Delgado, G. (1986). *Organizing the movement: The roots and growth of ACORN*. Philadelphia: Temple University Press.

————. (1994). *Beyond the politics of place: New directions for community organizing in the 1990s*. Oakland, CA: Applied Research Center.

Deming, W. E. (1986). *Out of the crisis*. New York: Random House.

Democratic Leadership Council. (1990). *The New Orleans declaration*. Washington, D.C.: Democratic Leadership Council.

DiNitto, D. (1991). *Social welfare: Politics and public policy* (3rd ed.). Englewood Cliffs, NJ: Prentice Hall.

DiNitto, D. M., & Dye, T. R. (1987). *Social welfare: Politics and public policy*. Englewood Cliffs, NJ: Prentice Hall.

Downing, J., Fasano, R., Friedland, P. A., McCullough, M. A., Mizrahi, T., & Shapiro, J. J. (1991). Computers for social change: Introduction. In J. Downing, R. Fasano, P. A. McCullough, M. A. Mizrahi, & J. J. Shapiro (Eds.), *Computers for social change and community organizing* (pp. 1–8). New York: Haworth Press.

Doyal, L., & Gough, I. (1991). *A theory of human need*. New York: Guilford Press.

Dunham, A. (1972). *The new community organization*. New York: T. Y. Crowell Co.

Dunkerley, D. (1988). Historical methods and organizational analysis: The case of a naval dockyard. In A. Bryman (Ed.), *Doing research in organizations* (pp. 82–95). London: Routledge.

Durning, A. (1989). Action at the grassroots: Fighting poverty and environmental decline. *Worldwatch Paper, 88*(January), 1–70.

Easterbrook, G. (1986). Ideas move nations. *Atlantic Monthly*, (January), 60–76.

Eley, G. (1992). Nations, publics, and political cultures: Placing Habermas in the nineteenth century. In C. Calhoun (Ed.), *Habermas and the public sphere* (pp. 340–354). Cambridge, MA: MIT Press.

Ellsworth, C., et al. (1982). Toward a feminist model of planning. In S. Vandiver & A. Weick, *Women, power, and change* (pp. 151–153). Silver Spring, MD: National Association of Social Workers.

Elshtain, J. B. (1994). *Democracy on trial*. New York: Basic Books.

Elton, G. R. (1967). *The practice of history*. London: Routledge & Kegan Paul.

Epstein, B. (1993). The Bay Area movement against the Gulf War. In R. Fisher and J. Kling (Eds.), *Mobilizing the community* (pp. 291–318). Newbury Park, CA: Sage.

————. (1990). Rethinking social movement theory. *Socialist Review, 90*(Jan.–Mar.), 35–65.

Erlich, J. L., & Rivera, F. G. (1994). Should today's community organizer use the tactics handed down from earlier generations? Yes. In M. J. Austin & J. I. Lowe (Eds.), *Controversial issues in communities and organizations* (pp. 112–127). Boston: Allyn & Bacon.

Esping-Andersen, G. (1990). The three political economies of the welfare state. *International Journal of Sociology, 20*(Fall), 93–123.

Etzioni, A. (Ed.). (1995). *New communitarian thinking: Persons, virtues, institutions, communities.* Charlottesville & London: University Press of Virginia.

――― . (1993). *The spirit of community: Rights, responsibilities, and the communitarian agenda.* New York: Crown Publishers.

Evans, S., & Boyte, H. (1986). *Free social spaces: The sources of democratic change in America.* New York: Harper & Row.

――― . (1979). *Personal politics.* New York: Vintage Books.

Evers, A., & Woolman, H. (1986). *Big city politics: New patterns and orientations on the local level of the welfare state.* Vienna: Eurosocial Research Papers.

Fabricant, M., & Burghardt, S. (1992). *The welfare state crisis and the transformation of social service work.* Armonk, New York: M. E. Sharpe.

Farber, H., & Kreuger, A. (1993). Union membership in the United States: The decline continues. In B. Kaufman & M. Kleiner (Eds.), *Employee representation: Alternatives and future directions* (pp. 105–134). Madison, WI: Industrial Relations Research Association.

Finn, J. (1994). The promise of participatory research. *Journal of Progressive Human Services, 5*(2), 25–42.

Fisher, J. (1980). *The response of social work to the Depression.* Cambridge, MA: Schenkman.

――― . (1936). *The history of the rank and file, 1931–6.* New York: New York School of Philanthropy.

Fisher, R. (1995). Political social work. *Journal of Social Work Education, 31,* 194–203.

――― . (1994). *Let the people decide* (2nd ed.). New York: Twayne Publishers.

――― . (1993). Grass-roots organizing worldwide: Common ground, historical roots, and the tension between democracy and the state. In R. Fisher & J. Kling (Eds.), *Mobilizing the community* (pp. 3–27). Newbury Park, CA: Sage.

――― . (1992). Organizing in the modern metropolis. *Journal of Urban History, 18,* 222–237.

――― . (1984). *Let the people decide.* Boston: Twayne Publishers.

Fisher, R., & Kling, J. (1994). Community organization and new social movement theory. *Journal of Progressive Human Services,* (5), 5–24.

――― . (Eds.). (1993). *Mobilizing the community.* Newbury Park, CA: Sage.

――― . (1991). Popular mobilization in the 1990s: Prospects for the new social movements. *New Politics, 3*(Winter), 71–84.

――― . (1987). Leading the people: Two approaches to the role of ideology in community Organizing. *Radical America, 21*(1), 31–46.

Fisher, J., et al. (1994). Empowerment-based curriculum design: Building a program in political social work. In L. Gutierrez & P. Nurius (Eds.), *Education and research for empowerment practice* (pp. 127–136). Seattle, WA: Center for Policy and Practice Research.

Flacks, R. (1990). The revolution of citizenship. *Social Policy,* (21), 37–50.

Floud, R. G. (1985). History. In A. Kuper & J. Kuper, (Eds.), *The social science encyclopedia* (pp. 358–361). London: Routledge & Kegan Paul.

Foucault, M. (1982). The subject and power. In H. Dreyfus & P. Rabinow (Eds.), *Michel Foucault* (pp. 208–226). Chicago: University of Chicago Press.

Frank, A. G., & Fuentes, M. (1990). Civil democracy: Social movements in recent world history. In S. Amin, et al. (Eds.), *Transforming the revolution: Social movements and the world-system,* (pp. 200–222). New York: Monthly Review Press.

Freedman, S. G. (1993). *Upon this rock: The miracles of a black church*. New York: Harper-Collins.

Freedman, S. G., & Medoff, J. (1984). *What do unions do?* New York: Basic Books.

Freire, P. (1985). *The politics of education: Culture, power and liberation*. Boston: Bergin & Garvey.

———. (1970). *Pedagogy of the oppressed*. New York: Seabury Press.

Freudenberger, H. (1974). Staff burnout. *Journal of Social Issues, 30*(Winter), 459–465.

Friedman, M. (1962). *Capitalism and freedom*. Chicago: University of Chicago Press.

Friedman, T. (1993). The designs behind the surprises. *New York Times*, (November 28), Sec. 4/1, 3.

Friedrich, O. (1990). Freed from greed? *Time*, (January 1), 58–60.

Future of the American Workplace. (1993). Conference handouts. Washington, D.C.

Geismar, L. L. (1982). Comments on the obsolete scientific imperative in social work research. *Social Service Review, 56*(2), 311–312.

George, V., & Wilding, P. (1976). *Ideology and social welfare*. London: Routledge & Kegan Paul.

Gil, D. (1984). Reversing dynamics of violence by transforming work. *Journal of International and Comparative Social Welfare, 1*(Fall), 5–17

———. (1981). *Unraveling social policy*. Boston: Schenkman.

Gilbert, N., Specht, S., & Terrell, P. (1993). *Dimensions of social welfare policy*. Englewood Cliffs, NJ: Prentice Hall.

Gilder, G. (1981). *Wealth and poverty*. New York: Basic Books.

Gilligan, C. (1982). *In a different voice*. Cambridge, MA: Harvard University Press.

Glaser, B. G., & Strauss, A. L. (1967). *The discovery of grounded theory: Strategies for quantitative research*. Chicago: Aldine Publishing.

Glazer, N. (1984). The social policy of the Reagan administration. *Public Interest*, (Spring), 85–99.

Glennester, H., & Midgley, J. (Eds.). (1991). *The radical right and the welfare state*. London: Wheatsheaf.

Goffman, E. (1965). *Asylums*. New York: Harper & Row.

Gortner, H., Mahler, J., & Nicholson, J. (1987). *Organization theory: A public perspective*. Chicago: Dorsey Press.

Gough, I. (1979). *The political economy of the welfare state*. London: Macmillan Press.

Gray, J. (1995). Does democracy have a future. *New York Times*, (January 22), Sect. 7/1, 24–25.

Greever, B. (1972). *Tactical investigations for people struggles*. Chicago: Midwest Academy.

Grinker, W. J. (1987). *Memorandum* to Stanley Brezenoff, First Deputy Mayor, Human Resources Administration, January 29, pp. 6–7.

Grosser, C. (1976). *New directions in community organization: From enabling to advocacy*. New York: Free Press.

Gulf Coast Tenants Organization. (n.d.). A short history of the Gulf Coast Tenants Organization. 1866 W. Grayson St., New Orleans, LA, 70119.

Gummer, B. (1988). Managing in the public sector: Privatization, policy deadlock, and the erosion of public authority. *Administration in Social Work*, (12), 27–25.

Gutierrez, L. M. (1990). Working with women of color: An empowerment perspective. *Social Work*, (35), 149–154.

Gutierrez, L. M., & Lewis, E. A. (1995). A feminist perspective on organizing with women of color. In F. G. Rivera & J. L. Ehrlich (Eds.), *Community organizing in a diverse society* (2nd ed.) (pp. 95–112). Boston: Allyn & Bacon.

———. (1992). A feminist perspective on organizing with women of color. In F. G. Rivera & J. L. Ehrlich, *Community organizing in a diverse society* (pp. 113–132). Boston: Allyn & Bacon.

Gutierrez, L. M., & Nurius, P. (Eds.). (1994). *Education and research for empowerment practice.* Seattle: Center for Policy and Practice Research, University of Washington.

Gutierrez, L. M., et al. (1992). Improving the human condition through empowerment practice. Paper presented at the NASW/IFSW World Assembly.

Gutman, H. G. (1977). *Work, culture and society in industrializing America.* New York: Vintage.

Habermas, J. (1989). *The structural transformation of the public sphere.* Boston: Harvard University Press.

Hamer, F. L. (1992). Jointness at GM: The cruel hoax. *Labor Page,* (October/November), 70.

Harney, K. (1992). While FHA gushes red ink mortgage crusaders see red. *San Francisco Examiner,* (June 7), p. C6.

Harrington, M. (1984). *The new American poverty.* New York: Basic Books.

———. (1962). *The other America.* New York: Penguin.

Harvey, D. (1989). *The condition of postmodernity.* Cambridge, MA: Basil Blackwell.

———. (1985). *Studies in the history and theory of capitalist urbanization.* Baltimore: Johns Hopkins University Press.

Harwood, R. C. (1991). *Citizen and politics: A view from mainstreet America.* New York: The Kettering Foundation, 1991.

Haworth, G. O. (1984). Social work research, practice, and paradigms. *Social Service Review, 58*(3), 343–357.

Haynes, K. S., & Mickelson, J. S. (1991). *Affecting change: Social workers in the political arena.* White Plains, NY: Longman.

———. (1985). *Politics and social policy: The hidden power base* (2nd ed.). Paper presented at the Council on Social Work Education, Annual Program Meeting, Kansas City, March.

Heckscher, C. (1994). Beyond contract bargaining: Partnerships, persuasion, and power. *Social Policy, 25*(2), 19–29.

———. (1988). *The new unionism.* New York: Basic Books.

Heinemann, M. B. (1981). The obsolete scientific imperative in social work research. *Social Service Review, 55*(3), 370–380.

Hergenroeder, R. (1994). *Making power visible.* Unpublished paper. Graduate School of Social Work, University of Houston, Houston, TX.

Hill, E. (1990). The S&L bailout. *Challenge,* (33), 40–56.

Homan, M. S. (1994). *Promoting community change: Making it happen in the real world.* Pacific Grove, CA: Brooks/Cole.

Hooyman, N. R., & Bricker-Jenkins, M. (Eds.). (1986). *Not for women only: Social work practice for a feminist future.* Silver Spring, MD: National Association of Social Workers.

Hopkins, H. (1936). *Spending to save: The complete story of relief.* Seattle, WA: University of Washington Press.

Hudson, W. H. (1982). Comments on the scientific imperative in social work research and practice. *Social Service Review, 56*(2), 246–258.

———. (1978). First axioms of treatment. *Social Work, 23*(January), 60–66.

Hyde, C. (1992). The ideational system of social movement agencies: An examination of feminist health centers. In Y. Hasenfeld (Ed.), *Human services as complex organizations* (pp. 121–144). Newbury Park, CA: Sage.

——— . (1989). A feminist model for macro-practice: Promises and problems. *Administration in Social Work*, (13), 145–181.

Jacoby, R. (1987). *The last intellectuals*. New York: Basic Books.

Jansson, B. (1988). *The reluctant welfare state*. Belmont, CA: Wadsworth.

Jayaratne, S., & Chess, W. E. (1984). Job satisfaction, burnout, and turnover: A national study. *Social Work, 29*(Sept/Oct), 442–452.

Jayaratne, S., Sacks, M. L., & Chess, C. (1991) Private practice may be good for your health and well-being. *Social Work, 36*(May), 221–232.

Jayaratne, S., Siefert, K., & Chess, W. (1988). Private and agency practitioners: Some data and observations. *Social Service Review, 62*(June), 325–338.

Johansson, S. (1976). "Herstory" as history: A new field or another fad? In B. A. Carroll (Ed.), *Liberating women's history*. Normal, IL: Illinois University Press.

Johnson, M. (1992). A latter-day Martin Luther. *Time*, (August 24), 37.

Judd, D. (1994). Enclosing the commons of the public city. In H. Liggett & D. Perry (Eds.), *Representing the city*. Newbury Park, CA: Sage.

Judge, C. (1995). Soul men. *In These Times*, (January 23), 35.

Judis, J. B., & Lind, M. (1995). For a new nationalism. *The New Republic*, (March 27), 19–27.

Kahn, S. (1994). *How people get power*. Washington, D.C.: NASW Press.

——— . (1991). *Organizing*. Silver Spring, MD: NASW Press.

Kallick, D. D. (1994). Toward a new unionism. *Social Policy, 25*(2), 2–6.

Karger, H. J. (1995). *The public good and the welfare state in Africa*. Paper presented at the School of Social Work, Harare, Zimbabwe, May 11.

——— . (1988). *Social workers and labor unions*. New York: Greenwood Press.

——— . (1984). The early unionization movement in social work, 1934–1947. *Social Development Issues, 8*(Winter), 73–78.

——— . (1983a). Reclassification and social work: Is there a future in public welfare for the trained social worker? *Social Work, 28*(November-December), 427–432.

——— . (1983b). Science, research, and social work: Who controls the profession? *Social Work, 28*(3), 200–205.

——— . (1981). Burnout as alienation. *Social Service Review, 55*(June), 270–283.

Karger, H. J., & Stoesz, D. (1994). *American social welfare policy: A pluralist approach* (2nd ed.). White Plains, NY: Longman.

Kasarda, J. (1988). Jobs, migration and the emerging urban mismatches. In M. Geary & L. Lynn (Eds.), *Urban change and poverty* (pp. 140–178). Washington, D.C.: National Academy Press.

Katz, J. (1980). *Action research: A guide to resources*. New Orleans: ACORN.

Katz, M. (1986). *In the shadow of the poorhouse*. New York: Basic Books.

Kauffman, L. A. (1992). The left attacks identity politics. *Village Voice*, (June 30), 20.

——— . (1990). Democracy in a postmodern world. *Social Policy*, (Fall), 6–11.

Keefe, T. (1980). Empathy, skill, and critical consciousness. *Social Casework*, (Sept.), 30–31.

Kirzner, M. L. (1985). *Public welfare unions and public assistance policy: A case study of the Pennsylvania Social Services Union*. Doctoral dissertation, University of Pennsylvania.

Kitzinger, C., & Perkins, R. (1993). *Changing our minds: Lesbian feminism and psychology*. New York: New York University Press.

Kleinkauf, C. (1982). Running for office: A social worker's experience. In M. Mahaffey & J. W. Hanks (Eds.), *Practical politics: Social work and social responsibility* (pp. 181–194). Silver Spring, MD: National Association of Social Workers.

Kling, J. (1993). Complex society/Complex cities: New social movements and the restructuring of urban space. In R. Fisher & J. Kling (Eds.), *Mobilizing the community* (pp. 28–51). Newbury Park, CA: Sage.

Kling, J., & Fisher, R. (1992). *New social movements, community organizing, and the condition of post modernity*. Paper presented at First Annual Conference on the Integration of Social Science and Social Work, University of Michigan, 1992.

Konopka, G. (1958). *Eduard C. Lindeman and social work philosophy*. Minneapolis, MN: University of Minnesota Press.

Kramer, R., & Specht, H. (1983). *Readings in community organization practice* (3rd ed.). Englewood Cliffs, NJ: Prentice Hall.

Kwasi, A. (1983). Impact of unionism on pension fringes. *Industrial Relations* (22), 419–425.

Laclau, E., & Mouffe, C. (1985). *Hegemony and socialist strategy: Toward a social democratic politics*. London: Verso.

Laliberty, R., & Christopher, W. I. (1986). *Health care labor relations: A guide for the '80s*. Owing Mills, MD: National Health Publishing Co.

Lamb, R. (1952). Suggestions for a study of your hometown. *Human Organization*, (Summer), 45–56.

Landsberg, M. (1995). Nation's social health declined in '93. *Houston Chronicle*, (October 16), 1C & 2C.

Lane, R. (1939). The field of community organization. In H. R. Knight (Ed.), *Proceedings*, National Conference of Social Work (pp. 27–59). New York: Columbia University Press.

Lappé, F. M., & Dubois, P. M. (1994). *The quickening of America: Rebuilding our nation, remaking our lives*. San Francisco: Jossey-Bass.

Lasch, C. (1991). *True and only heaven*. New York: Norton.

———— . (1978). *The culture of narcissism*. New York: Norton.

Lash, S., & Urry, J. (1987). *The end of organized capitalism*. Oxford: Basil Blackwell.

Leahore, B., & Cates, J. (1985). Use of historical methods in social work research. *Social Work Research and Abstracts, 15,* 22–27.

LeComte, R. (1990). Connecting private troubles and public issues. In B. Wharf (Ed.), *Social work and social change in Canada* (pp. 31–51). Toronto: McClelland & Stewart.

LeGrand J., & Robinson R. (Eds.). (1985). *Privatization and the welfare state* (pp. 86–97). London: Allen & Unwin.

Lehr, V. (1993). The difficulty of leaving "home": Gay and lesbian organizing to confront AIDS. In R. Fisher & J. Kling (Eds.), *Mobilizing the community* (pp. 246–269). Newbury Park, CA: Sage.

Leonard, P. (1990). Contesting the welfare state in a neo-Conservative era: Dilemmas for the left. *Journal of Progressive Human Services*, (1), 11–26.

Lewis, O. (1965). *La vida*. New York: Harper & Row.

Lightman, E. (1982). Professionalization, bureaucratization, and unionization in social work. *Social Service Review*, (56), 130–143.

Lipsitz, G. (1988). *A life in the struggle: Ivory Perry and the culture of opposition*. Philadelphia: Temple University Press.

Logan, J. R., & Swanstrom, T. (Eds.). (1990). *Beyond the city limits: Urban policy and economic restructuring in comparative perspective*. Philadelphia: Temple University Press.

Longres, J. (1996). Radical social work. In A. McNeece & P. Raffoul (Eds.), *Social work futures*. Boston: Allyn & Bacon.

——— . (1995). *Human behavior in the social environment*. Itasca, IL: F. E. Peacock.

Longres, J. F., & McLeod, E. (1980). Consciousness raising and social work practice. *Social Casework, 61*(May), 267–276.

Lord, S., & Kennedy, A. (1992). Transforming a charity organization into a social justice community center. *Journal of Progressive Human Services*, (3), 21–38.

Lubove, R. (1969 & 1975). *The professional altruist: The emergence of social work as a career, 1880–1930*. New York: Atheneum. Reprinted 1975, Pantheon.

Lum, D. (1992). *Social work practice and people of color* (2nd ed.). Pacific Grove, CA: Brooks/Cole.

Lyotard, J. (1979). *The post-modern condition: A report on knowledge*. Minneapolis, MN: University of Minnesota Press.

Mahaffey, M. (1987). Political action in social work. *Encyclopedia of Social Work* (18th ed., Vol. 2, pp. 283–294). Silver Spring, MD: NASW Press.

——— . (1982). Lobbying and social work. In M. Mahaffey & J. W. Hanks (Eds.), *Practical politics: Social work and social responsibility* (pp. 69–84). Silver Spring, MD: NASW Press.

Marston, S. A., & Towers, G. (1993). Private spaces and the politics of places: Spatioeconomic restructuring and community organizing in Tucson and El Paso. In R. Fisher & J. Kling (Eds.), *Mobilizing the community* (pp. 75–102). Newbury Park, CA: Sage.

Martin, G. (1990). *Social policy in the welfare state*. Englewood Cliffs, NJ: Prentice Hall.

Martin, P., & O'Connor, J. (1989). *The social environment*. White Plains, NY: Longman.

Masi, D. (1981). *Human services in industry*. Lexington, MA: D. C. Heath.

McCullough, M. F. (1991). Democratic questions for the computer age. In J. Downing, R. Fasano, P. A. McCullough, M. A. Mizrahi, & J. J. Shapiro (Eds.), *Computers for social change and community organizing* (pp. 9–18). New York: Haworth Press.

McMurtry, S. L., & Kettner, P. M. (1994). Is community organization dead and is the future organizational practice. Yes. In M. J. Austin and J. I. Lowe (Eds.), *Controversial issues in communities and organizations* (pp. 97–111). Boston: Allyn & Bacon.

Meenaghan, T. M., Washington, R. O., & Ryan, R. M. (1982). *Macro practice in the human services*. New York: Free Press.

Melucci, A. (1989). *Nomads of the present: Social movements and individual needs in contemporary society*. Philadelphia: Temple University Press.

Midgley, J. (1986). *Community participation, social development, and the state*. London: Methuen.

Miller, J. B. (1983). Women and power. *Social Policy*, (Spring), 3–6.

Mills, C. W. (1959). *The sociological imagination*. New York: Penguin.

Mohan, B. (1980). Human behavior, social environment, social reconstruction and social policy: A system of linkages, goals and priorities. *Journal of Education for Social Work, 16*(Spring), 83–98.

Mondros, J. B., & Wilson, S. M. (1994). *Organizing for power and empowerment*. New York: Columbia University Press.

Monk, A., & Newdom, F. (1976). The outposting method of community services: A multifaceted field experience. *Journal of Education for Social Work, 12*(Fall), 72–88.

Montgomery, D. (1995). What the world needs now. *The Nation*, (April 3), 461–463.

Moreau, M. (1987). *Practice implications of a structural approach to social work*. Montreal: University of Montreal.

Morgan, D. L. (1988). *Focus groups as qualitative research*. Newbury Park, CA: Sage.

Morris, A. (1984). *The origins of the civil rights movement: Black communities organizing for change*. New York: Free Press.

Moynihan, D. P. (1993). Defining deviancy down. *The American Scholar*, (Winter), 16–25.

Mullaly, R. (1993). *Structural social work: Ideology, theory, and practice*. Toronto: McClelland & Stewart.

Murray, C. (1984). *Losing ground*. New York: Basic Books.

Muwakkil, S. (1995). Color blind. *In These Times*, (March 6), 15–17.

Netting, F. E., Kettner, P. M., & McMurtry, S. L. (1993). *Social work macro practice*. White Plains, NY: Longman.

Northen, H. (1982). *Clinical social work*. New York: Columbia University Press.

O'Connor, J. (1973). *The fiscal crisis of the state*. New York: St. Martin's Press.

O'Donnell, S. (1995). Is community organizing the greatest job one could have? Findings from a survey of Chicago organizers. *Journal of Community Practice, 1*(2), 1–20.

Offe, C. (1987). Challenging the boundaries of institutional politics: Social movements since the 1960s. In C. Maier (Ed.), *Changing boundaries of the political: Essays on the evolving balance between the state and society, public and private in Europe*. Cambridge, UK: Cambridge University Press.

Okafor, A. (1985). White collar unionization. *Personnel*, (62), 17–21.

Ouchi, W. (1976). *Theory Z*. Reading, MA: Addison-Wesley.

Paget, K. (1990). Citizen organizing: Many movements, no majority. *American Prospect*, 7(Summer), 115–128.

Pappell, C., & Rothman, B. (1966). Social group work models: Possession and heritage. *Journal of Education for Social Work*, (2), 81–96.

Parsons, R., Jorgensen, J., & Hernandez, S. (1994). *The integration of social work practice*. Pacific Grove, CA: Brooks/Cole.

Pastor, M. (1995). PRRAN-LA: The Los Angeles poverty and race researcher & activist network. *Poverty & Race, 5*(4), 9–10.

Pecora, P. J., & Austin, M. J. (1983). Declassification of social service jobs: Issues and strategies. *Social Work, 28*(Nov/Dec), 421–426.

Peters, C. (1983). A new politics. *Public Welfare*, (18), 34–45.

Peters, T. J., & Waterman, R. H. (1984). *In search of excellence*. New York: Warner Books.

Phillips, K. (1990). *The politics of rich and poor*. New York: Random House.

Pierson, P. (1990). The "exceptional" United States: First new nation or last welfare state? *Social Policy and Administration, 23*(November), 15–21.

Piven, F. F., & Cloward, R. (1982). *The new class war: Reagan's attack on the welfare state and its consequences*. New York: Pantheon.

——— . (1971). *Regulating the poor*. New York: Vintage.

Pollitt, K. (1994). Subject to debate. *Nation*, (July 25/August 1), 118.

——— . (1992). Are women morally superior to men? *Nation*, (December 28), 799–807.

Pray, K. (1931). Where in social work can the concept of democracy be applied? In *Proceedings*, National Conference of Social Welfare (pp. 625–631). New York: Columbia University Press.

Putnam, R. (1994). *Making democracy work*. Princeton, NJ: Princeton University Press.

Rabushka, A., & Hanke, S. H. (1989). Getting ready for the global economy. *The Jerusalem Post*, (November 8), 9.

Ratner, L. (1985). Understanding and moving beyond social workers' resistance to unionization. *Catalyst*, (5), 70–81.

Rees, S. (1991). *Achieving power: Practice and policy in social welfare*. North Sydney, Australia: Allen & Unwin.

Reeser, L. C., & Epstein, I. (1990). *Professionalization and activism in social work: The sixties, the eighties, and the future*. New York: Columbia University Press.

Reich, R. (1983). *The next American frontier*. New York: Penguin.

Reid, W. J. (1987). Research in social work. *Encyclopedia of social work* (18th ed., Vol. 2, pp. 474–487). Silver Spring, MD: National Association of Social Workers.

Reisch, M. (1995). *If you think you're not political, guess again: The 1994 elections.* Keynote Address, NASW California Legislative Days Conference, February 12. Sacramento, CA, 1–4.

——— . (1993). The social worker in politics as a multi-role group practitioner. *Social work with groups: Selected papers* (pp. 187–201). New York: Haworth.

——— . (1988). The uses of history in teaching social work. *Journal of Teaching in Social Work*, (2), 3–16.

Remele, K. (1994). *Christianity and Western therapeutic culture.* Paper presented at the International Society for the Study of European Ideas, Vienna.

Reynolds, B. (1961). *An unchartered journey.* New York: Citadel Press.

Richardson, C. (1992). Employee involvement: Employee empowerment, total quality management. *Labor Page*, (October/November), 73.

Riesman, D. (1950). *The lonely crowd: A study of the changing American character.* New Haven, CT: Yale University Press.

Rips, G. (1994). COPS at 20. *The Texas Observer*, (June 17), 6–7.

Rivera, F. G., & Erlich, J. L. (1995). *Community organizing in a diverse society* (2nd ed.). Boston: Allyn & Bacon.

——— . (1992). *Community organizing in a diverse society.* Boston: Allyn & Bacon.

Roberts, R., & Northen, H. (1976). *Theories of social work with groups.* New York: Columbia University Press.

Robinson, B., & Hanna, M. (1994). Lessons for academics from grassroots community organizing: A case study of the Industrial Areas Foundation. *Journal of Community Practice*, *1*(4), 63–94.

Rose, S. (1990). Advocacy/empowerment: An approach to clinical practice for social work. *Journal of Sociology and Social Welfare, 17*(June), 41–51.

Rosenthal, B., & Mizrahi, T. (1994). Should community-based organizations give priority to building coalitions rather than building their own membership? Yes. In M. J. Austin & J. I. Lowe (Eds.), *Controversial issues in communities and organizations* (pp. 9–22). Boston: Allyn & Bacon.

Ross, M. G. (1967). *Community organizing.* New York: Harper & Row.

Rothman, J., & Tropman, J. (1987). Models of community organization and macro practice perspectives: Their mixing and phasing. In F. M. Cox, J. L. Ehrlich, J. Rothman, & J. E. Tropman (Eds.), *Strategies of community organization: Macro practice* (4th ed.) (pp. 3–26). Itasca, IL: F. E. Peacock.

Rubin, H. J., & Rubin, I. S. (1992). *Community organizing and development* (2nd ed.). New York: Macmillan.

Ruckdeschel, R. A., & Farris, B. E. (1981). Assessing practice: A critical look at the single-case design. *Social Casework, 62*(7), 413–419.

Rude, G. (1980). *Ideology and popular protest.* New York: Pantheon.

Russell, M., & Hornby, H. (1987). *National study of public child welfare job requirements.* Portland, ME: National Child Welfare Resource Center for Management and Administration.

Ryan, M. (1992). Gender and public access: Women's politics in nineteenth century America. In C. Calhoun (Ed.), *Habermas and the Public Sphere* (pp. 259–288). Cambridge, MA: MIT Press.

Salamon, L. (Ed.). (1989). *Beyond privatization: The tools of government action.* Washington, D.C.: Urban Institute Press.

Sandel, M. (1988). Democrats and community. *New Republic*, (February 22), 20–23.

Savas, E. S. (1987). *Privatization: The key to better government.* Chatham, NJ: Chatham House.

Saxton, P. (1991). Comments on social work and the psychotherapies. *Social Service Review,* 65(4), 314–317.

Schambra, W. (1991). Conservatives, liberals, and the principles of "public life." *Public Life,* 2(March), 4–15.

Schorr, A. (1985). Professional practice as policy. *Social Service Review,* (59), 178–196.

Schram, P. (1993). *Inverting political economy: Looking at welfare from the bottom up.* Paper delivered at the American Political Science Association meeting, Boston, MA, June.

Schuerman, J. R. (1982). Comments on the obsolete scientific imperative in social work research. *Social Service Review,* 56(1), 144–148.

Scott, A. (1990). *Ideology and the new social movements.* London: Unwin Hyman.

Sennett, R. (1990). *The conscience of the eye.* New York: Norton.

——— . (1974). *The fall of public man.* New York: Norton.

Shaffer, G. (1987). *Professional social worker unionization: Current contract developments and implications for managers.* Paper presented at the National Association of Social Workers, Annual Conference, New Orleans, Sept. 12.

——— . (1979). Labor relations and the unionization of professional social workers. *Journal of Education for Social Work,* (19), 83–94.

Shaffer, G., & Ahearn, K. (1982). *Current perceptions, opinions, and attitudes held by professional social workers toward unionization and the collective bargaining process.* Unpublished paper, School of Social Work, University of Illinois, Champaign.

Shapiro, D. (1974). Occupational mobility and child welfare workers: An exploratory study. *Child Welfare,* (53), 5–13.

Sherman, W., & Wenocur, S. (1983). Empowering public welfare workers through mutual support. *Social Work,* 28(Sept–Oct), 370–375.

Simon, B. L. (1994). *The empowerment tradition in American social work: A history.* New York: Columbia University Press.

——— . (1990). Rethinking empowerment. *Journal of Progressive Human Services,* (1), 27–40.

Skerry, R. (1993). *Mexican Americans: The ambivalent minority.* New York: Free Press.

Slaght, E. F. (1994). Are quick and dirty needs assessments better than no needs assessments? Yes. In M. J. Austin & J. I. Lowe (Eds.), *Controversial issues in communities and organizations* (pp. 142–148). Boston: Allyn & Bacon.

Smith, A. (1983). *The wealth of nations.* New York: E. P. Dutton.

Soja, E. (1985). The spatiality of social life. In D. Gregory and J. Urry (Eds.), *Social relations and spatial structures.* New York: St. Martin's Press.

Sorkin, M. (Ed.). (1992). *Variation on a theme park: The new American city and the end of public space.* New York: Noonday Press.

Souflee, F. (1977). Social work: The acquiescing profession? *Social Work,* (22), 419–421.

Specht, H., & Courtney, M. (1994). *Unfaithful angels: How social work abandoned its mission.* New York: Free Press.

Spradley, J. (1979). *The ethnographic interview.* New York: Holt, Rinehart, and Winston.

Starr, P. (1987). *The limits of privatization.* Washington, D.C.: Economic Policy Institute.

Steinfels, P. (1992). A political movement blends its ideas from left and right. *The New York Times,* (May 24), B16.

Stoesz, D., & Karger, H. J. (1996). *Small change: Domestic policy under the Clinton presidency.* White Plains, NY: Longman.

——— . (1992). *Reconstructing the American welfare state.* Savage, MD: Rowman & Littlefield.

Stout, K. D. (1993). Intimate femicide: Effect of legislation and social services. *Affilia 4*(Summer), 21–30.

Sundet, P. (1981). *If community organization is dead—why won't it stay buried?* Unpublished paper, University of Illinois, Champaign-Urbana, April.

Sundman, H. (1994). UNO: Taking organizing to a new level or leaving the community behind? *The Chicago Reporter,* (May/June), 1–2.

Tambor, M. (1988). The social service union in the workplace. In H. Karger (Ed.), *Social workers and labor unions* (pp. 83–96). New York: Greenwood Press.

——— . (1979). The social worker as worker. *Administration in Social Work, 3*(Fall), 289–300.

Tambor, M., & Shaffer, G. (1985). Social work unionization: A beginning bibliography. *Catalyst, 17–18*(Nov.), 131–136.

Tananbaum, S. (1994). *Public spheres and public needs: Late nineteenth century patterns of Jewish philanthropy in London.* Paper presented at the American Historical Association meeting, Washington, D.C.

Third Ward Community Cloth Cooperative. (n.d.). Flyer, Urban League, Houston, TX.

Tosh, J. (1991). *The pursuit of history.* White Plains, NY: Longman.

Touraine, A. (1985). An introduction to the study of social movements. *Social Research, 52*(Winter), 749–787.

Trattner, W. (1974). *From poor law to welfare state.* New York: Free Press.

True, J. A. (1989). *Finding out: Conducting and evaluating social research.* Belmont, CA: Wadsworth.

Tudiver, N. (1982). Business ideology and management in social work: The limits of cost control. *Catalyst,* (4), 25–48.

United States Department of Housing and Urban Development. (1995). *U.S. housing market conditions.* Washington, D.C.: U.S. Department of Housing and Urban Development, Office of Policy Development and Research, August 1995.

University of Houston, Graduate School of Social Work. (1991). Political social work. Leaflet, Houston, TX., n.p.

Vacek, M. S. (1994). *Secular priests in the church of individual repair.* Unpublished paper.

Van Den Bergh, N., & Cooper, L. B. (1987). Feminist social work. *Encyclopedia of social work* (18th ed., Vol. 2, pp. 611–627). Silver Spring, MD: NASW Press.

——— . (Eds.). (1986). *Feminist visions for social work.* Silver Spring, MD: NASW Press.

Vandenberg-Daves, J. (1992). The manly pursuit of a partnership between the sexes: The debate over YMCA programs for women and girls, 1914–1933. *Journal of American History, 78*(March), 1324–1346.

Vigilante, J. L. (1974). Between values and science: Education for the profession during a moral crisis or is proof truth? *Journal of Education for Social Work, 3*(10), 110–118.

Wagenaar, T. C. (Ed.). (1981). *Reading for social research.* Belmont, CA: Wadsworth.

Wagner, D. (1993). *Checkerboard square.* Boulder, CO: Westview Press.

——— . (1990). *The quest for a radical profession: Social service careers and political ideology.* Lanham, MD: University Press of America.

Wagner, D., & Cohen, M. (1978). Social workers, class, and professionalism. *Catalyst,* (1), 25–53.

Walker, A. (1990). The strategy of inequality: Poverty and income distribution in Britain 1979–89. In I. Taylor (Ed.), *The social effects of free market policies* (pp. 43–66). Sussex, UK: Harvester-Wheatsheaf.

Wallerstein, I. (1990). Antisystemic movements: History and dilemmas. In S. Amin, et al. (Eds.), *Transforming the revolution: social movements and the world-system*. New York: Monthly Review Press.

Warner, S. B. (1968). *The private city: Philadelphia in three periods of growth*. Philadelphia: University of Pennsylvania Press.

Weil, M. (1986). Women, community, and organizing. In N. Van Den Bergh & L. Cooper (Eds.), *Feminist visions for social work* (pp. 187–210). Silver Springs: NASW Press.

Weingartner, S. (1992). ACTWU's workplace agenda. *The Labor Page*, (October/November), 71.

Weitzman, J. (1975). *The scope of bargaining in public employment*. New York: Praeger.

Wenocur, S., & Weisner, S. (1992). Should community organization be based on a grassroots strategy? In E. Gambrill & R. Pruger (Eds.), *Controversial issues in social work* (pp. 288–300). Boston: Allyn & Bacon.

West, C. (1992). Learning to talk of race. *New York Times Magazine*, (August 1), 6–7.

Wharf, B. (Ed.). (1990). *Social work and social change in Canada*. Toronto: McClelland & Stewart.

Whyte, W. F. (1966). *Street corner society: The social structure of an Italian slum*. Chicago: University of Chicago Press.

Wignaraja, P. (Ed.). (1993). *New social movements in the south: Empowering the people*. London: ZED Books.

Wilensky, H., & Lebeaux, C. (1965). *Industrial society and social welfare*. New York: Free Press.

Wilson, P. A. (1981). *Community organization: An integrated approach to practice*. Paper presented at the Community Organization Symposium, Council on Social Work Education, APM, Louisville, Kentucky, March 6.

Wilson, W. J. (1987). *The truly disadvantaged*. Chicago: University of Chicago Press.

Withorn, A. (1984). *Serving the people: Social services and social change*. New York: Columbia University Press.

Wodarski, J., et al. (1986). Reagan's AFDC policy changes: The Georgia experience. *Social Work*, 31(July/August), 273–277.

Wolch, J. (1990). *The shadow state: Government and the voluntary sector in transition*. New York: The Foundation Center.

The World Bank. (1993). *World development report 1993: Investing in Health*. New York: Oxford University Press.

——— . (1990). *World development report 1990: Poverty*. New York: Oxford University Press.

Young, I. (1993). *Civil society and social change*. Paper presented at the American Political Science Association meeting, San Antonio, TX.

Zimbalast, S. E. (1977). *Historic themes and landmarks in social welfare research*. New York: Harper & Row.

——— . (1955). *Major trends in social work research: An analysis of the nature and development of research in social work, as seen in the periodical literature, 1900–1950*. Unpublished doctoral dissertation. Washington University, George Warren Brown School of Social Work, St. Louis, MO.

Index